DANTE'S *VITA NUOVA* AND THE NEW TESTAMENT

T0385011

Modeling knowledge as revelation and theology as poetry, this powerful new reading of the *Vita nuova* not only challenges Dante scholars to reconsider the book's speculative emphases but also offers the general reader an accessible yet penetrating exploration of some of the Western tradition's most far-reaching ideas surrounding love and knowledge. Dante's "little book," included in full here in an original parallel translation, captures in its first emergence the same revolutionary ferment that would later become manifest both in the larger *oeuvre* of this great European writer and in the literature of the entire Western canon. William Franke demonstrates how Dante's youthful poetic autobiography disrupts sectarian thinking and reconciles the seeming contraries of divine revelation and human invention, while also providing the means for understanding religious revelation in the Bible. Ultimately, this revolutionary unification of Scripture and poetry shows the intimate working of love at the source of inspired knowing.

WILLIAM FRANKE is Professor of Comparative Literature and Religious Studies at Vanderbilt University and Visiting Professor at the University of Navarra. He is a research fellow of the Alexander von Humboldt-Stiftung and has been Fulbright-University of Salzburg Distinguished Chair in Intercultural Theology and Study of Religions. His books include *Dante's Interpretive Journey* (1996), *On What Cannot Be Said* (2007), *Poetry and Apocalypse* (2009), *Dante and the Sense of Transgression* (2013), *A Philosophy of the Unsayable* (2014), *The Revelation of Imagination: From the Bible and Homer through Virgil and Augustine to Dante* (2015), *Secular Scriptures: Modern Theological Poetics in the Wake of Dante* (2016), *A Theology of Literature* (2017), and *On the Universality of What is Not: The Apophatic Turn in Critical Thinking* (2020).

DANTE'S *VITA NUOVA* AND THE NEW TESTAMENT

Hermeneutics and the Poetics of Revelation

With the original Italian text and a new English translation of the *Vita nuova*

WILLIAM FRANKE

CAMBRIDGE
UNIVERSITY PRESS

Shaftesbury Road, Cambridge CB2 8EA, United Kingdom

One Liberty Plaza, 20th Floor, New York, NY 10006, USA

477 Williamstown Road, Port Melbourne, VIC 3207, Australia

314–321, 3rd Floor, Plot 3, Splendor Forum, Jasola District Centre, New Delhi – 110025, India

103 Penang Road, #05–06/07, Visioncrest Commercial, Singapore 238467

Cambridge University Press is part of Cambridge University Press & Assessment, a department of the University of Cambridge.

We share the University's mission to contribute to society through the pursuit of education, learning and research at the highest international levels of excellence.

www.cambridge.org
Information on this title: www.cambridge.org/9781009013819

DOI: 10.1017/9781009031127

© William Franke 2021

First published 2021
First paperback edition 2023

A catalogue record for this publication is available from the British Library

Library of Congress Cataloging-in-Publication data
NAMES: Franke, William author, translator. | Dante Alighieri, 1265–1321. Vita nuova.
| Dante Alighieri, 1265–1321. Vita nuova. English.
TITLE: Dante's Vita nuova and the New Testament : hermeneutics and the poetics of revelation : with the original Italian text and a new English translation of the Vita nuova / William Franke, Vanderbilt University, Tennessee.
DESCRIPTION: Cambridge ; New York, NY : Cambridge University Press, 2021. | Includes bibliographical references and index.
IDENTIFIERS: LCCN 2021010761 (print) | LCCN 2021010762 (ebook) | ISBN 9781316516171 (hardback) | ISBN 9781009031127 (ebook)
SUBJECTS: LCSH: Dante Alighieri, 1265–1321. Vita nuova. | Dante Alighieri, 1265–1321 – Religion. | Religion in literature. | BISAC: LITERARY CRITICISM / European / General
CLASSIFICATION: LCC PQ4310.V4 F73 2021 (print) | LCC PQ4310.V4 (ebook) | DDC 851/.1–dc23
LC record available at https://lccn.loc.gov/2021010761
LC ebook record available at https://lccn.loc.gov/2021010762

ISBN   978-1-316-51617-1   Hardback
ISBN   978-1-009-01381-9   Paperback

Contents

Illustrations

Prologue

The revolution in literary theory in recent decades – since structuralism, post-structuralism, and deconstruction, since hermeneutics, reader-response theory, and various spin-offs in the critical styles labeled new-historicist, feminist, Marxist, postcolonial, queer theory, and the rest – has dramatically changed the landscape for reading literature in general. Some of the most salient specific consequences are to be seen in the modified relations between literature and religion. It used to seem that there was a clear line of demarcation between secular literature in novels, plays, or poems, on the one hand, and inspired texts of revealed religions such as the Bible and the Qur'an, or even the Vedas and Upanishads, on the other. But theoretical questionings and critical border crossings have altered that radically. What constitutes *revelation* has been re-envisioned and redefined in ways that leave secular literature no longer so securely isolated from the claims and modalities of what was formerly cordoned off as religious or was at least in principle not of human making. This is particularly true for an author such as Dante. While generally respecting the distinction between his own work and God's, he also pushes hard against its limits. He places his own literary production in a zone nearly continuous with revelation in the Bible by making it practically comparable in function: his poetry aims to induce a total existential conversion of humanity in light of a purportedly true vision coming down to him as conferred from heaven.

Central to my critical and cultural-historical project is the attempt to show how this effacing of boundaries between imaginative literature and religious revelation is brought about by modern authors beginning with Dante and following in his wake. Although he is recognized primarily for his literary achievements, Dante is all along oriented in an overtly theological direction. He is inspired by a declaredly theological vision and is confessedly motivated by an outspokenly religious faith from beginning to end of his literary *oeuvre*. My broader purpose in interpreting him here is to recover a deeper understanding of the theological sources and grounding of our cultural heritage and historical destiny in general.

Dante's *Vita nuova*, his first book and essentially the first book of the Italian literary tradition, is a uniquely privileged case in point for this broad-based endeavor to read literature for its eminently theological purport. The idea of literature as a vehicle of theological revelation – and even as itself an original, indispensable realization of it – can find a point of departure in this particular text initiating Dante's incomparably revelatory trajectory of authorship. Read in this way, the *Vita nuova* is emblematic of a new life and marks a new beginning for literature in the modern era. What we can see in this new role for literature emerging into tremulous self-consciousness in Dante's youthful *libello* is that literature, in many respects, takes over functions that were previously reserved for ecclesiastically authorized channels of religious revelation.

Even with the precipitous decline of institutionalized religion in the secularized West in the modern era, literature retains this role as revelation. Indeed, it is surely in part *because of* the decline of official religious practice that the revelatory vocation of literature in our time has again become resonant and may even be found to be accentuated and enhanced. However, this vocation is now likely to entail "revelation" in a broader phenomenological, existential, or spiritual sense rather than just a narrowly, or dogmatically, defined "religious" sense. Some such role for literature as revelatory of other worlds and of all imaginable possibilities of experience is attested by modern literary classics from Kafka and Pessoa to Joyce or Wolf and Morrison, Borges or Eliot, or . . . you name it.

The reading I propose here of the *Vita nuova*, accordingly, is meant to be exemplary of one of the richest and most comprehensive ways of reading literature that has become newly possible in our time, a type of reading that I call "theological" in a peculiar sense. It is "theological" because of its aiming at a comprehension open to the whole of culture and history, the alpha and the omega, and its opening them even beyond themselves to what they cannot comprehend. This type of reading is "theological," furthermore, because of its conceiving of such comprehension and incomprehension through metaphors of unlimited consciousness and personal agency. An expression's being "theological" can consist in its projecting to infinity structures and capacities of human existence such as personhood or loving engagement and ethical commitment. In such discourse, the unlimited and infinite function as figures of "the divine." The way of reading and writing developed here is accurately placed, accordingly, under the sign of religion and literature. Much of my own previous work can be productively contextualized within this galaxy of criticism, and the present work shines in full measure when set within the greater constellation of my own kindred and interconnected works – alongside those of others.[1]

In certain disciplines, moreover, it is now customary to designate our times as "post-secular."[2] This means that the typically secularist strictures defining the empirical and so-called real world as sealed off from anything otherworldly have become increasingly porous. Such a secular framework has been dominant throughout the modern era both at the university and in society at large, but it has begun to collapse and implode, at least in select spheres of the most radical critical thinking today.[3] Seismic activity along this cultural fault line between the secular and the religious has a large share of responsibility for bringing about the new configuration of religion and literature in scholarship and in critical reflection across disciplines.

Yet, despite this incipient shift in the orientation of theoretical reflection at the university, more broadly in the circumambient culture, these are times of eclipse for our overall understanding of the meaning of revealed religious truth. The dangers of this attenuated intelligibility have grown menacing and insidious. We are now constantly confronted with the untoward social and political consequences of this forgetting. We run up against the impasses of (post)modern democratic society left without any consensual basis for authority. We lack the infinite openness to one another in a dimension of self-transcendence that is requisite for free and effective self-governance. Especially in our advancing cyber age, the cultivation of literature, seconded by speculative inquiry into the literary bases of revelation or the disclosure of truth, is a crucial antidote to the unmediated, positive handling of religious

---

[1] I have previously contributed volumes to two series featuring religion and literature: *Dante and the Sense of Transgression: "The Trespass of the Sign"* (London: Bloomsbury [Continuum], 2013) in the New Directions in Religion and Literature series edited by Mark Knight and Emma Mason; and *Secular Scriptures: Modern Theological Poetics in the Wake of Dante* (Columbus: The Ohio State University Press: 2016) in the Literature, Religion, and Postsecular Studies series, edited by Lori Branch. Several other books of mine along a similar interdisciplinary trajectory, most explicitly *Poetry and Apocalypse: Theological Disclosures of Poetic Language* (Stanford: Stanford University Press: 2009), likewise form a background giving larger scope to the effort of the present book to elucidate religious revelation in poetic literature.

[2] One landmark here is Jürgen Habermas and Joseph Ratzinger, *The Dialectics of Secularization* (San Francisco: Ignatus Press, 2006). I outline this epochal shift in the Introduction to *On the Universality of What Is Not: The Apophatic Turn in Critical Thinking* (Notre Dame: University of Notre Dame Press, 2020).

[3] Graham Ward, ed., *The Postmodern God: A Theological Reader* (Oxford: Blackwell, 1998) registered this sea change, which has continued to deepen along lines lucidly surveyed in relation to contemporary literature by Paul T. Corrigan, "The Postsecular and Literature: A Review of Scholarship," https://corriganliteraryreview.wordpress.com/2015/05/17/the-postsecular-and-literature/ (accessed April 28, 2020).

revelation by the mass media and its filtering through digital informatics. These technically performative vehicles threaten to overpower and blend out other more complexly traditional and intellectually reflective means of communicating and disseminating culture.

This book, then, is an effort to continue to foster, with renewed cognizance of their transformative and perhaps even saving power, the literate forms and practices that were so crucial to the making of modern society, with its revolutionary fervors and its creative freedoms. National literatures and their founding narrations were constitutive of the emerging historical identities of peoples. More sweepingly still, poetic language was the key to opening a visionary experience of a revelatory dimension of the real. Such traditional resources are now at risk of being forgotten and discarded in an increasingly post-literate culture that is self-threatened with suicide or, in any event, propelled by certain self-destructive drives toward the brink of extinction.

Dante stands near the origin of the secularization of religion at the dawn of the modern age and even stands out as one of its primary progenitors.[4] And yet, he is also still fully in touch with and even a champion of a theological vision hailing from the Middle Ages and antiquity. Today we are facing a radicalization of secularization or a "second secularization" comprising a loss of faith even in the humanities,[5] which means in ourselves – in selves themselves and in their freedom and destiny. As if called forth on cue by our time and its crises, Dante demonstrates how theology can be crucial to the continuing intelligibility and viability of the humanities. Dante's translation of theological doctrine into poetic vision is key to our being able to continue to receive the saving graces of religion and humanities alike in our current twice-over secularized culture and technologized world. Dante is among our greatest guides to how we can still benefit from our human wisdom traditions and their spiritual vision. We can and need to be galvanized by these resources in their broader potential

---

[4] A milestone here is Erich Auerbach, *Dante: Poet of the Secular World*, trans. Ralph Manheim (Chicago: University of Chicago Press, 1961), originally *Dante als Dichter der irdischen Welt* (Berlin: Walter de Gruyter, 1929). My *Secular Scriptures: Modern Theological Poetics in the Wake of Dante* pursues this trajectory.

[5] Simon During, "Losing Faith in the Humanities: The Decline of Religion and the Decline of the Study of Culture Are Part of the Same Big Story," in "Endgame: Can Literary Studies Survive?" *The Chronicle Review*, December 18, 2019, pp. 20–24, persuasively analyzes this loss of faith in the humanities as extending the religious secularization of previous centuries. At first, he seems to equate radical secularization with extinction of religion rather than with its reconfiguring in more *worldly* terms, as the Latin word "saecularia" would suggest. In the end, however, his drift is to reconceive the humanities as still persistently at work in broader contexts beyond the walls of the academy.

for shedding a light of truth open to infinity in this unprecedentedly perilous situation for human culture susceptible to collapsing and succumbing to a "post-truth" condition.[6]

The modern period, with its belief in unlimited progress and even in a kind of human self-salvation by advances in technical fields such as medicine, genetic engineering, cybernetics, informatics, and robotics, may well prove to be the great exception in the history of humankind. Throughout the ages, the wisdom of salvation was almost always invested, on the contrary, not in striving after improvement in one's material conditions but rather in achieving relative indifference to them – or at least in the sovereignty of not being abjectly subject to merely external, material factors and circumstances.

Dante's "poetics of praise," in which praise of his lady constitutes its own sole and sufficient motivation and excludes seeking any other type of reward (*Vita nuova* XVIII. 6–9), is an express instance of such a self-reflective attitude. Generally speaking, such salvation consisted in knowing that, no matter how difficult things get, however intolerable, there is something that history and its tragedy cannot touch or destroy – some level of our being that remains immaculate and intact. We feel that we can be saved, or can at any rate go on (at least to perish with dignity), if we can just get back into relation with this inner, higher, more intense degree of being. The relentlessly accumulating disasters of the current era are taking us back perhaps toward making this kind of awareness, along with the "spiritual" being it embodies, meaningful, and even indispensable, once again.

In this register and in myriad other possible tonalities – particularly prophetic tonalities – the *Vita nuova* is an inauguration of a "new life" indeed, one that can make an existential appeal to readers today on grounds of its emergent modern subjectivity. Its novelty as a literary-historical phenomenon is assessed here anew. Most importantly, however, its implicit injunction to renew our existence is probed with an insistent urgency lent it by our postmodern predicament and by Dante's own self-conscious intention as formulated on the cusp of the modern era. My analysis and interpretation attempt to discern that intent through the kind of existential engagement out of which the *Vita nuova*'s implicit injunction to a new life itself speaks. Such existential commitment – and the performative linguistic act in which it crystallizes – is the "crease" in the page where literature and religion become inseparable and fold into one another.

---

[6] Myriam Revault d'Allonnes, *La faiblesse du vrai: Ce que la post-vérité fait à notre monde commun* (Paris: Seuil, 2019).

There is one further wrinkle. When I speak of redeeming theology and of the redemption of the humanities through theology, I am thinking of theology especially from the standpoint of *negative* theology – or theology as (negated by) poetry. Theology, *qua* negative, is the knowing of our own unknowing of divinity – or of whatever it is that most deeply bonds us together as humans and grants us our very existence together with everything else. Negative theology thus takes a purely critical stance with respect to all systems or ideologies – in effect, idolatries – that pretend to be able to articulate a foundational knowledge of existence in finite, human language. Negative theology is thus critical, first and foremost, of theology itself. Yet this critique does not exclude – nay, it may even foster and motivate – celebration *in a poetic mode* of theology as an unknowing knowing.[7]

Considered scientifically, such poetic knowing or wisdom seems not to be knowing at all. At least it is not an objective knowing of something such as ultimate reality or divinity. Still, while not claiming properly and positively to *know* anything, theological poetry can witness to the divine by articulating human experience in its passionate, existential relation to the infinite. Dante's "theology" offers compelling figures for imagining all reality in relation to what remains for us an ineffable mystery at its source. This also places all our human fields of knowing in their properly finite perspectives as delimited domains of objects bordering on something other than all that they can comprehend in the defined terms of our humanly forged concepts. This undefined territory beyond knowledge can, nevertheless, be *ac*knowledged. We can thereby project our knowledge of finite things into another dimension of the infinite and ineffable, which we do not know, but which can be poetically explored and intimated – as it is by Dante's otherworldly imagination. This, I propose, is how we might best understand Dante's testament today, with its witness to another world and life, and so elude cultural nihilism.

---

[7] I make this argument, marrying medieval apophatic theology and contemporary French deconstruction, in *Dante and the Sense of Transgression: "The Trespass of the Sign"*. I give it a historical grounding in Part II of *Dante's Paradiso and the Theological Origins of Modern Thought: Toward a Speculative Philosophy of Self-Reflection* (New York: Routledge, 2021).

Acknowledgments

My engagement with Dante's *Vita nuova* extends over several decades, beginning from graduate student days and reaching into current professional engagements in the present of writing and finalizing this manuscript. The earliest version of the essay on which the book is based was written for a seminar with Robert Harrison (Stanford University, Spring semester, 1988) and simultaneously for an independent study with Rachel Jacoff of Wellesley College, then visiting professor at Stanford. My long-sustained thanks are due to both mentors for their guidance and comments. The book vastly expands and thoroughly rewrites this essay, "Dante's New Life and the New Testament: An Essay on the Hermeneutics of Revelation," published originally at the suggestion of Zygmunt Barański in *The Italianist* 31 (2011): 335–66.

In 2017, I had the opportunity to develop and present, in German, a version of my *Vita nuova* interpretation, focusing specifically on the topic of the dream, under the title "Traum-Epistemologie und religiöse Offenbarung in Dantes *Vita nuova*." This presentation was invited as a guest lecture for the research project on European Dream Cultures, the *Graduiertenkolleg "Europäische Traumkulturen,"* of the Universität des Saarlandes, Saarbrücken, Germany, June 13, 2017. I thank Prof. Dr. Susanne Kleinert, Lehrstuhl für Romanische Philologie und Literaturwissenschaft, and Prof. Dr. Christiane Solte-Gresser, Lehrstuhl für Allgemeine und Vergleichende Literaturwissenschaft, for this invitation. I am particularly grateful to comparatist colleagues Karl-Heinz Stierle and Manfred Schmeling for their participation in the seminar and for helpful commentary and remarks.

The results of this encounter are distilled into the Epilogue on "Dreams and the Epistemology of Revelation in Dante's *Vita nuova*." This section translates from German into English my notes for the lecture/seminar and reworks them into essay form. Although not an organic part of my original essay on the *Vita nuova*, this reflection is highly pertinent to the hermeneutics of revelation in Dante's *prosimetron* masterpiece. This final segment of the book takes up a different angle of exposition based still on hermeneutic philosophy but blending in elements drawn from dream theory in anthropology and psychoanalysis. So it is offered here as a supplemental "Epilogue" that deepens the hermeneutic approach to illuminating the same theme as is expounded in the preceding chapters on religious revelation effected through creative employment of lyrical figures in poetic language.

Some pages from an earlier version of the first two chapters of the interpretive essay that has become this book were adapted and translated into German in order to appear as "Christliche Offenbarung mittels lyrischer Dichtung: Dantes *Vita nuova* und das Neue Testament" in *Christlicher Humanismus: Festschrift für Sigmund Bonk*, ed. Veit Neumann and Susanna Biber (Regensburg: Verlag Friedrich Pustet, 2019), pp. 117–38.

I am grateful also to the organizers – David Bowe and Valentina Mele – of a session on "Rereading Dante's 'Vita nuova' – Modes of Interpretation" at the Congresso Dantesco Internazionale: "Alma Dante 2019," in Ravenna, May 31, 2019, for the opportunity to participate in exchange on a wide range of current research concerning this most remarkable production of Dante's youth. This meeting, bearing the imprint of current scholarly ferment around the *Vita nuova*, gave the immediate impetus for my moving this work into the process of publication in anticipation of the seventh centenary commemorating Dante's death.

The text benefited considerably, in the concluding phase, from the counsel and suggestions of two anonymous readers. Finally, I thank Philippe Guérin for the invitation to present "*La Vita nuova* entre poésie et prose: Renouvellement de vie et révélation théologique" in his medieval lecture series at the Centre d'Études et de Recherches sur la Littérature Italienne (CERLIM), Université de la Sorbonne Nouvelle, Paris, on November 14, 2020.

Note on Text and Translation

The text of the *Vita nuova* is remarkably dense and needs to be constantly consulted and referred back to in any attentive and reflective reading. Dante's book of memory ("libro de la mia memoria," I. 1) challenges us to undertake an exacting exercise in the art of memory (*ars memoria*), and the Appendix furnishes a useful tool for building durable retention of the precise terms of his text. The original Italian is indispensable for researchers and readers of Italian, just as is an accurate, but also an enticing and inspiring, translation for those reading exclusively in English.

My translation was conceived as standing beside the original text and in the service of the critical essay. Now complete, however, it is potentially autonomous. Still, the *task* of translation is never completed. My purpose is not to stabilize and fix a definitive version but rather to keep translation always open to further conceivable possibilities. The translation of the whole work in the Appendix does not always correspond exactly to the renderings of the text improvised in the critical essay.

Initially, I had proposed to extract the passages most crucial for my critical exposition and speculative interpretation of Dante's work. These extracts comprised the following chapters of the book: I–V, IX–XII, XIV, XVIII–XX, XXIII–XXVI, XXIX, XXXIV–XXXV, XXXVIII–XLII.

This selection provided an outline referring especially to the themes of revelation, blessedness, and the dream, which serve as connecting threads for stitching the whole text together and as guidelines for its interpretation. Singling out some organizing motifs that mark crucial articulations of the story as a whole proved helpful in order to facilitate a synoptic grasp of Dante's work by setting its major lineaments into relief. There was, moreover, sufficient material in these extracts to represent something of the overall shape of Dante's story and its intricacy as witnessed to by his "little" book. The "witness" in question emerged in concentrated form as a testimony to an at least quasi-religious sort of experience through this selective compendium of choice flowers – this *florilegio* – of Dante's poetry and of the rhetorically elaborated prose that surrounds it.

I received, however, encouragement to translate and include the entire text of the *Vita nuova*. In the end, there is nothing in the text that does not contribute something of exquisite significance to the whole work, every feature and facet of which is interwoven with all the rest. Consequently, the volume now presents a complete translation. My method, generally, is to translate phrase by phrase, privileging linguistic cognates and trusting to cultural tradition rather than to one's own contemporary idiom to guide the recreation of the work in another language and culture. This approach is influenced by Friedrich Hölderlin's and Walter Benjamin's aims in translation – not to substitute for the original and stand in its way, but to let the light of its language shine as reflected through another language. The awkwardness of monotonously repeated, archaic expressions like "gentle lady" (*gentile donna*) can itself be very revealing. It is apt to signify a certain strangeness about language that opens especially in the gaps between languages. I like to be able to hear the Italian text behind the English translation, though this is not always possible, since the English words do not possess exactly the same elasticities as the Italian. In addition, the immediacy of the voice of a live subject, speaking in the present is crucial to this book in particular, given its clamoring with new life claimed for a particular human individual.

The Italian text follows the critical edition by Michele Barbi (Florence: Società Dantesca Italiana, 1960 [1932; 1907]). I thank the Società Dantesca Italiana and their publisher, Le Lettere, for kind permission to reprint from *Le Opere di Dante*, testo critico della Società Dantesca Italiana, a cura di M. Barbi, E. G. Parodi, F. Pellegrini, E. Pistelli, P. Rajna, E. Rostagno, G. Vandelli, con indice analitico dei nomi e delle cose di M. Casella. Introduzione di E. Ghidetti, Firenze, Le Lettere, 2011 (ristampa anastatica).

The Barbi text remains the basic reference for the more recent editions by Domenico De Robertis in *Opere minori* I, I (Milan: Ricciardi, 1984); Dino S. Cervigni and Edward Vasta (Notre Dame: University of Notre Dame Press, 1995); Stefano Carrai (Milan: BUR, 2009); Guglielmo Gorni in the Meridiano Mondadori of Dante's *Opere* I (2011); and Donato Pirovano and Marco Grimaldi in the "Nuova Edizione Commentata delle Opere di Dante" (Rome: Salerno, 2015–19). An online version of Barbi's entire text is available with a translation by Mark Musa on the website of the Princeton Dante Project: http://etcweb.princeton.edu/dante/pdp/vnuova.html. Barbi's earlier

1907 edition is archived at: https://archive.org/details/imgGI107Miscellanea Opal. Barbi's division into chapters or "paragraphs," further divided into subsections, has generated heated controversy.[8] These divisions prove, none-theless, useful for the study aid proposed here in the Appendix – which is *not* a new critical edition. The same rationale justifies my invented chapter titles.

Marco Grimaldi kindly offered guidance regarding the Barbi text. I have also consulted the translations of Andrew Frisardi, *Vita nova* (Evanston: Northwestern University Press, 2012) and A. S. Kline, *La Vita nuova/The New Life* (Delaware: CreateSpace Independent Publishing Platform, 2001).

Bible quotations throughout are from the Authorized King James Version (1611) checked against – and, where necessary, corrected by – *The Greek New Testament*, 2nd ed. (New York: United Bible Societies, 1968) and *Bibliorum Sacrorum iuxta Vulgatam Clementinam Nova Editio* (Vatican: Typis Polyglottis, 1959).

T. S. Eliot quotations in the epigraphs and elswhere are from *Four Quartets* (London: HBJ, 1943).

---

[8] Enrico Malato, *Per una nuova edizione commentata delle opere di Dante* (Rome: Salerno, 2004), pp. 36–40; Dino S. Cervigni, "Segni paragrafali, maiuscole e grafia nella *Vita nuova*: Dal libello manoscritto al libro a stampa," *Rivista di letteratura italiana* 13/1–2 (1995): 283–362; Guglielmo Gorni, "'Paragrafi' e titolo della *Vita Nova*," chapter V of *Dante prima della Commedia* (Fiesole: Cadmo, 2001), pp. 111–32.

Introduction: The Vita nuova as Theological Revelation through Lyrical Interpretation

> Footfalls echo in the memory
> Down the passage which we did not take
> Towards the door we never opened
> Into the rose-garden. My words echo
> Thus, in your mind.
>
> (T. S. Eliot, "Burnt Norton," I)

Salutation and Salvation

The *Vita nuova* claims to be the story of Dante's encounters with and love for the woman who became his "beatifier," namely, Beatrice. From very near the outset of the book, she is declared to be his "beatitude" ("Apparuit iam beatitudo vestra," II. 5) by his psychological faculties – his "animal spirit" ("lo spirito animale") speaking to his "spirits of sight" ("li spiriti del viso").[1] Despite this (for modern readers at least) weirdly objectifying personification of his own faculties, which are activated by his perception of her, this beatitude is a deeply and irreducibly personal experience ensconced in Dante's highly idiosyncratic autobiographical narrative. And yet he has already at this point noted that the woman in question was spontaneously called "Beatrice" – meaning "she who confers beatitude" – also by other persons, even by many who did not know her name ("fu chiamata da molti

---

[1] The doctrine of multiple "spirits" or "spiritelli" coexisting in the psyche of the lover and communicating with one another as subtle essences operating between the physical and the spiritual is based on Galen's medical theories. Robert Klein, "Spirito Peregrino," chapter 4 of *La forme et l'intelligibile* (Paris: Gallimard, 1970), pp. 31–57, especially pp. 44–48, trans. Madeline Jay and Leon Wieseltier as *Form and Meaning: Essays on Renaissance and Modern Art* (New York: Viking, 1979), pp. 62–85, offers a lucid account of this source. Galen's theories circulated in Latin Averroist spheres and were relayed by the Florentine physician Taddeo Alderotti (1210–95). The doctrine is deployed most conspicuously – and with a parodic air – by Dante's contemporary Guido Cavalcanti, whose sonnet "Pegli occhi fere un spirito sottile" employs the word "spirito" in subtly differentiated acceptations in every one of its fourteen lines.

Beatrice li quali non sapeano che si chiamare," II. 1). We are left to infer that they must, therefore, have guessed her name from their own experience of her as beatifying, or as giving them bliss, and that they were speaking as if inspired or prompted by this soul-transforming experience.

The question of the status of this woman, whether real or allegorical, and in what degrees, has bequeathed to Dante scholarship a crux for endless debate.[2] Nevertheless, the status of this claim can be determined by reference to a model that, in Dante's own cultural context, would have been quite inescapable. A person whose presence blesses (literally "beatifies") him, and whose greeting or "saluto" can constitute "the very limits of my blessedness" ("tutti li termini de la mia beatitudine," III. 1; echoed in XVIII. 4 and XIX. 20), is unmistakably Christ-like. Indeed, she is, for Dante anyway, salvation or blessedness itself and is, from the very first, identified as such. Her name alone says as much.

The figure of salvation ("salute") in the greeting ("saluto") continues to grace – or haunt – the work: it becomes an obsession. A few chapters later, Dante's phrase "when this most gentle [or kind or graceful] salvation saluted" ("quando questa gentilissima salute salutava," XI. 3) plays once again doubly on the double meaning of "salutare" as conferring both a "greeting" and "salvation." Dante tells us again that in his lady's "salutations" dwelt his "beatitude" ("ne le sue salute abitava la mia beatitudine," XI. 4).[3] Appearing to Dante in the image and in the salvific role of Christ, Beatrice leads Dante to, and even in some sense *is*, "the new life" – "la vita nuova" – just as the title of his book about her announces. Beatrice, in this regard, is strikingly like the one who proclaims himself "the way, the truth, and the life" (John 14: 6) – both protagonist and propagator of a new and blessed life. Beatrice's name and greeting concertedly announce such quasi-evangelical good news to Dante.

Of course, Dante himself, as the one who receives this new life through his relation to Beatrice, is also, and most actively, the protagonist of his own story. The "new life" in question is also his own. In fact, the words of the title *Vita nuova* can also mean simply "young life" and so might serve primarily just to designate Dante's youthful poetic autobiography. The title can surely be heard this way, too. Still, the relational and evangelical senses of the title's terms, echoing Saint Paul's injunction to "walk in

[2] Edward Moore, "Beatrice" (1891), in *Studies in Dante*, 2nd series (Oxford: Clarendon Press, 1899), pp. 79–151, parses the various approaches into Realist, Idealist, and Symbolist.
[3] Dante uses the feminine form "la salute" (salvation) interchangeably with "il saluto" (greeting) also to mean "salutation," for example, in XI. 1.

newness of life," contribute ineluctably to its richly suggestive and ultimately religious resonances. Less literally, but more plainly translated, Paul's
injunction is "to live a new life" through following Christ raised from the
dead "by the glory of the father" (Romans 6: 4).[4] These senses and
resonances belong irrevocably to the title's semantic range, no matter
what emphases are preferred and adopted for its critical interpretation.

Dante makes the analogy with Christ unmistakable and programmatic
in Chapter XXIV by casting Beatrice in a visionary procession as the one
who comes after Guido Cavalcanti's ladylove, Giovanna. This lady's name
is a feminized form of Giovanni or John, and Dante glosses it as coming
from "that John who preceded the true light" ("lo suo nome Giovanna è da
quello Giovanni lo quale precedette la verace luce").[5] This is what is said in
the Gospel According to John concerning John the Baptist as the precursor
or forerunner of Christ. This John was "sent from God" in order "to bear
witness to the Light," although he himself "was not that Light," not "the
true Light, which lighteth every man that cometh into the world" (1: 6–9,
23). The same name (with only the difference in gender) is suited to Guido
Cavalcanti's lady because of her position with respect to Dante's lady,
Beatrice. Giovanna is the one who precedes Beatrice, who is the be-all and
end-all, the cynosure, of feminine beauty and virtue that warrants even the
analogy to the divine Savior.

Dante embellishes this analogy further and unveils an even more cryptic
encoding of it by explaining that Giovanna, on account of her beauty, was
also called by the nickname "Primavera." As a word in ordinary parlance,
this name means "Spring" but, broken down, it can also be heard as saying
"prima verrà," or "will come first." This decrypting of a second nominative
for Cavalcanti's lady proves decisive on the day when she comes first in
a procession of ladies that includes also Beatrice. Love appears to Dante
and speaks to him in his heart saying that he, Love, moved the originator of
this *senhal* to impose it solely in consideration of the day on which Beatrice
would manifest herself to her lover's imagination accompanied by this lady
"Primavera," who would precede her ("Queste donne andaro presso di me
così l'una appresso l'altre, e parve che Amore mi parlasse nel cuore,

---

[4] The Latin Vulgate reads: "ut quomodo Christus surrexit a mortuis per gloriam Patris, ita et nos in
novitate vitæ ambulemus"; and the Greek New Testament: "ἵνα ὥσπερ ἠγέρθη Χριστὸς ἐκ νεκρῶν
διὰ τῆς δόξης τοῦ πατρός, οὕτως καὶ ἡμεῖς ἐν καινότητι ζωῆς περιπατήσωμεν."
[5] The analogy between Christ and Beatrice, from which this essay begins, constitutes a central axis of
the influential interpretation of the *Vita nuova* proposed by Charles S. Singleton, *An Essay on the
"Vita nuova"* (Cambridge, MA: Harvard University Press, 1949). Beatrice is fully unveiled as an
Advent of Christ in the Earthly Paradise by Singleton in *Journey to Beatrice*, Dante Studies 2
(Cambridge, MA: Harvard University Press, 1958).

e dicesse: 'Quella prima è nominata Primavera solo per questa venuta d'oggi; ché io mossi lo imponitore del nome a chiamarla così Primavera, cioè prima verrà lo die che Beatrice si mosterrà dopo la imaginazione del suo fedele," XXIV. 4).

Thus, everything about her and her name(s) says that Giovanna, alias Primavera, precedes Beatrice in a manner analogous to the way that John the Baptist comes before and prepares the way for the Christ. The Gospel According to Mark 1: 1–5 interprets John the Baptist as the messenger who is prophesied to come before – in order to prepare for – the birth of the Christ. Mark is referring to Malachi: "As it is written in the prophets, 'Behold, I send my messenger before thy face, which shall prepare thy way before thee'" (3: 1), and he draws also on Isaiah, who prophesies: "The voice of one crying in the wilderness, Prepare ye the way of the Lord, make his paths straight" (40: 3). The Gospel According to Matthew takes up exactly the same passages from the prophets, citing Isaiah's injunction (Matthew 3: 3) and repeating Malachi's proclamation (Matthew 11: 10), as Scriptural prophecies now fulfilled by John the Baptist in relation to Jesus as the Messiah.

This pattern of succession from precursor to fulfillment is, of course, incidentally and somewhat outrageously, also suggestive of a certain way of construing the relation between Dante and his "first friend" ("primo amico," XXIV. 6; XXV. 10; XXX. 3). After all, Guido Cavalcanti was not only Dante's "first" or best friend but also his chief rival for the coveted accolade of being recognized as the preeminent Tuscan poet of the age. The relative order of their ladies' appearance in Dante's imagining of the scene can hardly help but reflect, at least indirectly, on the two rival poets and their mutual positioning and standing, yet this reflection is subtly insinuated by Dante as if it were not his point at all. Any hint about the poets' own relations, in which the older and preeminent Guido would be cast as preparing the way for his more important, younger successor, is upstaged by the imperative incumbent on Dante to praise his own lady above all others. All else is overshadowed by the higher sort of religious significance that Dante attributes to Beatrice.

At times, the theological intensity of the *Vita nuova*'s affirmations concerning Beatrice as Dante's personal savior and beatifier becomes so palpable as to approach an idolatrous heterodoxy.[6] But this is not the only way to read Dante's insertion of certain topoi of courtly devotion to

---

[6] So Gertrude Leigh, *The Passing of Beatrice: A Study in the Heterodoxy of Dante* (London: Faber & Faber, 1932).

a beloved lady into his Christian-theological framework (actually placing them back into the matrix whence they derived). To read sympathetically and understandingly, we are better advised to interpret any virtual identification of Beatrice with Christ *not* as an idolatrous worshipping of the creature rather than the Creator (in the terms of Romans 1: 25) but simply as an instance of the one working in and through the other.[7]

Just as, in general, Christ works through the individuals who constitute his body, which is the Church, according to the Pauline doctrine of Christ as the head and the Church as his body (I Corinthians 12: 12–27), so Christ reaches Dante in particular through the blessed person of Beatrice. This need be no more difficult to account for theologically than as a particular instance of the mystical incorporation of the body of Christ by the members of his Church. The Church, taken as his metaphorical "body," consists in those who perform his redemptive work in the world. In this sense, Beatrice might actually incarnate Christ for Dante, who, as a youthful character in the story of his own progressive spiritual growth, may not yet be fully cognizant nor completely precise, theologically speaking, in his perception of her role as a mediator toward increate divinity. We find here the seed of a theological conception that was to be more fully developed later.[8]

Not only is Beatrice like Christ in Dante's life, but also Dante's book about the individual who saves and beatifies him bears a likeness to the Church's book about Christ, its Savior. Both Dante's *libello* and the Church's Gospel tell stories of the encounters in life, followed by death, and finally by glorification in heaven, of their respective savior-beatifiers. The Christian New Testament announces as its good news the new and greater life in Christ ("I have come that ye might have life, and that ye might have it more abundantly," John 10: 10). Similarly, the *Vita nuova*, the story of a new and more worthy life found through his relationship

[7] Gabriel Pihas, "Dante's Beatrice: Between Idolatry and Iconoclasm," *St. John's Review* 57/1 (2015): 84–116, explores a number of "traditional theological avenues for explaining the role of Beatrice" (95n), with reference to the orthodoxy of Aquinas, among others.
[8] Oliver Davies, "Dante's *Commedia* and the Body of Christ," in *Dante's "Commedia": Theology as Poetry*, ed. Vittorio Montemaggi and Matthew Treherne (Notre Dame: University of Notre Dame Press, 2010), especially pp. 171–74, further defines the relationship between Beatrice and Christ theologically in terms of Transfiguration and Ascension. Antonio Rossini, "L'*anakefalàiosis* di Beatrice a *Purg.* 28–33: Una Cristologia soteriologica di taglio sapienziale," in *Il Dante sappienziale: Dionigi e la bellezza di Beatrice* (Pisa: Fabrizio Serra, 2009), pp. 75–100, interprets Beatrice-Christ in a specifically sapiential guise as Solomonic Sophia, noting how the *Vita nuova* "is surreptitiously inserted into the number of the sacred texts" ("surrettiziamente inserita nel novero dei testi sacri") as a "prologue" and as "inspired, in a broad sense" ("*lato sensu* ispirati," p. 76). See, further, Mario Pazzaglia, *Il "mito" di Beatrice* (Bologna: Pàtron, 1998).

with Beatrice, is Dante's good news. And, to the extent that his experience is, in principle, universalizable and might be taken as exemplary, and thus as revealing possibilities for others, we could also reasonably call it "the good news according to Dante."

It is exactly from the moment of Beatrice's appearance to the nine-year-old Dante that he finds written in his memory the rubric "Incipit vita nova" (I. 1). This signpost tells us that in retrospect Dante understands his life to have been a new life from the time of Beatrice's entry into it – and precisely on that account. His story in the *Vita nuova*, notwithstanding its autobiographical character, does not start from his biological birth but rather from this spiritual *new* birth. This story of new birth begins, moreover, by explicitly marking its beginning with an "incipit." Its very first words are meta-narratologically self-reflective: "In that part of the book of my memory, before which little could be read, is found a rubric that says: *Incipit vita nova*" ("In quella parte del libro de la mia memoria dinanzi a la quale poco si potrebbe leggere, si trova una rubrica la quale dice: *Incipit vita nova*").

The life in question and the book about it – like Christian life and the New Testament – are inseparable: they fuse metaphorically. For a Christian, moreover, this new life cannot but have connotations of being a redeemed and a blessed life. Nonetheless, Dante's new life at this point might still have been, as yet, only provisional and proleptic. St. Paul (echoing Isaiah 65: 17 and 43: 18) had exclaimed, "If any man be in Christ he is a new creature; old things are passed away, behold all things are become new" (II Corinthians 5: 17). And yet, despite this accomplished fact, "the earnest expectation of the creation waiteth for the revealing of the sons of God" (Romans 8: 19).

In some sense fulfilling the anticipation of the "already" within the "not yet," which distinguishes Christian temporality, Beatrice, too, attains to a new life in the course of the events recounted in the *libello*. And this new life is unequivocally a glorified life with God, blessed forever ("colui qui est per omnia secula benedictus," XLII. 3). This glory has already been anticipated as early as Chapter II by Beatrice's being called "the glorious lady of my mind" ("la gloriosa donna de la mia mente," II. 1). That she is already dead from the outset of Dante's writing of the book is confirmed explicitly just afterward in Chapter III, where Dante recounts her bestowing on him her salvific greeting. He mentions in passing that her unspeakable graciousness merits her being rewarded presently in heaven: "and by her ineffable courtesy, which is rewarded today in the great age [of eternity], she greeted/ saluted me most virtuously" ("e per la sua ineffabile cortesia, la quale è oggi meritata nel grande secolo, mi salutoe molto virtuosamente," III. 1).

Part of the meaning of the fact that she already *is* such blessedness and salvation ("tanta salute," XXXI. 10) is that Beatrice is called to new life in high heaven ("l'alto cielo"), or in the new and eternal age ("secol novo," XXXI. 15). Indeed, her death, if anything, is the event around which the whole book revolves. Yet, we will see that it occupies this pivotal position especially by dint of its virtual *absence* from the narrative, except through allusions of the type just cited.

In sum, a crucial component of my contention is that "new life" in Dante's *Vita nuova* must be heard primarily in a Christian evangelical register – with its New Testament resonances of a new and resurrected life. This connotation sometimes comes up in critical discussion of the meaning of the words "Vita nuova" as they occur already from the very title of the book.[9] Of course, as we have already noted, they can be translated also as "young life."[10] In *Purgatorio* XXX. 115, Beatrice uses "vita nova" in just this sense to describe Dante in his youth, with its great promise ("questi fu tal nella sua vita nova"), which she accuses him of having squandered and betrayed. And again, in line 7 of his sestina "Al poco giorno e al gran cerchio d'ombra," Dante uses the word "nova" clearly to mean simply "young" in the expression "nova donna" ("young woman").

Nevertheless, such a meaning cannot be taken to fix and delimit the sense of the word in the title of the *Vita nova* (often preferred by scholars as the original spelling rather than the modern Italian *Vita nuova*) or in the references to "vita nova" within Dante's work. That the Christian connotations of the resonant phrase "new life," especially considering its ritualization in the sacrament of baptism, should have been irrelevant for such an author as Dante is not credible. As Vittore Branca observes: "It is enough to peruse the works of Saint Augustine to find repeated in those pages about ten times that 'the new life is that of the man who knows God.'" Branca recalls also the pages of Richard of Saint Victor, whom Dante defines as "more than man through contemplation," in *Paradiso* X. 132. It is Richard, finally, who "ties also 'the new poetry' to precisely the 'new life'; 'The new life in justice and love creates the new poetry.'"[11]

---

[9] See, for example, Mario Pazzaglia, "Vita nuova," in *Enciclopedia dantesca*, ed. Umberto Bosco, 6 vols. (Rome: Istituto dell'Enciclopedia Italiana, 1970–78), V, pp. 1086–96, especially p. 1088.

[10] Guglielmo Gorni, "Vita Nova, Libro delle 'amistadi' e della 'prima etade,'" in *Dante prima della Commedia* (Florence: Cadmo, 2001), pp. 133–47.

[11] "Basta del resto scorrere le opere di Sant'Agostino per trovare nelle loro pagine ripetuto una decina di volte 'la vita nuova è quella dell'uomo che conosce Dio'; o quelle di Riccardo da San Vittore ('che a considerar fu più che viro', come lo definisce Dante nel *Paradiso* X, 132) il quale proprio alla 'Vita nuova' lega anche la 'poesia nuova'; 'La Vita nuova nella giustizia e nell'amore crea la nuova poesia.'" Vittore Branca, *Il sole 24 Ore*, March 26, 1995, p. 36.

Even if these Christian resonances of "new life" could be considered obvious and might generally be taken for granted (certainly in Dante's cultural context more than in our own), still the comparisons implied in them are far from having been exploited to the full.[12] An enormous amount has been learned about Gospel writing in well over a century of the most intensive, painstaking, and ingenious critical study of the New Testament.[13] Many of the surprising aspects of the process that have come to light can make puzzling features of Dante's testament of new life much more limpid. My reading of the *Vita nuova* proposes to use the Gospels as the model of a book written in loving memory of a person whose significance is – and must remain – central in the life of the author(s). Dante's book witnesses to the miraculousness of that person realized in full only after the person's death. Yet, in the re-telling, this realization is reflected retrospectively over every episode of the hallowed individual's existence on earth.

This approach through the model of the New Testament will help us to resolve, or at least to displace on to a philosophically deeper ground, some well-known difficulties in the interpretation of Dante's "New Life," notably the crux concerning the reality or actual historical existence of Beatrice. It will also help to open up new perspectives on provocative meanings of certain of the book's enigmatic features such as its relentless rhetoric of appearance and its saturation with uncanny look-alikes and unlikely repetitions of events and their descriptions. Heretofore, some of these conundrums have scarcely been placed under the scrutiny they deserve. At least, they have not yet been fully sounded in their far-reaching implications for Dante's implicit hermeneutics and ontology.

---

[12] Suggestive remarks on the New Testament model for figural interpretation in the *Vita nuova* are made by Michelangelo Picone, "La *Vita nuova* fra autobiografia e tipologia," in *Dante e le forme dell'allegoresi*, ed. M. Picone (Ravenna: Longo, 1987), p. 65. In her *Assembling the Lyric Self: Authorship from Troubadour Song to Italian Poetry Book* (Minneapolis: University of Minnesota Press, 2000), Olivia Holmes highlights in Dante's *libello* "a figural reading of literary history that he learned from the Gospels, especially the Gospel of John" (p. 120) and notes "Dante's superimposition of the Gospel story onto the conventional love story of the vernacular lyric sequence" (p. 126). Guglielmo Gorni, *Il nodo della lingua e il Verbo d'Amore* (Florence: Olschki, 1981), pp. 39–45 and 155–58, documents the book's Scriptural and especially Johannine echoes, as does also, and most exhaustively, Domenico De Robertis, *Il libro della "Vita nuova,"* 2nd ed. (Firenze: Sansoni, 1970).

[13] For an overview of basic results of the critical approach to the synoptic Gospels, see Carl R. Holladay, *A Critical Introduction to the New Testament: Interpreting the Meaning and Message of Jesus* (Nashville: Abingdon Press, 2005); Étienne Charpentier, *Pour lire le Nouveau Testament* (Paris: Les Éditions du Cerf, 1983); and Roland Meynet, *New Introduction to the Synoptic Gospels* (Rome: Gregorian University Press, 2010). Some radical hermeneutic perspectives are argued for by Thomas Sheehan, *The First Coming: How the Kingdom of God Became Christianity* (New York: Random House, 1986).

All of this centrally concerns the mysterious significance of Beatrice and of the book itself as "revelation."

Lyrical Exaltation and Theological Revelation

Of particular concern for what follows is the role of those resources of self-reflective language and affective imagination customarily called "lyrical" (in consideration especially of their songlike characteristics) in the process by which books like the Gospels and the *Vita nuova* come to be composed. A principal aim of the ensuing reflections is to suggest the paramount importance – and something of the specific workings – of this lyrical dimension in religious consciousness, as well as in literary experience generally. This, in itself, is a compelling reason for us to study with acute attention Dante's youthful collection of lyric poems and the hybrid work that he created out of it – a *prosimetrum* (prose narrative plus metered compositions, or poems). For in our contemporary cultural climate, the lyrical, along with many other traditional literary and religious values, runs a risk of extinction. Even the very concepts "poetry" and "literature" as such – and then *a fortiori* dependent notions such as "lyric" – can in academic contexts all too easily be "deconstructed" and discarded as nothing but illusory metaphysical idealizations. Yet the rapturous verbal enchantment and heightened existential attunement experienced through the mediation of poetic language, especially in lyrical forms such as those found in religious liturgy, should not be allowed to succumb completely to aggressively rational or narrowly cognitive critique – and, with even less justification, to ideological dismissal or condemnation.

The lyrical will be presented here as a vital constitutive moment of religious revelation and as crucial to a poetics of revelation conceived in terms of hermeneutic theory. This approach will establish the premises and the parameters for a debate in Chapter 4 with one remarkable contemporary contribution to Dante studies in this area of research. An arresting and enticing approach to interpreting the *Vita nuova* was inaugurated by *The Body of Beatrice*, an original and masterful book by Robert Harrison.[14] Guided by the insights and methods of phenomenology in the manner of Edmund Husserl and Martin Heidegger, this book raises speculation on the meaning of Dante's prosimetric masterpiece to a level of reflection where it can become philosophically and religiously relevant for us today.

---

[14] Robert Pogue Harrison, *The Body of Beatrice* (Baltimore: The Johns Hopkins University Press, 1988).

I find *The Body of Beatrice*'s argumentation to be profound and compelling and its rhetorical presentation exquisite, yet I remain unpersuaded by its conclusions, as well as by its premises.[15]

For Harrison, the *Vita nuova* originates in and from the experience of a woman, which he would have to be an irreducible reality neither needing nor admitting of explanation, around which barrages of hermeneutic assault accumulated only later. This not-to-be-interpreted origin is complemented, in Harrison's view, by an equally self-transcending and irreducible, interpretation-resistant destination. For Dante's book issues in an opening toward the temporality of narrative, and this entails projection into an as yet unrevealed future. An inviolable mystery is supposedly left intact at either end, harboring in the unaccountable experience that generates the necessarily indecipherable *libello*. In the middle – that is, across the whole of the *Vita nuova* – what happens in one way or another constitutes an overcoming of the lyric obsession that so possessed (and by implication stunted) Guido Cavalcanti and Francesco Petrarca. They are dubbed cases of "lyric stubbornness" and are set up as foils to Dante. Only Dante, by virtue of his book's opening to narrative, with its projection of a future, defers disclosure and preserves the mystery of what, according to Harrison, the lyric's epiphanic insistence is bent on making manifest.

A kindred reading of the *Vita nuova* (making explicit reference to Harrison's treatment) as fundamentally about overcoming "poetic solipsism" is proposed by María Rosa Menocal. "Above all, the *Vita nuova*, the story so charmingly called the 'New Life,' is in fact the story of the death – the purposeful and necessary death – for Dante of the old ways of reading and writing, the old kind of Literature, that had proved so disappointing." What Dante would have rejected by this account, and what in any case has become a motive of rejection in our day, is the fact that "the greatest obsession of troubadour poetry is itself."[16] This self-reflexive, essentially lyrical structure is what Menocal and Harrison alike reject, claiming that in doing so they are following Dante's cues.

I argue that Harrison has vastly underestimated the absolutely fundamental and perduring, the original and life-affirming, role of the lyric mode in Dante's inspiration as a writer. The acknowledged lyricism of the *Paradiso* is read by Harrison as part of Dante's falling away from the authentic encounter registered in the *Vita nuova* into a more conventional

[15] My critical "Note" on the book appears in *Rivista di studi italiani* 6/2 (1988): 78–82.
[16] María Rosa Menocal, *Writing in Dante's Cult of Truth: From Borges to Boccaccio* (Durham, NC: Duke University Press, 1991). Quotations from p. 18 and p. 22.

and inevitably falsifying form of language. But I maintain that Beatrice, as the phenomenon of transcendence that Harrison so convincingly shows she was for Dante, is possible only by the instrumentality of the lyric, specifically by virtue of its powers to express registers of personal experience in which subjective response and feeling are constitutive parts or aspects of objective events, not secondary and less real. Furthermore, I maintain that at the other end of the *Vita nuova*'s trajectory, at its *finis*, the narrative dimension that Dante discovers or projects is not the overcoming, but the fulfillment, of the lyric mode.[17]

Harrison endeavors to chart the trajectory of Dante's career as directed to the surpassing not only of the courtly lyric of his time, but also of the lyric mode per se, and as culminating in the emergence of "the epic alternative." I contend, in contrast, that if the narrative poetry of the *Commedia* exists to tell a story, it exists to tell it in such a way as cannot dispense with the lyrical sensibility. Instead, the *Vita nuova* owes its incomparable visionary power in great measure to the non-chronological, non-cognitive, musical, and emotional qualities of lyric that make things happen within the souls of readers. This interior theater is as much the scene of the action and is, in any case, inseparable from what happens on the narrative scene of the supposedly objective events that the book's story recounts.

These arguments will constitute a defense, in some respects, of the "revelo-centric" reading of the book that Harrison, in a word, rejects.[18] They will also constitute a certain assessment, informed especially by existential theology, of what revelation is and of how it is achieved historically and literarily. This assessment amounts to the rudiments of a hermeneutic theory of revelation.[19] Such a theory, as presented here, trains attention particularly on the lyrical dimension of religious revelation. This topic has wide-ranging application in religiously revelatory literature. It concerns what

---

[17] Teodolinda Barolini, "'Cominciandomi dal principio infino a la fine' (V.N., XXIII, 15): Forging Anti-Narrative in the Vita nuova," in *"La gloriosa donna de la mente": A Commentary on the "Vita nuova,"* ed. Vincent Moleta (Florence: Olschki, 1994), pp. 119–40, likewise argues for a dialectical *contaminatio* between lyric and narrative, resulting in narrativized lyric and lyricized (dechronologized) narrative, from the *Vita nuova* to the *Paradiso*.

[18] Such a "Singletonian," revelation-centered view is advocated very ably also by Barbara Nolan, "The Vita nuova and Richard of St. Victor's Phenomenology of Vision," *Dante Studies* 92 (1974): 35–52: "We can also confirm the function of all the visions of the *libello* as prophetic inscriptions commenting on the narrator's *historia* and predicting its issue in a final blinding revelation of beatitude" (p. 35).

[19] Similar in this regard is Paul Ricoeur, "Hérmeutique de l'idée de révélation," chapter 1 of *La révélation* (Bruxelles: Facultés Universitaires Saint Louis, 1977), pp. 15–53, trans. as "Toward a Hermeneutic of the Idea of Revelation," in *Essays in Biblical Interpretation*, ed. Lewis S. Mudge (Philadelphia: Fortress Press, 1980), pp. 73–118. However, Ricoeur's comparable theoretical inferences are drawn from analysis of the interaction of literary and legal genres in the Torah.

William Blake in his prophetic poetry calls "the Auricular Nerves of Human Life. Which is the Earth of Eden" (*The Four Zoas*, I, 18).[20] As the terms of this statement from a cultural milieu far removed from Dante's own confirm, the prophetic and revelatory powers of poetry are intimately bound up with the rapture engendered by the lyrical and musical – or, even more pertinently, the *aural* and *oracular* – qualities of poetic language. Hearing or audition, when realized in its fully poetic and sensuous potential, as well as in its intellectual resonance, can unveil human existence as a Paradise of the senses *and* of sense (or meaning). The sense of hearing opens into an attention to the wholly other that is not yet given and that is nowhere localized in space, whereas the sense of sight as it operates in vision, image, and dream tends to be circumscribed by definite, finite, locatable, concrete objects represented to a subject. Therefore, I maintain that lyric opens into a dimension of theological revelation.

Giuseppe Mazzotta, Harrison's erstwhile teacher, likewise understands the *Vita nuova*'s poetry as aiming at a kind of theological revelation. Despite their difference on this crucial issue, virtually all of the distinctive emphases of Harrison's reading can be found already in Mazzotta's essay "The Language of Poetry in the *Vita nuova*."[21] Mazzotta flags the enigmatic nature of the *Vita nuova*; "the narrative's stubborn refusal to yield its secret"; "the irreducible particularity of the oneiric experience"; Beatrice's body in its materiality and mortality; the fatal rivalry with Cavalcanti; and "the openness of the *Vita nuova*'s end," making it "the book of the future." Harrison's anti-theological reading shows up in this light as originating in Mazzotta's (and Dante's) theological vision. Ironically, the *Vita nuova*'s theological inspiration turns out to lie at the generating source of even some of the readings that are most stubbornly hostile to theology, not least Harrison's own.

The vital importance of specifically theological approaches to Dante has, in fact, made a remarkable comeback and been strongly vindicated in some of the more recent critical literature. Theology has again become the key to interpreting Dante's poetry for a new generation of scholars.[22] An earlier

---

[20] *The Complete Poetry and Prose of William Blake*, ed. David W. Erdman (Berkeley: University of California Press, 1982).

[21] Giuseppe Mazzotta, "The Language of Poetry in the *Vita nuova*," *Rivista di studi italiani* 1/1 (1983): 3–14.

[22] See especially the introduction to Vittorio Montemaggi and Matthew Treherne, eds., *Dante's "Commedia": Theology as Poetry* and, as a follow-up, Claire E. Honess and Matthew Treherne, eds., *Reviewing Dante's Theology*, 2 vols. (Bern: Peter Lang, 2018). What I baptize the "theological turn" is the subject of a separate monograph of mine in course of preparation: "Dantologies: Critical Encounters after the Theological Turn in Dante Studies." Some parts are available in preliminary form in "Religion and Representation: Dante Studies after the Theological Turn," *The Year's Work*

version of a certain core of the present work, originally written partly in reaction to Harrison's book shortly after it appeared in 1988 (as recorded in the Acknowledgments), proves to have been itself prophetic of what might be called the theological turn in Dante studies and, more broadly, of the theological turn in phenomenology. Having broached this line of inquiry in my early essay on the *Vita nuova*, I developed and applied it to a reading of the *Divine Comedy* in the more concerted and elaborated argument of *Dante's Interpretive Journey.*[23] That book already, explicitly and programmatically, makes the case for a theological turn in philosophical hermeneutics. It does so, among other ways, by absorbing deconstructive methodologies, even while contesting and reversing their typically anti-theological self-understanding. That book's invention of a "dialogue between the *Divine Comedy* and modern thought" applies Heidegger's hermeneutic phenomenology, taking it in precisely the theological direction that the Teutonic master so nervously eschewed.

Hermeneutic phenomenology has, in recent decades, been extended much further in directions receptive to religious revelation in a theological sense, notably in the work of Michel Henry, Jean-Luc Marion, Jean-Louis Chrétien, and Jean-Yves Lacoste. This "theological turn" in phenomenology entails a turn from the perhaps over-rigorous insistence on the immanence of the phenomenon to a focus on the transcendent and invisible, or even concealed, aspects of phenomena that indirectly show up as folded into them. The movement is delineated, even if with a large measure of dissent, by Dominique Janicaud in *Le tournant théologique de la phénoménologie française.*[24]

The *Vita nuova* offers one of the most enlightening exemplifications imaginable of how a theological phenomenology can be concretely incarnated in a poetic text. I undertake in what follows to elucidate exactly how the *Vita nuova* does this in light of phenomenological inquiry and hermeneutic theory. Both prove key to our comprehension of a too-little-understood mode of

---

in *Critical and Cultural Theory* 26/1 (2018): 86–105. Of special pertinence in the present context is the liturgical cast of Dante's theology, for which see Treherne's *Dante's Commedia and the Liturgical Imagination* (Berne: Peter Lang, 2020).
[23] William Franke, *Dante's Interpretive Journey* (Chicago: University of Chicago Press, 1996), Religion and Postmodernism series edited by Mark C. Taylor.
[24] Dominique Janicaud, *Le tournant théologique de la phénoménologie française* (Combas: L'Eclat, 1991). In English, see Dominique Janicaud, Jean-François Courtine, Jean-Louis Chretien, Paul Ricoeur, Michel Henry, and Jean-Luc Marion, eds., *Phenomenology and the "Theological Turn": The French Debate* (New York: Fordham University Press, 2000). A clarifying engagement with the movement is offered by J. Aaron Simmons and Bruce Ellis Benson, *The New Phenomenology: A Philosophical Introduction* (London: Bloomsbury, 2013).

"theological" revelation in literature that is indispensable for the life and perpetual renewal of our culture, especially in its highest aspirations and subtlest effects.

In these theological optics, the incomparable importance of Dante's youthful *libello* resides chiefly in its opening to view an anatomy of religious revelation as issuing from poetic composition in response to a life-transforming event. The *Vita nuova* exposes such revelation as consisting in moments of lyric inspiration and expression followed by reflection rendered in prose concerning its enabling conditions in personal existence. Dante's unique and hybrid composition is marvelously, not to say miraculously, perspicuous in showing us how this process works. The *Vita nuova* offers an invaluable model and case study for helping us to understand the nature and mysteries of divine revelation in terms of its human presuppositions in poetic making. The *Vita nuova* suggestively illustrates and opens to view this endlessly fascinating process of revelation "in the making." Dante's "little book" thereby discloses in miniature this process as it applies not least to its own most important generator text, the Bible. Opening up insight into the role of poetic making in religious revelation is the overarching purpose of the comparative analysis and reflections proposed in these pages.

Conspectus

The present exposition, according to the structure of its argument, unfolds in six steps and their corresponding chapters. It begins, following this introduction (Chapter 1), by observing the power of lyric core texts to generate narrative in the New Testament as a model of theologically revelatory literature (Chapter 2). It then apprehends this same generative logic as it operates in the *Vita nuova* and produces the work's most characteristic and uncanny effects, which are amplified through proliferating repetition and mirroring (Chapter 3). This sets up a comparative analysis of phenomenological and hermeneutic methods, a detailed countering of Harrison's theses, and a defense of the lyric as possessed of interpretive resources for revealing specific registers of human life and spirit where the divine may be encountered and expressed (Chapter 4). The same model of the generative powers of interpretation carries over into the history of the work's effects in later ages (Chapter 5) and leads finally to envisaging an original poetics of religious revelation as an existential and theological hermeneutic (Chapter 6).

The Epilogue then takes up the topic of the dream as an interpretive form of revelation, a theme which was only dealt with obliquely in the foregoing chapters. This final reflection serves to return the discussion to a crucial origin of Dante's revelatory experience in his initial dream vision. This dream, issuing in writing, in effect, initiates Dante into his poetic project and introduces him to his circle, which perhaps became something of a cult, the *fedeli d'Amore* (III. 9; cf. VII. 7; VIII. 7; XXXII. 4).

Dante's extraordinary dream in *Vita nuova*, Chapter III, together with its sequels, thus opens up another angle of vision for contemplating the implication of religious revelation in the mysteries of interpretation as realized in poetic making and transmission. Reciprocally, the literary construction of a dream text is made to reflect back on revelation's true meaning as projected from the ordinarily inaccessible depths of human existence and the psyche. Certain strange, not to say miraculous, aspects of existence turn out to be revealed with surrealistic éclat through being oneirically surfaced and then literarily refracted.

CHAPTER 2

The New Testament Model of Salvific Reminiscence

I have said before
That the past experience revived in the meaning
Is not the experience of one life only
But of many generations – not forgetting
Something that is probably quite ineffable . . .

(T. S. Eliot, "The Dry Salvages," II)

The most prominent and obvious model of autobiographical *prosimetrum* for Dante was surely Boethius's *De consolatione philosophiae* (ca. 524), seconded by Alain de Lille's twelfth-century *De planctu naturae* (1168–72) and perhaps by Brunetto Latini's *Tesoretto* (ca. 1271–72), if indeed this uncompleted work was originally designed to include prose passages elucidating its more difficult verses.[1] One might also bring the *Vita nuova* into comparison with Metchthild of Magdeburg's *The Flowing Light of the Godhead* (*Das fliessende Licht der Gottheit*) and Marguerite Porete's *The Mirror of Simple Souls* (*Le mirouer des simples ames*) since all are hybrid compositions of poetry and prose.[2] Both late-thirteenth-century female mystics, moreover conjugate oracular revelations in poetry with prose statements of an empirical, autobiographical "I" in highly prophetic tones that illuminate how Dante's exploitation of the prosimetron form turns it into a type of theological revelation.

Nevertheless, in a more fundamental way, it is primarily the Bible that Dante is imitating in his book on the "new life."[3] A new life

---

[1] Stefano Carrai, "Introduzione" to Brunetto Latini, *Poesie* (Turin: Einaudi, 2016), pp. x–xiv.

[2] Peter Dronke, "The Poetic and the Empirical 'I'," chapter IV of *Verse with Prose from Petronius to Dante: The Art and Scope of the Mixed Form* (Cambridge, MA: Harvard University Press, 1994), pp. 95–114.

[3] The fundamental importance of the Bible as prosimetric model for Dante's youthful literary masterpiece has been emphasized by Zygmunt Barański. In "'Lascio cotale trattato ad altro chiosatore': Form, Literature, and Exegesis in Dante's *Vita nova*," in *Dantean Dialogues: Engaging with the Legacy of Amilcare Iannucci*, ed. Margaret Kilgour and Elena Lombardi (Toronto: University of Toronto Press, 2013), Barański maintains that "the Bible is without doubt the *Vita nova*'s primary

beyond death can be sought on the basis of the promises of Christian revelation and may even be deliciously foretasted through the delectation of Christian literature. The reading of this literature necessarily begins from the verses and narratives of the Bible itself together with their often embedded hymns and canticles. The New Testament is the eminent and – for Dante – inescapable model of the combined use of prose and poetry, or of narrative and lyric, for the rememoration of an individual in whom divinity has been revealed and in whom new life is found after an event of death-glorification. The canticles – notably the *Magnificat*, the *Benedictus*, the *Nunc dimittis* – and the *Pater noster*, the "Lord's Prayer," are perhaps the most conspicuous examples of poetic compositions finding narrative settings in the synoptic Gospels and, in important ways, setting the tone for the whole story. Their use in the liturgy also serves to underscore their independent life as poems or prayers for recitation, thereby publicly shaping a community's collective worship and spiritual life.[4]

The beatitudes (to hew close to Dante's central thematics), as pronounced by Jesus at the opening of his Sermon on the Mount (Matthew 5: 1–12), are themselves intensely lyrical in form, as well as in inspiration and effect. They condense the whole thrust of the Christian life into edifying images that aim to pierce the heart profoundly with their urgent ethical demands and their call to holiness.

[3] Blessed are the poor in spirit: for theirs is the kingdom of heaven.
[4] Blessed are they that mourn: for they shall be comforted.
[5] Blessed are the meek: for they shall inherit the earth.
[6] Blessed are they which do hunger and thirst after righteousness: for they shall be filled.
[7] Blessed are the merciful: for they shall obtain mercy.
[8] Blessed are the pure in heart: for they shall see God.
[9] Blessed are the peacemakers: for they shall be called the children of God.
[10] Blessed are they which are persecuted for righteousness' sake: for theirs is the kingdom of heaven.

source" and proposes re-visioning "the special relationship between God's book and Dante's *libro*" (pp. 19–20). Starting from the phrase "the book of memory" in the *incipit* of the *Vita nuova*, Barański finds a key to "the *libello*'s fundamental dependence on Scripture" in Augustine's *De civitate Dei* 18, 35, 1, which interprets Malachi's *librum memoriae* as signifying the New Testament (p. 26). Barański develops similar theses also in "The Roots of Dante's Plurilingualism: 'Hybridity' and Language in the *Vita nova*," in *Dante's Plurilingualism, Authority, Knowledge, Subjectivity*, ed. S. Fortuna, M. Gragnolati, and J. Trabant (Oxford: Legenda, 2010), pp. 98–121, especially pp. 111ff.
[4] P. Mauro Láconi, *La preghiera di Gesù e la liturgia cristiana, nei vangeli sinottici* (Rome: Associazione Biblica Italiana, 1985) contains pertinent reflections on the re-deployment of lyric traditions in the Gospel narratives.

The beatitudes are seminal texts for Jesus's teaching and for the entire Christian vision of living with God. They must surely count in determining the semantic field for Dante's sense of the bliss and blessedness conferred on him by his personal beatifier. They lend themselves, furthermore, to liturgical recitation and serve as kernels inviting supplemental elaboration in the form of illustrative narratives or parables and edifying doctrinal discourses. In this regard, they could serve as models for Dante's lyrics concerning his own being blessed through Beatrice. As with the biblical beatitudes, Dante's beatitude is first distilled into lyrical verses and is then decanted into the *Vita nuova*'s prose narratives and commentaries. There is at least a logical and a literary rationale for this order of precedence, whether or not it holds in a strictly chronological sense as well, as it demonstrably does for other biblical texts. In the New Testament's own model, the Old Testament, the *incipit* of Moses's Song in the book of Exodus stands as such a narrative-generating liturgical core text:

> I will sing unto the LORD, for he hath triumphed gloriously:
>   horse and rider hath he thrown into the sea. (Exodus 15: 1–21)

> ("Cantemus Domino: gloriose enim magnificatus est,
>   equum et ascensorem dejecit in mare.")

These verses can be shown by critical textual archeology to have preceded the narrative context in which they occur. We cannot but imagine this song to have existed first in a presumably liturgical mode. On the evidence of linguistic and stylistic analysis, this sequence of verses appears to be among the oldest materials of the Pentateuch and verisimilarly the generative source for much, if not all, of the Exodus narrative. Something equivalent could be said about numerous other passages, for example, Deborah's Song (Judges 5: 1–31) and the corresponding narrative in the book of Judges.[5]

Beyond what can be learned through objective historical research and direct analysis of documents, there is also a literary logic to this order progressing from poetry to prose in the evolution of tradition. There are mnemonic reasons why metrical forms of written expression come first in the literary history of a nation, a phenomenon that is widely manifest across cultures. This goes for verse in ritual or in magical formulas, whether

---

[5] Other examples include 1 Samuel 2: 1–10 (Hannah's Prayer); Isaiah 38: 10–20; 44: 23–28; Jeremiah 15: 15–25, Daniel 2: 20–23; 3: 26–45 (Prayer of Azariah) and 3: 52–90 (Song of the Three Young Men); Jonah 2: 2–9; Tobit 13 (Tobit's Prayer of Rejoicing). See Étienne Charpentier, *Pour lire l'Ancien Testament* (Paris: Cerf, 1993).

in the Old German *Merseburger Zaubersprüche* or in the "oracle bones" and the inscriptions on tortoise carapaces that record the earliest writing, used for divination, in pre-dynastic China.[6] A narrative language of culture that can ground a certain sense of nationhood originates first in versified forms similarly in the Homeric epics of archaic Greece and in the Vedas of ancient India. Most ancient in the latter are the *Samhita* – the prayers, benedictions, and mantras in which letters are "joined together" (*sam*, together + *hita*, put) into verses. Dante himself already, at the outset of Book II of *De vulgari eloquentia*, explicitly theorizes the priority of poetry to prose in the development and cultivation of a literary language:

> But, because prose writers seem mainly to have received it [the illustrious Italian vernacular] from the ones who bind it into verse, and because what has been bound into verse seems to remain as a model for prose writers (but not the reverse) – which seems to accord a certain primacy – we first disentangle what meters the illustrious vernacular uses in poetry, following the order of treatment that we promised at the end of the first book. (*De vulgari eloquentia* II, i, 1)

> (Sed quia ipsum [latinum vulgari illustre] prosaycantes ab avientibus magis accipiunt, et quia quod avietum est prosaycantibus permanere videtur exemplar, et non e converso – que quendam videntur prebere primatum – primo secundum quod metricum est ipsum carminemus ordine, pertractantes illo quem in fini primi libri polluximus.)

The progressive narrativization of verse specifically in the refashioning and transmutation of biblical poetry into epic narration is reconstructed by Robert Alter.[7] He describes a natural evolution starting from poetry, as the original form of literary expression, and moving to prose as its extension and elaboration. A section of *The Art of Biblical Poetry* entitled "From Line to Story" traces the metamorphosis of literary stem cells from the single poetic verse into the fully elaborated prose narrative. Alter pays attention particularly to "the narrative development of metaphor" and finds a similar developmental dynamic at work in other aspects of poetic language. He emphasizes how narrative can be inherent in and arise from the poetic functions of focusing, heightening, or concretizing through the form of repetition characteristic of biblical verse, namely, parallelism.

---

[6] The magical chants of the *Merseburger Zaubersprüche* were first published by Jacob Grimm in 1841. For oracle bones, see David N. Keightley, *These Bones Shall Rise Again: Selected Writings on Early China* (Albany: State University of New York Press, 2014).
[7] Robert Alter, *The Art of Biblical Poetry* (New York: Basic Books, 1985).

In somewhat more technical terms, Alter explains that "what we very frequently find in biblical verse is the emergence of the syntagmatic from the paradigmatic: as the poet offers an approximate equivalent for an image or idea he has just invoked, he also begins, by the very logic of specification or intensification of the system in which he works, to push the initial image or idea into action, moving from one image to another that is temporally subsequent to and implied by the first."[8] This dynamic of expansion and externalization inherent within the poem manifests itself in the form of prose accretions that arise from and accumulate around verse seeds or kernels: these outgrowths culminate finally in full-blown narrative elaboration.

Poetic core texts recording something of the transformative intensity of an originating event of the divine generate a plethora of narrative texts that, after the fact, help explain the sense of the miraculous that poetry is most apt initially to register and express. Among the oldest residues preserved within the New Testament are doxologies and hymns discovered by using the instruments of Source Criticism (*Quellenkritik*) and Form Criticism (*Formgeschichte*, literally "history of form"). Critical study has been able to isolate verse forms embedded within the earliest extant Christian texts, particularly in certain Pauline and pseudo-Pauline epistles. Most notably, verses 6 to 11 of Philippians, chapter 2, comprise a primitive Christian canticle that pre-dated and was incorporated into the epistle:

> [5]Let this mind be in you, which was also in Christ Jesus:
> [6]*Who, being in the form of God, thought it not robbery to be equal to God [or: thought not divinity a thing to be grasped:]*
> [7]*But made himself of no reputation, and took upon him the form of a servant, and was made in the likeness of men:*
> [8]*And being found in fashion as a man, he humbled himself, and became obedient unto death, even the death of the cross.*
> [9]*Wherefore God also hath highly exalted him, and given him a name which is above every name:*
> [10]*That at the name of Jesus, every knee should bow, of things in heaven, and things in earth, and things under the earth;*
> [11]*And that every tongue should confess that Jesus Christ is Lord, to the glory of God the Father.* (Philippians 2: 6–11)

> ([5]Hoc enim sentite in vobis, quod et in Christo Jesu:
> [6] *qui cum in forma Dei esset, non rapinam arbitratus est esse se æqualem Deo:*
> [7] *sed semetipsum exinanivit, formam servi accipiens, in similitudinem hominum factus, et habitu inventus ut homo.*

---

[8] Alter, *The Art of Biblical Poetry*, chapter 2, pp. 37, 39.

⁸ *Humiliavit semetipsum factus obediens usque ad mortem, mortem autem crucis.*

⁹ *Propter quod et Deus exaltavit illum, et donavit illi nomen, quod est super omne nomen:*

¹⁰ *ut in nomine Jesu omne genu flectatur cælestium, terrestrium et infernorum,*

¹¹ *et omnis lingua confiteatur, quia Dominus Jesus Christus in gloria est Dei Patris.*)

The koine Greek is also important in this case for recapturing the original rhythms and sonorities of the hymn:

⁵ τοῦτο φρονεῖτε ἐν ὑμῖν ὃ καὶ ἐν Χριστῷ Ἰησοῦ,

⁶ ὃς ἐν μορφῇ θεοῦ ὑπάρχων οὐχ ἁρπαγμὸν ἡγήσατο τὸ εἶναι ἴσα θεῷ,

⁷ ἀλλὰ ἑαυτὸν ἐκένωσεν μορφὴν δούλου λαβών, ἐν ὁμοιώματι ἀνθρώπων γενόμενος · καὶ σχήματι εὑρεθεὶς ὡς ἄνθρωπος

⁸ ἐταπείνωσεν ἑαυτὸν γενόμενος ὑπήκοος μέχρι θανάτου, θανάτου δὲ σταυροῦ ·

⁹ διὸ καὶ ὁ θεὸς αὐτὸν ὑπερύψωσεν, καὶ ἐχαρίσατο αὐτῷ τὸ ὄνομα τὸ ὑπὲρ πᾶν ὄνομα,

¹⁰ ἵνα ἐν τῷ ὀνόματι Ἰησοῦ πᾶν γόνυ κάμψῃ ἐπουρανίων καὶ ἐπιγείων καὶ καταχθονίων,

¹¹ καὶ πᾶσα γλῶσσα ἐξομολογήσηται ὅτι κύριος Ἰησοῦς Χριστὸς εἰς δόξαν θεοῦ πατρός.

Such poetic sequences and images gave the faith community its first capability of verbalizing the extraordinary, life-transforming experience of the miraculous individual who was the founder of its collective life – Jesus of Nazareth. The followers who remained after Jesus's death believed that he lived in glory on the right hand of God the Father, as stated in Peter's sermon on Pentecost in Acts 2: 14–36 (compare also 7: 56). They believed that they themselves were living a new life made possible for them because their lives had been touched and transformed by Jesus. The story of their encounters with Jesus before his death and resurrection/ascension, as recorded in the canonical Gospel narratives appearing some forty to sixty years later, was elaborated subsequently out of an assortment of memories. Composition of the narratives was guided by controlling images such as the pastoral Good Shepherd or the apocalyptic Son of Man. Particularly the binary oppositions between high and low, abasement and exaltation, are fixed in the lyrical and liturgical formulas of this canticle. It seems likely that the narratives could be produced in the first place only on the basis of paradigms like the trope of *kenosis* or "self-emptying," which is, in effect, a self-humbling or self-abasement. The narrative sequences or "syntagms"

of the New Testament should perhaps be seen chiefly as further developments elaborating on such lyric paradigms.[9]

Along similar lines, the Resurrection and the Ascension, upon careful
formal analysis, turn out to be readable as two complementary faces or
symbolic idioms for the same event of glorification-exaltation. Jesus's new
and glorified life is imaged convertibly in terms of a rising up or an
ascending above. This double-image, accordingly, would have generated
two different clusters of narratives condensed into images and expressing
this never adequately representable experience of the risen and glorified
Lord. When Dante, in his premonitory fantasy, or "imaginazione," of her
death, envisions Beatrice's ascension in a "nebuletta bianchissima" ("most
white little cloud") escorted by a multitude of the heavenly host singing
"Hosanna in excelsis" (XXIII. 7), he has in fact made recourse to one of
these image clusters familiar from Mark 11: 9–10.

Not only do tropes, or what I have just called lyric paradigms, seem to
have first enabled the revelation of Jesus as glorified Lord to be verbalized:
they also function as the enabling conditions of the very perception of the
event. And they do so, moreover, in a different, more musical, non-
conceptual or ultra-conceptual key, one that operates anteriorly to the
binary structures of significance that have already been described. The
advent of Jesus as the Christ in the lives of the first Christians in the Easter
experience was prepared for and made possible by an assortment of figures
or types contained in certain verses of the Jewish Scriptures that suddenly,
in the light of Easter, came to be understood in a new way as having been
fulfilled by Jesus. This literature lived in the minds of the faithful through
regular public celebration of the liturgy, as well as in private devotional
practices, and it can be seen to have pre-programmed, pervasively and
decisively, the story of Jesus that later came to be told in the Gospels.

The weaving of narratives around these core prophetic-poetic texts
begins right from the tradition that a Messiah for Israel would come out
of Bethlehem, a fact that counts as remarkable, since the town was
otherwise not particularly significant. Matthew 2: 6 cites this tradition:
"And thou, Bethlehem, in the land of Juda, are not least among the princes
of Juda: for out of thee shall come a Governor, that shall rule my people
Israel." Matthew is reproducing verbatim the prophecy in Micah 5: 2
foretelling that Jesus was to be born in Bethlehem.

---

[9] The distinction between the syntagmatic and the paradigmatic that is so crucial to structural
linguistics as practiced and applied by Roman Jakobson is based on Ferdinand de Saussure, *Cours
de linguistique générale*, ed. Charles Bally and Albert Sechehaye (Paris: Payot, [1916] 1955), pp. 170–75.

The Psalms, from which so many of the prophecies fulfilled by Jesus according to the Gospels are drawn, were Israel's hymnal. The twenty-second Psalm, for example – "My God, my God, Why hast thou forsaken me?" – is the text on Jesus's lips in the Gospel tradition just before his expiration. Together with this hymnic poetry, the often intensely lyrical (and mnemonic) poetry of the prophets furnished the language of an expectation within which alone the whole Christ event could become intelligible, and so could significantly occur.

Following in this tradition, it is not surprising that the earliest formulations in language on the part of Christians of what had occurred in the Christ event should have been cast into lyrical forms – like the canticle in Philippians 2 – in order to be recited in the liturgy of the primitive Church. The wonder and exaltation experienced by the Church at its origin was expressed in poetry, and this poetic and more specifically lyrical dimension would remain indispensable to the experience, even when it came to be narrativized. This ordering entailed that the narrative of Jesus's life and ministry would inevitably be, at the very same time, a narrativization of the mystical experience within the Church community of the risen Lord. The Lord's presence in liturgical song would inspire and animate the narrative reconstruction of events.

The story of the disciples on the road to Emmaus after the Crucifixion is emblematic and eloquent in this regard. The wayfarers in the Gospel According to Luke recognize the apparent stranger accompanying them as Jesus only at the Eucharistic moment of the *breaking of bread* (Luke 24: 13–35). This is a hint that Jesus may actually be recognized as Lord and God only in the Holy Sacrament and specifically through its employment of the words of the liturgy, in which he can be imagined and sung as present in his glory even long after his physical presence on earth. This liturgical, lyrical celebration in the Eucharist makes an original experience of him possible – and for many concerned (all besides Jesus's direct disciples), this would be the first and perhaps the only type of experience possible, barring some exceptional miracle. Such liturgical experience, moreover, can be the basis for further experience of Christ revealed as working through his Spirit in acts of charity performed by the Church as his body.

Some such posterior re-experiencing and reformulation of events in the light shed by Easter seems to be alluded to and even to be authorized by Jesus's promises in the Gospels to his disciples that the Holy Spirit will inspire their memory and establish the record of him and his words. "These things have I spoken unto you, being yet present with you. But the Comforter, which is the Holy Ghost, whom the Father will send in my name, he shall teach you all things, and bring all things to your remembrance, whatsoever I have said unto you" (John 14: 25–26). In saying this, Jesus implies that the disciples' actual memories of the past need not be exclusively relied on, nor even necessarily be privileged, in reconstructing the story of his words and deeds.

The narratives of the Gospels, then, may be seen as generated in good part by inspired retrospective remembrance. Of prime importance here are the lyrical crystallizations that first precipitated, linguistically and conceptually, the forms for apprehending the extraordinary significance of the person Jesus of Nazareth. Only when the evangelist (and, behind him, the evangelical community) had grasped in faith who Jesus *is* could the account of who he *was*, in an historical life lived on earth, be worked out in narrative terms. This means that who Jesus is *for them* presently, as experienced in the lyrical transports of poetry performed in liturgy and in the creedal Symbol and in the sacraments, as well as in Christian works of love, is an indispensable key to the disciples' recognition of anything that is recounted about Jesus in the Scriptures as truly revealed. Revelation has to take place essentially *in the present* as the moment of living truth.

The nativity scenes in Luke and Matthew provide a provocative case study of the way in which narrative is prone to spring up around figural cores and poetic epitomes. The Gospel According to Luke's story of the virgin birth seems to have been in part an accident engendered by (mis)translation of the Hebrew word *almah* for "young girl" by the Greek word for "virgin" or "maiden" (παρθένος, *parthenos*) in the Septuagint, the Greek translation of the Hebrew Bible, which was used by Luke. The word "virgin," in its connotative suggestiveness, already contains in itself a poetic universe – what can appropriately be called a "myth."[10] And Luke's whole story might well be thought to have originated simply as a sort of Midrash in narrative form expanding upon this mistranslated verse from Isaiah 7: 14.[11] Whether or not this is actually the case, its plausibility is suggestive of how prose narratives can develop from, and elaborate on, linguistic hints contained in lyrical hymns and oracles.

---

[10] I use the term "myth" to mean the representation of a fundamental condition of existence in a sense informed by the theology of Rudolf Bultmann, *Theologie des Neuen Testaments*, 9th ed. (Tübingen: J. C. B. Mohr, [1948] 1984). In English, see especially *New Testament and Mythology and Other Basic Writings*, ed. S. Ogden (Philadelphia: Fortress Press, 1984).

[11] See Raymond E. Brown, *The Birth of the Messiah: A Commentary on the Infancy Narratives in the Gospels of Matthew and Luke*, new ed. (New York: Doubleday, 1999), pp. 143–53. I treat this passage in greater detail in *The Revelation of Imagination: From the Bible and Homer through Virgil and Augustine to Dante* (Evanston: Northwestern University Press, 2015), pp. 33–34.

This process of *a posteriori* narrativization of poetic prophecy becomes almost explicit in the Gospel According to John when the evangelist cites a passage from the book of the prophet Zechariah 9: 9 about Zion's king coming to Jerusalem, riding on an ass:

> And Jesus when he had found a young ass, sat thereon; as it is written, "Fear not, daughter of Sion: behold thy King cometh, sitting upon an ass's colt." These things understood not his disciples at the first: but when Jesus was glorified then remembered they that these things were written of him, and that they had done these things unto him. (John 12: 14–16)

Although a sufficiently ambiguous veil remains drawn between remembering and inventing, John nevertheless exposes unmistakably the tendency of elaboration in narrative prose to take core verse texts – here a prophetic revelation in the form of an oracle – as their point of departure. Whatever the actual event may or may not have been, clearly its precise significance was imposed retrospectively under the influence of the prophecy avowedly recognized as such only later.

Thus, Gospel writing must be sharply distinguished from historiography because its primary purpose is not to record facts, but to witness to faith. Even when it invokes the rhetoric of factuality, as in the miracle stories, the facts are presented always as signs, and their meaning is given only within a horizon of belief. The Gospels are really about a miracle of faith within the lives of individuals in the Christian community, and only when they are taken as such is the outward "history" that they tell susceptible of being comprehended.

Dante, of course, had no idea of the Gospel stories such as I have delineated here with the help of modern synoptic criticism and literary analysis. Nevertheless, the evangelical model was unavoidable for any Christian author writing about new life, and Dante himself insists on the association of Beatrice with Christ. He does so most ostentatiously in *Vita nuova* XXIV, with its procession positioning Beatrice as coming after Guido Cavalcanti's Giovanna in the place of "that John" (the Baptist) who cries in the wilderness: prepare the way of the Lord ("Ego vox clamantis in deserto: parate viam Domini," John 1: 23). But also in *Vita nuova* XXIII, the apocalyptic signs announcing Christ's death are evoked as prefiguring Beatrice's death. In fact, this parallel is insinuated and developed all through the *libello* in subtle and incidental fashion. My suggestion is that certain principles of hagiography most apparent in the most intensively studied hagiographical documents of all, those of the New Testament, are operative in Dante's hagiographical work as well.[12]

The basis for such an analogy lies in a common existential condition. One's whole life can miraculously take on new meaning by one's loving a certain individual who then becomes no longer accessible in the flesh, at least not as an individual body. Still, this person may be found to give a new significance to one's life on an ongoing basis indefinitely into the future. Works recording such experience need to express the ecstatic awakening and accession of life communicated by this person's presence and memory, and for this purpose poetry is paramount. A chronicle of facts alone about such persons could not reveal their extraordinary significance. The "biographical" narratives subsequently elaborated are keyed to texts that do not just state facts; instead, they convey figuratively and lyrically the meaning of a new life.

The poetic and especially the lyrical heightening of life must first capture the extraordinary significance of the individual in question and the impact of his or her event on the lives of witnesses, including the life of the witness who becomes the writer. This existentially verified, lived miracle, which is the presupposition for beginning the story, must first be cast into a symbolic form "lyrically" felt to embody and communicate this new and heightened life.[13] Transposing this figural/lyrical core into a temporal dimension of narrative, the book begins, then, appropriately, with a miracle story or an account of a dream vision. Such is the annunciation of the angel to Mary, or the apparition of Beatrice to Dante.

Corollaries from the *Convivio*

As a corroborating corollary, it is well worth noting that Dante again subtly evokes the Gospel as his model in his next book – which happens likewise to be composed of poetry and prose. The prose, moreover, again stands – now

---

[12] In a different way, this is suggested also by Mario Pazzaglia, "La *Vita nuova* fra agiografia e letteratura," *Letture classensi* 6 (1977): 189–210, and by Vittore Branca, "Poetica del rinnovamento e tradizione agiografica nella 'Vita nuova,'" in *Studi in onore di Italo Siciliano* (Florence: Olschki, 1966), pp. 123–48.

[13] William Paden, ed., *Medieval Lyric: Genres in Historical Context* (Urbana: University of Illinois Press, 2000) evidences something of this potential of medieval lyric in the Latin, Troubadour, Old French, and Italian traditions on which Dante principally drew. Maureen Barry McCann Boulton, *The Song in the Story: Lyric Insertions in French Narrative Fiction, 1200–1400* (Philadelphia: University of Pennsylvania Press, 1993) focuses specifically on northern France in the thirteenth and fourteenth centuries and on lyric interludes in narrative in which song is inserted into story. Dante's originality in his intensification of the revelatory capacities of lyric as deployed within prose narrative emerges all the more strongly from these comparisons.

explicitly – in the "service" ("servigio") of the poetry (*Convivio* I. v. 5–7). The prose is now figured, in a well-garnished image, as explanatory "bread" ("pane") served up to accompany the "meat" ("vivanda") of the songs or *canzoni* in order to make the latter more digestible (*Convivio* I. i. 11–18). There are already several recognizable New Testament motifs folded into these metaphors.

Dante promises that this new cultural barley bread of the vernacular in his *Convivio* will satiate thousands and yet leave him still with overflowing baskets ("Questo sarà quello pane orzato del quale si satolleranno migliaia, e a me ne soverchieranno le sporte piene," I. xiii. 12). His images here implicitly evoke Luke 9: 11–17 recounting the miraculous multiplication of the five loaves and two fish, in which five thousand were satiated and after which twelve teeming "baskets" (echoed by Dante's "sporte piene") of fragments were gathered up.

Switching metaphors from nurture to light, and blending in another Gospel motif, the evangelical overtones of Dante's entire poetic and cultural project resound in the *Convivio*'s annunciation of the new light of a rising sun that is destined to replace the old one, which is now setting. "This will be a new light, a new sun, which will rise where the old one sets and will give light to those who are in shadows and in darkness because of the worn-out sun that does not shine for them" ("Questo sarà luce nuova, sole nuovo, lo quale surgerà là dove l'usato tramonterà, e darà lume a coloro che sono in tenebre e in oscuritade per lo usato sole che a loro non luce," *Convivio* I. xiii. 12).[14] This new light and life of an emerging culture, like Dante's new personal life in relation to Beatrice, is decked out with allusions to and echoes of the Gospels. Both of the liturgical songs *Benedictus* and *Nunc dimittis* taken from the Gospel According to Luke, respectively Luke 1: 68–80 and 2: 29–32, portray the new birth of the Messiah as the rising of a new light. They reflect their light on Dante's proposal for a new vernacular culture, transposing it into a New Testament key promising altogether new life.

A luminous verse from the *Benedictus* contains Zechariah's prophecy of salvation that begins with the birth of his son, who will become John the Baptist and go before the Lord to prepare his way. It rings out in an exultant announcement: "the dayspring from on high hath visited us, to give light to them that sit in darkness and in the shadow of death" ("in quibus visitavit nos, oriens ex alto: illuminare his qui in tenebris et in

---

[14] I quote and translate from *Convivio*, ed. Caesare Vasoli, in *Opere minori* (Milan: Ricciardi, 1988), vol. 5, tome I, pt. II.

umbra mortis sedent," Luke 1: 78–79). Using similar imagery, another lyrical passage in verse from the *Nunc dimittis*, known liturgically also as "Simeon's Canticle," records the words of Simeon, a devout man waiting in the temple in Jerusalem to see Israel's salvation in the person of the Messiah. He was not to see death before seeing the Christ, according to a prophecy vouchsafed him by the Holy Spirit. When Jesus is presented in the temple for circumcision, Simeon takes the baby up into his arms and declares:

> Lord, now lettest thou thy servant depart in peace, according to thy word:
>   For mine eyes have seen thy salvation,
>   Which thou hast prepared before the face of all people;
>   A light to lighten the Gentiles, and the glory of thy people Israel.
>   (Luke 2: 29–32)
>
> (Nunc dimittis servum tuum, Domine, secundum verbum tuum in pace:
>   Quia viderunt oculi mei salutare tuum
>   Quod parasti ante faciem omnium populorum:
>   Lumen ad revelationem gentium, et gloriam plebis tuae Israel.)

Noteworthy for the thematic attunement of the text in the present context, and for imagining how it might have sounded to Dante's ears, is not only the use of "salutare" in Latin to mean "salvation" but also the use of the word "revelation" in the final verse of the Vulgate version, literally: "A light of revelation to the gentile peoples."

It can hardly be overlooked, then, that Dante uses Christian evangelical imagery and pronouncements in order to introduce his own program for a new life – the dawn of a new form of existence. He understands this new life as a kind of fulfillment of Christian messianic promises, but also as inaugurating some unprecedented, or at least as yet unexploited, innovations in the human ways of being and loving – as well as of writing lyric poetry. He presents the writing of lyric poetry in a revelatory combination with autobiographical narrative prose. The role of the experience of the singular individual, both in the subjective register of lyrical expression and in the actual facts of his existence recorded in prose, is discovered here in a revolutionary guise that serves to announce and usher in the modern age.

The "new sun" ("sole nuovo") is presumably the vernacular language that Dante proclaims is now replacing the old, worn-out sun of the Latin language and its culture. A new culture based on the rediscovery of Aristotle's philosophy in its full amplitude brings the natural light of reason to bear in illuminating the world that is now discovered in its undissimilated secularity.[15] Within this new horizon, Dante's *Convivio* articulates a Neo-Platonic philosophy that integrates Aristotle into its total vision of the cosmos from the very beginning of the treatise (*Convivio* I. i. 1) with the words "all humans desire by nature to know" ("tutti li uomini naturalmente desiderano di sapere"), taken expressly from the *incipit* to Aristotle's *Metaphysics* (Book I, chapter 1, 980a).

And yet, Dante sees the new day dawning for human reason as the fulfillment of evangelical promise rather than as its rejection and supplanting. The new life or "renaissance," literally "rebirthing," of the world is envisaged by Dante in the frame of the New Testament, with its promise of new life for all. Dante's inauguration of modernity is predicated on a new dispensation for revealed religion rather than on a discarding of it. The revolutionary ferment of the modern age is born from the seeds of theological revelation as Dante directly experiences and re-imagines it, beginning from his *Vita nuova*.

---

[15] Sonia Gentile, *L'uomo aristotelico alle origini della letteratura italiana,* preface by Peter Dronke (Rome: Carracci, 2005), renders this received view more complex and rich.

CHAPTER 3

From Appearing and Imagining to Revealing through Interpreting: The Vita nuova's Hermeneutics of Witness

In that open field
If you do not come too close, if you do not come too close,
On a summer midnight, you can hear the music
Of the weak pipe and the little drum
And see them dancing around the bonfire
The association of man and woman
In daunsinge, signifying matrimonie –
A dignified and commodiois sacrament.

(T. S. Eliot, "East Coker," I)

The *Vita nuova* tells the story of how the lyrics it includes came to be written as a result of Dante's encounters with Beatrice and their aftermath in his life. It presents itself as a prose narrative woven around lyric cores and as commentary on the lyric poems. The commentary becomes explicit in the glossatological sections, notably the so-called "divisioni," which some critics ever since Boccaccio have been at pains to explain – or edit – away.[1] Such *divisioni*, nevertheless, are not unprecedented and can be better understood as to their function in light of models such as Catalan grammarian Raimon Vidal's prose tractate on grammar, *Las razos de trobar* (ca 1200), which employs such divisions for commentary on existing exemplary poems divided into parts for purposes of analysis.[2] The presentation of poems along with the lives or *vidas* of the poets was well known in

---

[1] See Jason M. Houston, "'Maraviglierannosi molti': Boccaccio's *Editio* of the *Vita nuova*," *Dante Studies* 126 (2008): 89–107. This history is recapitulated and analyzed by Antonio D'Andrea, "La struttura della *Vita nuova*: Le divisioni delle rime," in *Il nome della storia: Studi e ricerche di storia e letteratura* (Naples: Liguori, 1982), pp. 25–58. Steven Botterill defends the *divisioni* as a vital analytic component showing form to be essential to content in "'Però la divisione non si fa se non per aprire la sentenzia de la cosa divisa' (*Vita nuova* XIV, 13): The *Vita nuova* as Commentary," in "*La gloriosa donna de la mente*": *A Commentary on the "Vita nuova*," ed. Vincent Moleta (Florence: Olschki, 1994), pp. 61–76.

[2] See Elizabeth Wilson Poe, *From Poetry to Prose in Old Provençal: The Emergence of the Razos, the Vidas, and Razos De Trobar* (Birmingham, AL: Summa Publications, 1984), especially chapter 5 on the *Vita nuova*. Scholastic exegesis, of course, also commonly practiced such detailed division in the analysis of texts.

Troubadour tradition and an obvious precedent for Dante's autobiographical framing of his poems in the prose sections of the *Vita nuova*.

The pre-existence of the poems with respect to the prose text of the *Vita nuova* is thus presupposed by the text itself, which often specifies the junctures of time in the past when the poems came to be written.[3] Taking the book on its own terms, then, the lyrics would form the first core of verbalization of Dante's miraculous experience. All of the various matters broached in the prose sections cluster around and attend upon the poems. The prose *ragioni* or "explanations" purportedly interpolate the "real life" situations surrounding each lyric and form the connecting tissue of a plot leading from one episode to the next. It is conceivable, however, and perhaps even likely, at least in certain instances, that these prose *ragioni* are indeed literally "rationalizations" and expansions of what the lyrics imply or project – rather than being actual memories of things that happened as they are said to have happened. This is exactly what has been found to be the case for the *razos* on the lives of the Troubadours.[4] Far from being rhetorical ornaments for the story, the lyrics would, then, in important respects, generate it. Of course, the prose, in turn, gives its own spin to the antecedent facts recorded in the lyrics, recontextualizing and repurposing the poems according to its own story line.[5]

Poetic Epiphany as Life-Transforming Theophany

The event of Beatrice conveyed in the *Vita nuova* is something that could never even in principle be adequately related by mere prose as a sequence of even quite extraordinary facts. Encountering Beatrice is inspirational and induces in Dante an otherwise unattainable state: it leads to and issues in the writing of poetry that bears witness to his total transformation. The poetry that Beatrice inspires – or at least the fact that encountering her is inspirational and is irresistibly expressed in poetry – underlies all that can be recounted about her as Dante's *beatrice*, literally his "beatifier." This epithet, which coincides with his lady's proper name used as a common noun beginning with a lower-case letter, is central to and even epitomizes

---

[3] Toby Levers, "The Image of Authorship in the Final Chapter of the *Vita nuova,*" *Italian Studies* LXII (2002): 5–19 meticulously collates the tenses of Dante's statements in prose and poetry, as narrator and as commentator (glossator) and as practicing poet, underlining how only the final chapter brings the work's fragmented authorial voices together into unity.

[4] Lucia Lazzerini, *Letteratura medievale in lingua d'oc* (Modena: Mucchi, 2001).

[5] Teodolinda Barolini, ed., *Dante's Lyric Poetry: Poems of Youth and of the Vita nuova* (Toronto: University of Toronto Press, 2014) investigates in detail and with ingenuity Dante's re-managing of his lyrics in the *libello* in comparison with their presumable original forms.

the book's "argument." We have already dwelt on the capital importance of
Dante's designating Beatrice as his "beatitude" ("la mia beatitudine") from
the book's outset, specifically in II. 5 and III. 1. This designation of her is
repeated in V. 1, IX. 2, X. 2, XII. 1, twice again in XI and four times in
XVIII. In all such instances, Dante's sense of her being his beatitude is
communicated to him directly by his lady's greeting.

Chapter XI is devoted entirely to describing the effects of Beatrice's
greeting on Dante and gives the most elaborate account of how, when she
was on the point of greeting him ("quando ella fosse alquanto propinqua al
salutare"), the spirit of love ("spirito d'amore") would destroy his own
sensory spirits ("spiriti sensitivi") and drive his own visual faculties away in
order to remain in their place. Dante becomes as if possessed by a spirit of
love. He is, in effect, beside himself and "out of his mind," so to speak –
that is, out of his normal senses. He is so overcome by sentiments of charity
and humility surging up in him that he can consider no one to be his
enemy ("nullo nemico mi rimanea"). He would immediately pardon
whoever had offended him. Might he be heard here as suggesting that
this was not generally his temperament? At least his other works attest to
his sometimes cantankerous proclivities. In contrast, here Dante is
inhabited and inspired not just by a particular love passion but by universal
love or charity, exempt from libido. He is transformed, not only morally,
but also physically, by Beatrice's greeting – to such an extent that his body,
under her sway, becomes as if numb and inanimate, so that he cannot
contain his bliss:

> E quando questa gentilissima salute salutava, non che Amore fosse tal mezzo
> che potesse obumbrare a me la intollerabile beatitudine, ma elli quasi per
> soverchio di dolcezza divenia tale, che lo mio corpo, lo quale era tutto allora
> sotto lo suo reggimento, molte volte si movea come cosa grave inanimata. Sì
> che appare manifestamente che ne le sue salute abitava la mia beatitudine, la
> quale molte volte passava e redundava la mia capacitade. (XI. 3–4)

> (And when this most gentle salvation saluted, Love did not come between us
> as overshadowing and tempering my intolerable beatitude, but he by excess
> of sweetness became such that my body, which was entirely under his sway,
> often moved as a sedated and inanimate thing. So that it became manifest
> that in her salutations dwelt my beatitude, which many times exceeded and
> overwhelmed my capacity.)

If she did not affect Dante in this way so as to translate him into a new,
normally inaccessible, dimension of existence, she would not be "Beatrice."
For no mere sequence of external events, without the witness of a subject,

as expressed in lyrical transports, could contain the miraculous meaning which she manifestly had – and was – for Dante. The text's self-interpretive lyrical intensity further evinces and articulates this subjective grounding of its own generative event.[6]

We saw, in the preceding chapter, that the revelation of Jesus as the Christ in the Gospels could not be given in the form of an objective, historical fact. Instead, this revelation of divinity is inextricably bound up with the disciples' personal experience in relation to Jesus and with their lyrical-poetic expression of it. What their testimony witnesses to is a faith that Jesus inspired in them, and this faith was never compulsory in reaction to who Jesus was or to what he did: it was, rather, a free response requiring a willing and total commitment of self. Even "seeing him" after the Resurrection, on the previously designated mountain in Galilee, where he was "worshipped," among the disciples there were some who doubted: "And when they saw him, they worshipped him: but some doubted" (Matthew 28: 17; καὶ ἰδοντες αὐτον προσεκύνησαν, οἱ δὲ ἐδίστασαν).

The stories about Jesus witness not just to mere outward happenings but, most fundamentally, to the miraculous transformations worked within the lives and hearts of the individuals who encountered him. Such is the deep significance, for instance, of the Virgin Birth – namely, what it says about the miraculous nature of Jesus of Nazareth for those who experienced him. To make of Jesus's divinity something more objective than this is to mythologize it – in the sense of "myth" expounded by existentialist theologian Rudolf Bultmann. For Bultmann, myth is no longer a viable form of knowledge in the modern scientific age. Supposedly, nothing that is not measurable in natural physical terms can be held veritably to exist in the scientific worldview. In another sense, however, myth is not incompatible with truth, and especially not with the truth of biblical revelation. Meant here is a sense of *mythos* that hews closer to the word's original meaning simply as "story." Such a sense is closer to the spirit of C. S. Lewis's dictum that "The heart of Christianity is a myth which is also a fact." "By becoming fact it does not cease to be myth: that is the miracle."[7]

The fact in question here, I submit, is not so much of the order of a first-degree empirical fact, a sensory perception, but rather a fact that is

---

[6] Gregory B. Stone, "Dante's Averroistic Hermeneutics (On 'Meaning' in the *Vita nuova*)," *Dante Studies* 112 (1994): 133–59, emphasizes that "the implied hermeneutic theory formulated in the *Vita nuova*" results in a "radical subjectivism" (p. 134).

[7] C. S. Lewis, "Myth Become Fact," in *God in the Dock*, ed. Walter Hooper (Grand Rapids, MI: Eerdmans, 1970), pp. 66–67.

constructed through the commitment of a life. A life can – *in fact* – be built on a "myth" or story that is believed in and is made to become the truth of an individual's own existence. This unconditional life commitment occurs with varying degrees of integrity and authenticity. In such terms, the *Vita nuova* can be read as Dante's "founding myth."[8] Such a myth can, moreover, be either individual or collective – a fact of personal existence or of historical communities and institutions. In reality, these two dimensions prove to be interdependent and inextricable.

Dante's experience of Beatrice was an experience of the miraculous and divine – of something that is beyond all finite experience of objects and that cannot be adequately expressed in reductively objectivizing terms. This is why Dante had need of a subjective language, the language of lyric, which, apart from what it says about any specific objective referent or content, expresses feeling by form.[9] Like the New Testament writers, Dante did, of course, express his sense of the miraculous in objectifying terms, but as his allusion to Homer in the prose of Chapter II betrays, he senses that he is veering into myth when he tries to state the miraculousness of Beatrice as a simple fact. That she should be the daughter not of a mortal, but of god – "'Ella non parea figliuola d'uomo mortale, ma di deo'" (II. 8) – also happens to be the central claim (adjusting for gender) made concerning Christ in the New Testament. But it is not a claim that could be proved objectively or even be intelligibly interpreted on a strictly factual basis. Dante's claim can be given a verifiable meaning only as expressing the marvel he felt and projected onto Beatrice, the object of that marvel, in the form of a hyperbolic attribute of divinity.

While it is natural, and fulfills certain emotional needs, that Dante should express the experience of Beatrice in the hyperboles and wish-fulfilling fantasies of myth, they must be understood to be interpretations revealing his personal experience as a subject. And this means that, in crucial ways, the truest or most authentic expression of this emotionally overwhelming experience must remain the lyric. Dante's lyrical language about Beatrice directly embodies his emotional exaltation and the existential reality of his ecstatic self-transcendence in relation to her. Lyrical

---

[8] Andrew Frisardi makes this suggestion in the introduction to his translation of the *Vita nova* (Evanston: Northwestern University Press, 2012), p. xx.

[9] Broadly indicative of Dante's aesthetic legacy in this regard, Susanne K. Langer, in *Feeling and Form: A Theory of Art* (New York: Charles Scribner's Sons, 1953), channels much linguistic reflection, together with experience of various art forms, into elucidating art as expressive of feeling along lines indicated by Ernst Cassirer's philosophy of symbolic form (*Philosophie der symbolischen Formen*, 1923–29).

language can effect this in and by its formal-aesthetic properties, its musical qualities, and its expressiveness in excess of all representational content or objective reference.[10]

Just as in the New Testament, so in the *Vita nuova,* the lyric form is indispensable for expressing what was felt and experienced in relation to the miraculous, divinity-revealing individual. Without lyrical expression and crystallization, there could have been no more than a passing, individual illumination, not a historical, life-transforming revelation, because the transcendent meaning of the event could not have been communicated or even formulated. The miracle of Beatrice lies in what her presence works within the hearts and minds of others, not in what is factually documentable about her.[11] Actual physical detail of her appearance is neglected – just as is physical description of Christ in the Gospels. We are told only a few symbolic features, principally pertaining to her eyes as the beginning of love ("principio d'amore") and her smile as the end of love ("fine d'amore," XIX. 20), and even these features are described not objectively but rather stereotypically and, most significantly, in terms of their love-inspiring effects on whomsoever should behold them. This is patent in probably their most telling description, the one given in "Donne ch'avete intelletto d'amore":

> De li occhi suoi, come ch'ella li mova,
> escono spirti d'amore inflammati,
> *che feron li occhi a qual che allor la guati,*
> *e passan sì che 'l cor ciascun retrova:*
> voi le vedete Amor pinto nel viso,
> la 've *non pote alcun mirarla fiso.*
>
>   (XIX. 12; italics added)

> (From her eyes, when she moves them,
> issue spirits of love inflamed,
> *that wound the eyes of whoever then beholds her,*
> *and penetrate, so that each attains the heart:*
> you see love depicted on her face,
> there where *no one can fix their gaze.*)

[10] Benedetto Croce, notably in *Estetica come scienza dell'espressione e linguistica generale: Teoria e storia* (Bari: Laterza, 1912), famously developed a theory of art as lyrical intuition and expression in more modern philosophical terms that, nevertheless, still resonate with the tradition Dante transmits and, in some ways, even originates.

[11] As suggested by Erminia Ardissimo and Silvana Scarinci, "Fenomenologia do maravilhoso na literatura italiana," *Per Musi* 24 Belo Horizonte (2011): 21–29, "Beatrice is, therefore, the prodigy or the supernatural event that enters into Dante's daily life in order to reveal to him an unexpected dimension of existence" ("Beatriz é, portanto, o prodígio, ou o evento sobrenatural que entra no cotidiano de Dante para lhe revelar uma dimensão inesperada da existência," p. 24).

Dante's experience of Beatrice actually steps outside of historical experience altogether into what is not describable in any prosaic terms. Accordingly, Dante is able to write that in Beatrice he saw "all the ends of my beatitude" ("tutti li termini de la mia beatitudine," III. 1). This phrase perhaps unwittingly evokes eschatological time – or rather the *eschaton*'s obliteration of historical time. There can be no objective descriptive language – objects being given always within the parameters of a given world – to describe what Dante experiences in that condition. But there is lyrical language and expression, and this is what Dante employs. This subjective and personal dimension harboring the effect Beatrice had on Dante can be conveyed only indirectly and lyrically to another person, a reader. Lyrical language does this specifically by suggesting the quality of feeling or the level of existence that was touched in the experience. Without such a lyrical language, all that could be said would be, "We had the experience but missed the meaning" (Eliot, *The Dry Salvages*, II). Yet thanks to the expressive power of lyrical language, another possibility arises, namely, that "approach to the meaning restores the experience / In a different form" (T. S. Eliot, *The Dry Salvages*, II).

It is remarkable that the same basic scheme of exalted humility as provided a first-order figuration in lyrical form of Jesus as the Christ in the hymn of Philippians 2 is operative also throughout the *Vita nuova*'s presentation of Beatrice as this glorious, yet humble, lady: she is paradoxically "crowned" with humility ("coronata ... d'umilitade"). In a certain manner, the purest lyrical expression of this leitmotif occurs in what could be considered the consummate poem of the *dolce stil novo*, "Tanto gentile e tanto onesta pare":

> Ella si va, sentendosi laudare,
>   benignamente d'umiltà vestuta;
>   e par che sia una cosa venuta
>   da cielo in terra a miracol mostrare.

(XXVI. 6)

> (She goes along, hearing herself praised,
>   beneficently dressed in humility;
>   and seems to be a thing come
>   from heaven to earth to show a miracle.)

Beatrice's manifestation takes on a sacramental aura here with this miraculous self-showing, as if she were come from heaven. The effects of this showing are embodied in the sigh (the sonnet's last word) that she inspires by the emotion she elicits from the one who, utterly transformed and in-spirited, beholds her:

> Mostrasi sì piacente a chi la mira,
>   che dà per li occhi una dolcezza al core,
>   che 'ntender no la può chi no la prova:
> e par che de la sua labbia si mova
>   un spirito soave pien d'amore,
>   che va dicendo a l'anima: Sospira.
>
> (XXVI. 7)

> (She shows herself so pleasing to whoever beholds her,
>   that she confers a sweetness through the eyes to the heart,
>   which cannot be understood by one who does not feel it:
> and it seems that from her lips there moves
>   a gracious spirit steeped in love
>   that goes along telling the soul: Sigh.)

The motif of paradoxically high humility accompanies virtually every mention of the "gloriosa donna," starting from her very first appearance "dressed humbly and modestly in a most noble crimson color" ("vestita di nobilissimo colore, umile e onesto, sanguigno," II. 3). Humility defines something unmistakable about her significance in no matter what circum-stances she appears. Yet, even more essentially, this quality defines Dante in relation to her. The humility that constitutes an essential characteristic of Beatrice turns out to correspond to, or even to be convertible with, something experienced in his own being by Dante in her presence, or by anyone who sees her: "The sight of her makes every being humble" ("La sua vista fa onne cosa umile," XXVI. 12). This correspondence between purportedly objective per-ceptions and the states that they produce within the perceiving subject is wrought to the point of becoming virtually a kind of convertibility between the two – with the proviso that this is so within the subject's experience.

Dante's subjective experience here is modeled on the religious experi-ence of the Gospels specifically at the point where Christ, reappearing after the Crucifixion to the disciples in a locked room, breathes his spirit on them and says, "Receive the Holy Spirit" ("insufflavit et dixit eis: Accipite Spiritum Sanctum," John 20: 22). He therewith sends them out on their salvific mission into the world as the continuation of his own sending as Savior by the Father ("sicut misit me Pater, et ego mitto vos," 20: 21). This passage suggests the higher spiritual purpose and destination to which Dante's amorous sighing is turned by the end of the book. Dante picks up the breathing of the lover's spirit as a sorrowful sighing and converts it into a pilgrim spirit ("lo peregrino spirito," XLI. 11) in quest of the beatific vision. The book's final sonnet specifies that a new intelligence of love placed in the lover by the weeping god, Love, now draws him upward:

> Oltre la spera che più larga gira
> passa 'l sospiro ch' esce del mio core:
> intelligenza nova, che l'Amore
> piangendo mette in lui, pur su lo tira.

(XLI. 10)

> (Beyond the sphere that turns most widely
> passes the sigh that issues from my heart:
> a new intelligence that Love in weeping
> puts into it draws it ever upward.)

Dante's forlorn and worldly sigh takes flight, exiting the physical universe altogether, in order to embark on a pilgrimage, purposing to rejoin, as its source, the divine spirit communicated from Christ. Communicated analogously from Beatrice in inspiring Dante, the sigh becomes his vehicle to heaven.[12] The *Vita nuova*'s final poetic flourish in this manner celebrates "the Eternal Feminine that draws us on high" ("Das Ewige-Weibliche / Zieht uns hinan"), much as in the Chorus Mysticus that concludes Goethe's *Faust* – except that in the *Vita nuova* this ascension is transposed into specifically New Testament terms.

Dialectic of Subjective Appearing and Visionary Revealing

The *Vita nuova* and the Christian Gospel are both predicated on a common assumption that there is a subjective dimension of experience in which alone the deep reality and meaning of history, or of a life history, or even just an event, can be perceived. Such salvific meaning as is reconstituted in both works declares itself to memory and can be adequately represented only by a form of witness that projects an inner experience of miracle onto the idiosyncratic diction of poetic language.[13]

---

[12] See, further, Bernard S. Levy, "Beatrice's Greeting and Dante's 'Sigh' in the *Vita nuova*," *Dante Studies* 92 (1974): 53–62. In an interreligious spirit, the sigh's opening a path from the finite to the infinite is explored by Franco Masciandro and Peter Booth, *Dante/Hafiz: Readings on the Sigh, the Gaze, and Beauty* (Pinsapo Press, 2017), pp. 1–56.

[13] I develop a focused reading of the Gospel along these lines in "Gospel as Personal Knowing: Theological Reflections on Not Just a Literary Genre," *Theology Today* 68/4 (2011): 413–23. A revised version in "The Gospel Truth: Personal Knowing and Miracle," chapter 6 of *A Theology of Literature: The Bible as Revelation in the Tradition of the Humanities* (Eugene, OR: Wipf and Stock, 2017), pp. 83–95, places this reading in the wider context of the Bible as witness.

Dante's acute awareness of this irreducibly subjective and personal aspect of the advent of divinity and salvation shows through clearly in his constant recourse to categories of dream, vision, and imagination in relating every one of Beatrice's epiphanies to himself.[14] From the first occasion, when he sees her plainly, he uses the rhetoric of appearing – "apparvemi" (II. 2) – and this rhetoric recurs with intensive redundancy in every one of his visions and dreams and memorable fantasies or "imaginations."[15] Even for an encounter with Beatrice strolling between two older gentlewomen ("due gentili donne," III. 1) in the public space of the streets of Florence, Dante employs the same language, with its vaguely psychologizing, subjectivizing implications: "this marvelous lady *appeared* to me dressed in purest white" ("questa mirabile donna apparve a me vestita di colore bianchissimo," III. 1).

The exceeding marvelousness of this woman seems to make it impossible to speak of her in purely objective, matter-of-fact terms. The state of excitement that she automatically induces evidently renders Dante's perceptions incommensurable with any common norm. Consequently, he can only speak about how she *appeared* to him, since his experience of her is abnormal, enhanced, and unique. When he discovers that she has similar effects on others (cf. "Tanto gentile" and "Vede perfettamente," XXVI. 5–7 and 10–13), that realization simply makes them, too, witnesses of what ordinarily would not be believed, for they, too, are beside themselves, dumbstruck with admiration and inwardly overwhelmed by an accession of virtue in their hearts. "And when she was near anyone, their hearts were filled with so much virtue that they dared not to raise their eyes, nor to respond to her greeting; and many who had experienced it would be able to testify to me about this to whoever might not believe" ("E quando ella fosse presso d'alcuno, tanta onestade giungea nel cuore di quello, che non ardia di levare li occhi, né di rispondere a lo suo saluto; e di questo molti, sì come esperti, mi potrebbero testimoniare a chi non lo credesse," XXVI. 1).

[14] A concise guide to the vast critical literature on dreams, visions, imaginings, fantasies, etc., with its fine distinctions between degrees and kinds of reality and with special attention to their reflexive properties as all this relates to Dante, is Zygmunt G. Barański, "Il carattere riflessivo dei tre sogni purgatoriali," in *"Sole nuovo, luce nuova": Saggi sul rinnovamento culturale in Dante* (Turin: Scriptorium, 1996), pp. 255–79. The extensive work of Jean-Claude Schmitt on dreams and visions in the broader medieval context will be brought to bear on this topic in the Epilogue (see footnotes 4–6 therein).

[15] Dino S. Cervigni, *Dante's Poetry of Dreams* (Florence: Olschki, 1986), pp. 39–70, exhaustively inventories and minutely analyzes this rhetoric in the *Vita nuova*. He posits the "physical reality" of six *apparimenti* to Dante as basic and as leading to visionary forms of appearing (p. 59), which he acknowledges as higher forms of experience. Along this line, but in reverse, I give precedence to poetic appearing as (re)constituting the reality of Dante's "new life."

Although somewhat oblique, an allusion to the Gospel pericope about the doubting Thomas and his serving as a foil for those who believe without seeing ("blessed are they that have not seen, and yet have believed," John 20: 29) can be detected in this passage.[16] It serves to further reinforce the New Testament background and framing of Dante's witness concerning Beatrice. In effect, Dante dons the mantle and creatively adapts the vocation of an evangelist. He resolves to write a poetry of praise in order to publish and spread the word about his miraculous lady so that "even those who were not able to see her sensibly," or experience her in the flesh, might nevertheless "know as much about her as words are able to convey" ("acciò che non pur coloro che la poteano sensibilmente vedere, ma li altri sappiano di lei quello che le parole ne possono fare intendere," XXVI. 4). With this purpose firmly in mind, he sets about to compose his banner sonnet "Tanto gentile e tanto onesta pare" (XXVI. 5).

The meaning that Beatrice took on within Dante's experience is described in terms of personal testimony or faith and is constitutive of all that he was able actually to see about her. What he *in fact* saw is bracketed within what he *believed* he saw, or seemed to see – or perhaps rather thought – about her. Dante expresses this in an episode which, in exemplary fashion, typifies all his encounters with Beatrice, by suggesting that his seeing of Beatrice was a seeing through love. Love supplants his visual faculties ("spiriti del viso") and takes over their function "because Love wanted to remain in their most noble place so as to behold the marvelous lady" ("però che Amore volea stare nel loro nobilissimo luogo per vedere la mirabile donna," XIV. 5; cf. also XI. 2). Thus Dante becomes "other than before" ("altro che prima"), indeed, to such an extent as to warrant speaking of his "transfiguration" ("trasfigurazione"). Such language recalls Jesus's transfiguration in the Gospels (Matthew 17: 1–8, Mark 9: 2–8, Luke 9: 28–36): it transfers the supernatural aura of a divine being to Dante's own existential condition, hinting at the intimate connection, indeed the inseparability, of the two.

The rhetoric of appearing consistently evokes a subjective dimension of experience in all the accounts of his encounters with this miracle of a woman. This rhetoric is so relentless in its recurrence as to demand to be accounted for in itself. Employing the various permutations of *pareami*, *mi parea vedere*, *m'apparve*, and *mi era apparuto*, in Chapter III. 3–7, Dante manages to repeat these formulaic expressions eleven times in the course of

---

[16] Levy, "Beatrice's Greeting and Dante's 'Sigh'," pp. 58–60, analyzes this discernible allusion to the Gospel passage concerning St. Thomas.

a description of his dream that is not even a page long. The same density of occurrence of this language of appearing characterizes the dream-description of Love as a young man dressed in white (XII. 3–8), who comes to help Dante change his course and win back Beatrice's favor after she denies him her "salute" ("greeting"). She does so because of his reputation's having been compromised through an imperious rumor that viciously defames him ("soverchievole voce che parea che m'infamasse viziosamente," X. 2) and that has been brought on by his feigning of devotion to a second screen lady.

Sometimes such expressions serve to introduce what Dante felt only interiorly, as in "I seemed to feel a marvelous tremor begin within my breast" ("mi parve sentire uno mirabile tremore incomminciare nel mio petto," XIV. 4). But the appearance idiom has a highly labile meaning, as it slides from qualifying a perception, to a belief, to a "look" – not an individuated object of perception per se, but an air giving a certain impression. Such slippages occur typically in the following phrase about the god Love: "Then *it seemed to me* that I recognized him, since he was calling me as he had already done often enough in my dreams: and looking at him it *seemed to me* that he was piteously weeping, and *it appeared* that he was waiting for a word from me" ("Allora *mi parea* che io lo conoscesse, però che mi chiamava così come assai fiate ne li miei sonni m'avea già chiamato: e riguardandolo, *parvemi* che piangesse pietosamente, e *parea* che attendesse da me alcuna parola," XII. 4). In each instance, the subjective conditioning of whichever type of cognition (sense perception, dream, fantasy, reflection, or imagination) is signaled, and the chain of association that is established links everything reported to the speaking subject and his existential condition.

Dante uses the same word when he wants to refer to what exists only in his imagination. Of Love, he writes that "in my imagination he *appeared* as a pilgrim" ("ne la mia imaginazione *apparve* come peregrino," IX. 3). And similarly, when Dante witnesses in a feverish dream the series of apocalyptic signs, they are governed by an identical semantics: "the darkening of the sun appeared to me" ("pareami vedere lo sole oscurare"); "it appeared to me that the birds flying in the air fell dead and that there were tremendous earthquakes" ("pareami che li uccelli volando per l'aria cadessero morti, e che fossero grandissimi terramuoti," XXIII. 5). All of these instances are dismissed by being ascribed to "erroneous fantasy" ("la erronea fantasia"), since they are impressions produced by Dante's feverish delirium. Nonetheless, in a symbolic register, they prove to be foreboding, revelatory signs of the impending and devastating death of Beatrice. That death itself will be announced shortly thereafter, in XXVIII. 1, as having already occurred.

However, there is one juncture at which Dante deliberately dispenses with the language of appearance. It occurs where he is speaking not of any sort of presence of Beatrice or of attendant figures. He tells us that, according to infallible truth ("secondo la infallabile veritade"), Beatrice *was* herelf the number 9 ("questo numero fue ella medesima" – XXIX. 3). He can be certain about her not as a phenomenon in space and time, but only as a mathematical symbol, for this is a question not of facts, but of significance. The certainty he has about her significance, moreover, is an ontological certainty. It is a certain truth for him not because of what he knows objectively, but because of what he *is* – namely, transformed in his own being through his relation to her.

Even his having new life, in Latin his being "novus," bespeaks his own belonging, alongside her, to this number *novem* (= 9). Of course, while her being participates in absolute Being and makes his own being do so likewise, she is not herself this absolute Being. Dante recognizes this when he says that he "speaks in similitude" ("per similitudine dico") in arriving at his conclusion that she was a miracle ontologically rooted in divinity, indeed in the Christian Trinity: "she was a nine, in other words, a miracle, whose root – that is, of the miracle – is only the wondrous Trinity" ("ella era uno nove, cioè uno miracolo, la cui radice, cioè del miracolo, è solamente lo mirabile Trinitade," XXIX. 3).

All this talk of appearance might induce us to make a distinction, as Robert Harrison does, between the phenomenal and the noumenal. But against this, I submit that Dante's language has not an epistemological, but rather a hermeneutic import (as will be discussed more thoroughly in the next chapter). Dante's reporting always of what *appears* to him does not indicate that Beatrice *herself* has a noumenal being that does not appear. And it does not mean that he is less than certain, or that this experience cannot be verified. It means, rather, that Dante is not simply reporting an act of perception of an object so much as expressing and actualizing an episode of personal witness. He is himself directly involved in what he experienced. It questioned his own very being and existence, just as much as he in turn may have questioned what he saw. Indeed, the implication is not that he in any degree doubted what he saw, but rather that it was an intensely personal and visionary sort of seeing.

It is this connotation of "pareami" ("it seemed to me") that has been felt by readers in all ages who have expressly recognized the book's pervasive "visionary" quality. Especially when we consider how this language is used to modulate fluidly from the domain of perception to that of belief – and thence to that of decision about meaning, and possibly also to action – we begin to sense its value for testifying to a personal susceptibility or sensibility. It serves as witness to a subjective transformation undergone in an encounter with a superlatively significant individual rather than for defining epistemologically the objective content of the entity or event in question. Whereas a priori the language of appearing qualifies as subjective and limits the validity of the perceptions it conveys, here such language signals a superior degree of truth: it reveals a higher reality.

It is remarkable that, after the disappearance of Beatrice, in the scene where the consoling "gentile donna" appears to Dante, the *pareami* idiom re-occurs only rarely and has not at all the same valence as in every instance of his encounters with Beatrice, or even with Love – which is to say, in every *revelatory* experience. In relation to the "lady at the window" in Chapter XXXV, the language of appearing occurs only twice. The principal occurrence is in relation to this gentle lady herself, who takes pity on Dante in his grief. Dante notices the woman gazing at him from a window "so piteously, *judging from her appearance,* that all pity seemed to be gathered into her" ("la quale da una finestra mi riguardava sì pietosamente, *quanto a la vista,* che tutta la pietà parea in lei accolta," XXXV. 2, italics added). This is carefully qualified as a strictly external appearing – *quanto a la vista* or "inasmuch as such a thing can be seen." The other mention of appearing occurs in reference to how *he,* Dante, looked *from the outside* and not to the inward quality of his apprehension of anything. His sad thoughts, he says, "made me appear on the outside to be terribly dismayed" ("mi faceano parere di fore una vista di terribile sbigottimento," XXXV. 1).

Here Dante becomes self-conscious and concerned lest his consternation be observed by others. This preoccupation is far removed from the total involvement in relation to an Other that distinguishes his encounters with Beatrice and that makes "parere" ("to appear" or "to seem") signal a particular sort of existential testimony. Indeed, when Dante encounters this gentle lady, who is young and very beautiful ("gentile donna giovane e bella molto"), not to say tempting, he is vulnerable to seduction precisely because he thinks of Beatrice as belonging to past time rather than to an immediate, phenomenal appearing in the present. "Sometime afterwards, it happened that I was in a place where I remembered past time, and I remained long in meditation and in painful thoughts" ("Poi per alquanto tempo, con ciò fosse cosa che io fosse in parte ne la quale mi ricordava del passato tempo, molto stavo pensoso, e con dolorosi pensamenti," XXXV. 1; cf. XXXIX. 2).

This sinking into nostalgic melancholia allows Dante's true vision of Beatrice's eternity and of her revelation of a new life in the present of his personal existence to weaken and fade. He is treating what Beatrice reveals to him in a visionary present as merely a past fact, but by this means he necessarily misses its true significance and its ultimately religious meaning. This liability to forgetting perhaps inheres in his framing of his vision from the outset of his narrative within the book of memory (I. 1). Nevertheless, the *present* sight of his eternally present beloved is what Dante has to recover and finally does recover at the end of the book, with its closing vision of "that blessed Beatrice" as "gloriously beholding the face of him who *is blessed throughout all ages*" ("quella benedetta Beatrice, la quale gloriosamente mira ne la faccia di colui *qui est per omnia secula benedictus*," XLII. 3). The eternal blessedness of the unnamed divinity reflects itself in Beatrice's being blessed. Her blessedness, as recalled all along in her very name, is sublated into God's in the book's final word "benedictus," which now applies to God himself. This is the sort of self-reflective structure that actualizes an inexpressible, transcendent reality and becomes the basis for revelation in Dante's book as a verbal mirror.

Memory, far from being simply the recalling of past time, can also be a vitally intense way of actualizing in the present what remains for all time, and indeed for eternity. So understood, "memory" transpires in a presentness that pervades – and yet also evades – consciousness, save in exceptional moments of grace. This is what Eliot's *Four Quartets* are steering toward as "the still point of the turning world" ("Burnt Norton," II and IV). Eliot writes, "To be conscious is not to be in time," but "only in time can the moment in the rose-garden . . . / Be remembered. . . . / Only through time is time conquered" ("Burnt Norton," II).

Eliot's verses are a veritable treasure trove for elucidating this elusive state of consciousness in and out of time that is so seldom conscious of itself. Especially the concluding verses of "The Dry Salvages," movement V, warrant being cited here. They imagine and potentially even enact a time consciousness that escapes the ordinary, mundane division of the tenses. They present, instead, a visionary awareness of the eternal in the "now." Of course, these verses can do so only by means of drawing a contrast with the more mundane state that alone is generally known but that can be apprehended as being inflected at its margins with something else that is strangely other. This otherness is evoked through what turn out to be uncannily familiar and perhaps even ordinary experiences, or at least aspects of them that are ordinarily scarcely noticed:

For most of us, there is only the unattended
Moment, the moment in and out of time,
The distraction fit, lost in a shaft of sunlight,
The wild thyme unseen, or the winter lightning
Or the waterfall, or music heard so deeply
That it is not heard at all, but you are the music
While the music lasts. These are only hints and guesses,
Hints followed by guesses; and the rest
Is prayer, observance, discipline, thought and action.
The hint half guessed, the gift half understood, is Incarnation.

Eliot's mystical intuitions evoked from everyday experience are also filtered through an inchoate philosophy of time that the continuation of this passage (to the end of "The Dry Salvages," V) works into lyrical verse. The "incarnation" of eternity in time, which is also at the heart of Dante's vision, and already in the *Vita nuova*, is for Eliot a realization of "the impossible." It becomes present in Eliot's poem as a supersensual, trans-spatial "here":

Here the impossible union
Of spheres of existence is actual,
Here the past and future
Are conquered, and reconciled,
Where action were otherwise movement
Of that which is only moved
And has in it no source of movement –
Driven by daemonic, chthonic
Powers. And right action is freedom
From past and future also.
For most of us, this is the aim
Never here to be realised;
Who are only undefeated
Because we have gone on trying;
We, content at the last
If our temporal reversion nourish
(Not too far from the yew-tree)
The life of significant soil.

This impossible union of spheres of existence can be glimpsed in exceptional moments of consciousness, but most people will never consciously realize it at all. It can, however, be unconsciously realized through right actions in their freedom from compulsion by merely "temporal," fateful ("demonic"), and earthly ("chthonic") determinants. We can act in obedience to an ideal, even while failing to grasp in its furthest consequences the meaning of our action as a free initiative and origin of good. Even while succumbing unenlightened to our mortality ("temporal reversion"), we may nevertheless materially leave behind us something of significance to be used by others coming after. Without being fully cognizant of it, we will have participated in a transcending of the normal segregations of past from future and will have moved into a greater fullness of time and existence.

As this passage suggests, moments of unitive experience are inevitably followed by relapse into the usual oblivion that is all that most of us consciously experience in any case. In the epiphanies in which Beatrice appears to him, Dante has anticipated what he clearly unveils as a visionary mode of seeing her in eternity in the "mirabile visione" (XLII. 1) of the *Vita nuova*'s final chapter. Still, the direct vision of eternity, of God himself, he attributes only to Beatrice herself "gloriously beholding the face of him *who is blessed throughout all ages*" ("Beatrice, la quale gloriosamente mira ne la faccia di colui *qui est per omnia secula benedictus*," XLII. 3).

Assisted by the modern poet's experience of transcending time translated into some more contemporary registers, we can now return to the phenomenological differentiation of Dante's modes of perception in their declension from the visionary or epiphanic mode that characterizes his experiences of Beatrice. By the time we reach the final chapter, we are reminded that we have been invited to imagine that this visionary mode characterizes, even more essentially, Beatrice's own vision of the divine one who is blessed for all eternity. Ordinary empirical vision shows up in light of this supremely potent degree of vision as a defective mode of perception.

In the earlier instance in Chapter XXXV, Dante simply "sees," as a matter of fact, the compassionate lady: "Then I saw a gentle lady, young and very beautiful, who was looking at me from a window" ("Allora vidi una gentile donna giovane e bella molto, la quale da una finestra mi riguardava," XXXV. 2). The window serves as an image for the objective, outward-turned perception that characterizes the scene. As a framing device, the window separates and cordons off the object from the perceiving subject. It implies a logic of objectification, even of self-objectification, which is the very antithesis of a captivating relation to a superlatively significant Other in self-oblivion and self-transcendence such as occurs in almost every instance in which Dante enters into relation with Beatrice.

The main occurrence of the telltale idiom of appearing in connection with the "gentile donna," the lady at the window, as we saw, comes in the phrase: "all pity appeared to be received in her" ("tutta la pietà parea in lei accolta"), which does *not* serve to suggest anything unique and indefinable about *Dante*'s personal experience. There is no "me" here (as there *is* in the reflexive form "pareami" so frequently used in speaking about Beatrice), and the phrase hews about as close to stating a plain, objective fact as any judgment about compassion in another person possibly could.

The contrast becomes all the more striking when we compare this scene of seeing and being seen by the pitying "gentile donna" with the re-apparition of Beatrice four chapters later (XXXIX) in an "imaginazione." Here the language of witness reappears in full force with all the personalized intensity of "mi parve" and "pareami." Dante has come to understand this pitying lady as the adversary of his love and loyalty to Beatrice, and he requires a visionary intervention in order to be reaffirmed in his original faithfulness. "Against this adversary of reason there arose one day, at about the ninth hour, a *strong imagination in me*, in which *I seemed* to see this glorious Beatrice in that crimson clothing in which she *appeared to my eyes*; and she *appeared to me* young and in the same age as when I first saw her" ("Contro questo avversario de la ragione si levoe un die, quasi ne l'ora de la nona, una *forte imaginazione in me*, che *mi parve* vedere questa gloriosa Beatrice con quelle vestimenta sanguigne co le quali *apparve a gli occhi miei*; e *pareami* giovane in simile etade in quale io prima la vide," XXXIX. 1, italics added).

Here we are back in the epiphanic mode, and it emphatically personalizes and subjectivizes perception. Somewhat surprisingly, at least at first, Dante aligns his imagination of Beatrice with "reason" and pits it against the "appetite" drawing him to the newly intruding *gentile donna*. Reason here rescues Dante, coming to him in a sort of apparition of Beatrice in his imagination. In fact, Dante has vouched all along for the rationality of his passion for Beatrice. He has maintained that, for all the obsessive intensity of his imagination of his lady, Love's impetuosity was governed by a noble virtue and never allowed him to overstep the faithful counsel of reason in any matter that it is appropriate for reason to adjudicate and regulate ("E avvegna che la sua imagine, la quale continuatamente meco stava, fosse baldanza d'Amore a segnoreggiare me, tuttavia era di sì nobilissima vertù, che nulla volta sofferse che Amore mi reggesse sanza lo fedele consiglio de la ragione in quelle cose là ove cotale consiglio fosse utile a udire," II. 9). Dante repeatedly insists that Love commanded him in accordance with the counsel of reason ("Amore, lo quale mi commandava secondo lo consiglio de la ragione," IV. 2), which thereby aligns with and supports his visionary penchants. Rather than simply serving as a principle of restraint, reason stands for a source of higher moral vision and symbolic insight into the inner unity of things. This level of insight belongs to that exalted mode of vision that I call "revelation" and endeavor to educe from Dante's book. Such vision deploys a typological logic of the "figure" and can include perceiving the coincidence of opposites.

The Figurative Logic of the Unique and Its Multiple Repetitions

Alongside the rhetoric of appearance stand other indicators that the story of the revelation to Dante via Beatrice is being told not so much in terms of plain, simple facts but rather as a meaningful event grasped figuratively in lyrical forms and then narratively objectified in retrospect. A figurative or symbolic logic must be discerned in the really quite peculiar sequence of incidents that Dante relates: it covers over and dissembles anything that might otherwise resemble historical contingency. That Beatrice's death should be so closely preceded by that of her father (Chapter XXII) – which itself parallels in important respects that of a young companion of hers (Chapter VIII) – cannot but create a configuration of happenings that reciprocally reflect one another. They interconnect as variants rather than merely following up on one another sequentially. The language used to describe the deceased young woman is indistinguishable from the style of language that Dante uses of Beatrice: "After the departure of this gentle lady, it pleased the Lord of the angels to call to his – or her – glory a young lady of very gentle aspect" ("Apresso lo partire di questa gentile donna fue piacere del segnore di li angeli di chiamare a la sua gloria una donna giovane e di gentile aspetto molto," VIII. 1). We cannot but think, for example, of the words calling Beatrice to heaven ("Angelo clama in divino intelletto . . ., " XIX. 7) so as to remedy what is purportedly Paradise's only deficiency. And this language has been anticipated by the references to the "glorious lady" of Dante's mind (II. 1), who is already being rewarded in heaven (III. 1) in the early stages of his story.

The reader might well think here in Chapter VIII that Dante is already telling, with the sort of circumlocutions to which he is habitually disposed, of Beatrice's own death. This seems plausible, if not likely, until one arrives at the mention of the deceased lady's having often been seen accompanying "quella gentil*issima*," that *most* gentle lady. This superlative can designate only Beatrice. Only now is it perfectly clear that Dante has been talking about someone else who *accompanied* her. What is more, Dante's great grief is wholly determined by the relation that this early victim had to his own lady. He resolves to write about this young victim in "recompense" expressly for the several occasions on which he had seen her in the company of his lady ("in guiderdone di ciò che alcuna fiata l'avea veduta con la mia donna," VIII. 2).

The fact that Beatrice is not the only beautiful young woman who dies tragically in the little book devoted to her, even though such a death is not to be taken as common but as catastrophic, is oddly redundant. It exemplifies the numerous structures of doubling which raise the narrative from the level of facts ingenuously reported to that of an ingeniously crafted exposition purposefully shaping the meaning of an event. In this narrative hall of mirrors, everything turns up double or multiple, including the visions of Beatrice and of *Amore.* Where the doublings seem gratuitous, for instance, with the *two* screen ladies (as if one of these were not already a sufficiently twisted turn of the plot), the effect is to diminish their weight as unique historical realities and turn them into tropes with a translucently literary function. They show up as uncanny equivalences and replicas such as would be unlikely to occur in reality. Without being motivated by some kind of artistic intent, or at least without our imagining them to be steered by a providential purpose, such occurrences are highly improbable, hardly to be believed as simple, straightforward facts.[17]

The multiple versions that Dante gives of his basic experiences heighten the sense of the narrative's constructedness. This is patent, for example, in the several parallel accounts of his bouts of *psychomachia.* We can compare the four "pensamenti" or thoughts of Chapter XIII with the "four things" ("quattro cose") offered as reflections on love's effects in Chapter XVI. These are very different constructions of similar material concerning love's often pathological effects on Dante, but they share in a common schematic structure. Even just the fact that he anticipates in dream what will actually happen, or that he gives both a prose account and a poetic version of each episode, inevitably calls attention to the different modes of framing the same contents of the experience that he wishes to communicate.

All these structures of duplication and redoubling indicate that the truth is not simply in the facts themselves, but that such facts as are related are rather variations on a theme and illustrations of a deeper meaning that cannot as such be unequivocally expressed once and for all. This meaning remains ineffable like the ineffable courtesy ("ineffabile cortesia") of Beatrice's greeting, which transports Dante to the very limits of his beatitude (III. 1; cf. XXXI. 15-16). The major figures of women, whether positive or negative, are all forged in the image of the book's one all-important figure – Beatrice herself. And similarly, all of the deaths in the book are in

[17] Robert Hollander, in "*Vita nuova*: Dante's Perceptions of Beatrice," *Dante Studies* XCII (1974): 1–18, considers Dante's mode of treating his perceptions in the *Vita nuova* to be "medieval *argumentum*," as distinguished from both *historia* and *fabula*. This is the mode of the *Commedia* as well and entails not believing that the actions recorded occurred in history "but only that this is their fictional convention" (p. 7).

one way or another versions of the book's central event – Beatrice's death. Where one central significance is established, everything else becomes subordinated to it and is reduced to the status of so many reverberations or partial manifestations of a master signified, whether in a positive or in a negative key.

Unique persons and events become multiple images in memory because of the plurality inherent within the sign, which is not *per se* a unique occurrence but is, instead, interchangeable with an infinity of other possible signs of the same thing. Paradoxically, a sign is one and the same sign only by virtue of its own iterability.[18] The same semiological dynamic also enables numerically different episodes to become unified as singular – yet multiply signifying – events. In this manner, similarly, the Gospels (especially as the Middle Ages read them) turn on a typological linking together of all things as signs: all incidents and items become mirrors of the one truly crucial event and person – which can never be apprehended as such or in themselves, but only through their many different multi-perspectival refractions.

It is difficult to determine how far the effect in question is calculated by Dante, but we are in a universe governed by a central transcendental Signified ("signifié"), which turns everything else into signifiers of itself. Beatrice, in Dante's book, turns into a mosaic of appearances because no single one of them can render her absolutely. The same must be said of the Gospels' manifold portraiture of Jesus by the *four* canonical evangelists – each with their own very distinctive cultural backgrounds and theological agendas. Perhaps this is also a reason why the art of the mosaic seems to be so exceptionally well suited for representing the Christ of Christian spirituality. This can be seen to great effect in the shimmering of so many diverse, crazily cut pieces, with their differently oriented surfaces and reflections, in the polychromatic mosaic vaults of the ceiling of Saint Apollinaris in Classe (near Ravenna). This multi-valent art form reflects images from the Gospels through to the *Commedia*, signally to its heaven of Mars.[19]

In the *Vita nuova*, Dante figures this structure of the many equivalencies for the one meaning or unique Signified in terms of a geometrical metaphor.

18 Jacques Derrida frequently brought this semiological paradox to light in his works, perhaps most influentially in "Signature événement context," in *Marges de la philosophie* (Paris: Minuit, 1972), most precisely pp. 390–93 on "Signature." The essay was reprised in English as the opening chapter of Derrida's debate with John Searle on speech act theory in *Limited Inc.*, trans. Samuel Weber and Jeffrey Mehlman (Evanston: Northwestern University Press, 1988).
19 Jeffrey T. Schnapp, *The Transfiguration of History at the Center of Dante's "Paradiso"* (Princeton: Princeton University Press, 1986), pp. 170–238, brings into effulgent historical focus the mosaics of Ravenna (and much else) in order to illuminate the heaven of Mars and its central symbol, the Greek Cross.

The god of Love – however remotely – can in truth be nothing but a dim, distorted image of the God who *is* Love. He is himself like the center of a circle, the parts of whose circumference are all similar, or equidistant. Dante, however, is emphatically "not like that" ("Ego tanquam centrum circuli, cui simili modo se habent circumferentie partes; tu autem non sic," XII. 4). The reproach is all the more to the point and strikes dead center, inasmuch as Dante should be in a uniquely privileged position to be able to comprehend his own center after the revelation of Beatrice. Nevertheless, while castigating Dante for not yet having found and established his center, the god's deliberately and pointedly reproving message at the same time announces that Dante is *not* his own center but must rather read the signs pointing him to his own authentic significance, the unifying love of his life. Love's pronouncement aims to interrupt the circuit of Dante's narcissism and break him open to the true source of his beatitude.

The uncanny similarities which structure the episodes of Dante's life finally become comprehensible when they are viewed retrospectively from the standpoint of the center, or, in other words, as centered on "the glorious lady of my mind" ("la gloriosa donna de la mia mente," II. 1). Viewed retrospectively, all the episodes of Dante's life are illuminated by the central significance for him of Beatrice. All occurrences in the story similarly point to her as to their deeper meaning. Their intrinsic similarity generates a whole constellation of look-alikes and seeming repeats which, from outside of this perspective, appear to be bizarre coincidences and pointless redundancies. Apart from this one, unifying significance, they would be totally inimical to Dante's rigorous and wasteless aesthetic. Dante is already beginning, in some respects, to anticipate Renaissance theories in which art imitates nature, and "Nature does nothing in vain" – "Natura nihil frustra facit," according to the Aristotelian dictum (*Politics* 1253a) embraced by Dante in *Convivio* III.xv.8 and in *Monarchia* I.xiv.2 ("omne superfluum Deo et nature displiceat"). Yet, for Dante, all this doubling is not just a re-duplication through re-presentation but has, instead, a much deeper significance as intimating a higher kind of revelation than all that straightforward, merely factual narration could deliver.

The Reflected Image and Its Being Broken Open to Transcendence

Dante's *libello* symbolizes itself by means of the metaphor of the book of memory as an emblem of the new meaning that is revealed in personal existence and that cannot be conveyed by a mere chronicle of facts. This metaphor governs the book from its very first sentence: "In that part of the book of my memory . . ." ("In quella parte del libro de la mia memoria . . ., " I. I). We are dealing thus from the start with a *reflected image* rather than with events themselves. The strategy of Dante's book will be to exploit the disparity between the meaning its events can have for Dante as a character in the story who encounters them one after the other for the first time and the sense they eventually assume for him as the scribe of memory rendering just their "essential purport" ("sentenzia," I. I). In this latter capacity, Dante works from their totalized configuration as fully realized events in the book of memory and, most importantly, with full cognizance of the final end of the story. In some sense, of course, any autobiographical narrative stands also in relation to an unknown ending, that of the writer's own death, which remains as a crucial dimension of mystery subtending and overshadowing any of the meanings that can be deliberately assigned and completely controlled by the author. This penumbra of death and, hopefully, salvation remains indeed crucial to the sense of Dante's entire narrative.

Dante raises his existential narrative in this way to a higher level of significance as a hermeneutic of revelation through techniques such as those being inventoried here. This heightening of his hermeneutic technique unfolds in tandem with and by means of a critical progression through successive historical forms of knowing associated with the writing of poetry and specifically of love lyrics in homage to a lady perceived in her overwhelming beauty and erotic attractiveness. This experience evolves through stages that can be associated with the courtly love tradition as it developed first in the Troubadours and Sicilians and then in Guittone d'Arezzo and further, in a new and different style, with Guido Guinizelli, and, finally, nearest of all to Dante, in Guido Cavalcanti. These four stages of his development are summarily recapitulated in the sonnet (lines 2–6) in Chapter XIII: "Tutti li miei penser."[20] In the outlook he reaches by means of such narrative synthesis, Dante's theologizing of this experience is achieved through a differentiated critique of the forms of experience that lead from the courtly scenario to the higher, visionary vantage point opened up to him by a hermeneutics of revelation.[21]

---

[20]   Teodolinda Barolini, starting with *Dante's Poets: Textuality and Truth in the Comedy* (Princeton: Princeton University Press, 1984), has contributed detailed study to distinguishing the various phases in Dante's surpassing of his predecessors. She deals particularly with this sonnet in her more recent *Dante's Lyric Poetry: Poems of Youth and of the* Vita nuova (Toronto: University of Toronto Press, 2014), pp. 143–45.

[21]   An overview of Dante's evolution through and beyond preceding lyric traditions is provided by Lino Leonardi, "Dante et la tradizione lirica," in *Dante*, ed. Roberto Rea and Justin Steinberg (Rome: Carocci, 2020), pp. 345–93.

While his love for Beatrice is presented as Dante's salvation, much of the complexity and subtlety of the work consists in showing how that over-whelming experience subjects Dante to severe tests and turns out to be not at all as easy as simply falling in love. Dante has to pass through an excruciating dismantling of his own self and through grief over the death of his beloved in order to fully experience the salvific power of love in this person. He can be lifted out of his general human misery temporarily by the transports of the infatuated love described at the outset of the story, but it is only through the privation of this enrapturing love in her physical person that Dante finds himself enduringly oriented to God. This comes about only through a torturing brokenness in his own life and self that exacts from him much spiritual toil in the effort to cope. Not just self-affirmation through the other's recognition of him in the "salute" or greeting, which, as he continues to reflect on it, becomes fundamentally a narcissistic satisfaction, but also the devastation of knowing his own frailty and limits belongs to Dante's discovery of love and salvation through his passion for Beatrice.

When Beatrice first appears to him at nine years old, she causes the "vital spirit" in his heart to tremble and pulsate violently ("orribilmente") with love. He is seized by the apprehension that, thenceforth, he is going to be frequently obstructed and a wretch ("Heu miser, quia frequenter impedi-tus ero deinceps!" II. 6). These words are uttered in Latin, which in this book is generally a superior, more revelatory idiom used by the god of Love and for citing the Bible. Curiously, these words are ascribed to the "natural spirit" dwelling in Dante's stomach ("spirito naturale, lo quale dimora in quella part ove si ministra lo nutrimento nostro," II. 6). They convey a "gut reaction" that is recognized for its power of revealing hidden truth about the deep secrets of the heart.

Dante's experience of his own limits and dependency in love, leading him finally to transcend himself in self-offering to another person, runs parallel to his progressive, step-by-step development at the level also of his artistic apprenticeship. First, he becomes critical of courtly modes and manners, with their deceptions and dissimulations. In Chapter XII, after the feint of the two screen ladies has discredited him, tainting his reputa-tion and causing Beatrice to deny him her greeting, Love bids him to put off such pretendings: "My son, it is time for us to lay aside our simulations" ("Fili mi, tempus est ut pretermictuntur simulacra nostra," XII. 3). He will have to put behind him the other outmoded poetic styles that vie within him and thereby produce a confusing battle among different, irreconcilable thoughts. They only plunge him into consternation and set him up to be ridiculed by the ladies in Beatrice's entourage in the episode of the *gabbo* or mocking (XIV–XVI) before he comes to forge his own personal style of poetry based purely on the praise of his lady (XVII–XIX).

By such measures, Dante is also forced to pass beyond rational artifices for pretending to control love and to keep it within the morally legitimate limits of religion that Guittone, the converted friar (of the *frati gaudenti*), imposed on his "canzoniere," recanting his early poems of unbridled erotic love. Dante moves thenceforth through the Cavalcantian tragedy of self-lacerating passion and finally beyond the "angelized woman" ("donna angelicata") of Guinizelli to an experience of being broken open to a future that transcends him, but a future toward which his own poetry of praise opens the way. Dante's being visited in his chamber by a young man dressed in white proffering words exceeding his comprehension (Chapter XII) is not without some evocations of the Annunciation to Mary (Matthew 1: 18–25; Luke 1: 26–28), thus projecting this distinctive new poetry into an evangelical key. All this, profoundly considered, represents Dante's conversion to a hermeneutics of revelation open to and dependent on an ultimate Other.

Dialectical Interpenetration of Inspiration and Reflection

In just this spirit, Dante announces as his new and more noble matter for poetry ("matera nuova e più nobile che la passata," XVII. 1) a poetry achieving beatitude strictly through words praising his lady ("In quelle parole che lodano la donna mia," XVIII. 6) and having no ulterior motives. This new and more noble matter is superior in that he can give it to himself and control it entirely: it is simply the praise that he gives to his lady without expecting anything in return. This makes poetry a totally self-reflexive operation. Deprived of Beatrice's greeting, mocked by the ladies, and routed by his own uncontrollable emotions, Dante performs a feat of rendering poetry a purely self-reflective act and yet one directed toward a beloved other, and he finds in this act alone his blessedness and salvation. In this way, he can be sure of his success, for he seeks nothing further than the offering of praise to his lady, and this is what the words of the poem are and achieve in and of themselves. Dante has invented a perfectly self-referential system and self-fulfilling project – and yet still one wholly directed toward an inspiring Other.

Dante thus stages a close coinciding between his own self-reflection and his being inspired from beyond himself – or his being beholden to a mysterious otherness – in his description of how he comes to this original style of praise poetry. He is made to stop and reflect by the fact of his own consternation about how to answer the ladies who mock him. He is confronted with his confusion as to why he seeks Beatrice's presence, even though he cannot sustain it without losing his public composure and becoming completely distraught inwardly. He then remains in suspense for a period of several days ("alquanto dì," XVIII. 9). *Reflecting much* ("pensando molto") on how to proceed (XVIII. 9), *conversing with himself* ("dicendo fra me medesimo," XVIII. 8), he reaches a resolution to seek his blessedness in nothing other than in the words that praise his lady (XVIII. 6). But then he unaccountably *receives* the first words for what was to become the manifesto poem of a new style and manner of poetry. Walking by a clear river ("uno rivo chiaro molto," XIX. 1), an appropriate and enticing image for a pure source of poetic inspiration, he is overwhelmed by a spontaneous upsurge of words. His tongue speaks "as if of its own accord" ("la mia lingua parlò quasi come per se stessa mossa," XIX. 2), enunciating the *incipit* of his breakthrough poem, the banner *canzone* of the sweet new style: "Ladies, who have intelligence of love" ("Donne ch'avete intelletto d'amore," XIX. 2).

Dante's experience of new life and of a miracle in relation to the presence of Beatrice, experienced as wholly other than any ordinary presence, comes to him as given from beyond himself. Yet, striking in these descriptions is how this experience of otherness is yoked to his own explorations of his art and to a conscious practice of self-reflection. Religious revelation or inspiration here goes hand in hand with Dante's own disciplined and deliberate development of his poetic technique. After receiving the inspired *incipit*, he spends several more days reflecting ("pensando alquanti die," XIX. 3) before beginning the *canzone* and therewith launching the *dolce stil novo*. Dante adumbrates here the far-reaching theme of revelation as realized concretely *in and through* reflection. Dante's descriptions of his way to this new conception of his lyric art in *Vita nuova* XVIII–XIX thus present it as an especially intense exercise in self-reflection, and yet this juncture in the story is at the same time precisely where he is overtaken by inspiration in a manner that surpasses his own agency. This hybridization of inspiration and reflection opens to view what is at stake at the heart of the *Vita nuova* in its immense, inaugural significance. Foreshadowed here is the historical destiny of literary inspiration to take up the relay from religion in revealing to us our own deeper reality as something inscrutably other than and in excess of ourselves.

This intimate union of inspiration and reflection is much later reaffirmed and articulated in the precise terms of Dante's answer in Purgatory to Bonagiunta da Lucca, who designates him as the inventor of the sweet new style. Dante explains that he is one who, when inspired by Love, takes note and then goes about signifying accordingly. The insistently self-reflexive language ("I' mi son un") that Dante uses reinforces the moment of "noting" plus "signifying" as a subjective mediation of what is, at the same time, an inspired gift. Dante writes here, to be exact, of his carefully noted reception of an inner "dictation" from an inspiring Love ("I' mi son un che quando / Amor mi spira noto, e a quel modo / ch'è ditta dentro vo' significando," *Purgatorio* XXIV. 52–54).[22]

Not to be overlooked, then, about this self-reflectiveness is its strict dependency on and orientation to what is other than and outside or beyond it. Paradoxically, Dante's prescription for a poetry that would be perfectly self-referential is wholly turned toward transcendence. His strategy is to make the poetry its own fulfillment in a reflexive movement, and yet it can accomplish this only by incorporating its transcendent inspiration, Beatrice, as its sole and central focus. Dante's momentous resolve, on the threshold of finding or inventing his own personal style of poetry, is to make his poetry its own fulfillment so that it no longer depends on Beatrice's greeting or on any other contingent factor outside the poetry itself. And yet, this poetry consists in nothing but praise for Beatrice, his beatifier.

From this point on, his blessedness is placed in nothing that can be taken away from him or come to nothing ("posto tutta la mia beatitudine in quello che non mi puote venire meno," XVIII. 4). Yet still Dante takes as his poetry's essential content precisely his devotion to the (w)hol(l)y Other, his revered lady, who is revealed to him in dazzling and elusive apparitions placed already under the sign of ineffability (III. 1). The new poetry's content and Dante's beatitude consist, as we have repeatedly emphasized, in nothing but "those words that praise my lady" ("quelle parole che lodano la donna mia," XVIII. 6). Nevertheless, and as a stubborn indicator of its transcendence, it is the divinity, Love, Dante's lord, who is said, by his grace, to place Dante's beatitude in that which cannot falter or be taken away from him ("lo mio segnore Amore, la sua merzede, ha posto tutta la mia beatitudine in quello che non mi puote venire meno," XVIII. 4).

---

[22] A source for Dante's wording here is commonly traced by commentators to Richard of St. Victor's treatise on mystical theology, *De IV gradibus violentae caritatis*. This passage states that only words composed according to what the heart dictates are worthily uttered ("Solus proinde de ea digne loquitur qui secundum quod cor dictat verba componit"). *Patrologia Latina*, ed. J.-P. Migne, CXIV, col. 1195. *Patrologiae Cursus Completus, Series Latina* (Paris: 1844–64). Available online at: http://patristica.net/latina/ (accessed August 19, 2020).

Dante constantly plays up the role of reflection in extending the inspiration wrought by Beatrice through his own reflective remembrance of her. He notes about Beatrice that not only her presence but also *the memory of her* in his thought worked miracles or operated efficaciously ("e non solamente ne la sua presenzia, ma ricordandosi di lei, mirabilmente operava," XXVI. 15). By this route, his reflection can make itself independent of her actual presence. Indeed, the next time Dante speaks of "new matter" ("nuova materia," XXX. 1) for his poetry, he uses the phrase to introduce his poems written for Beatrice *in morte* under the sign of the widowed city as announced by Jeremiah's Lamentation (*Quomodo sedet sola civitas*) in Chapter XXVIII. 1.

Exemplarily, Chapter XXXIV, about the anniversary of Beatrice's death, depicts Dante as plunged deep into thought about her. His meditation, which again becomes equivalent to receiving something of a visitation (to be discussed further in Chapter 5), illustrates how memorialization can function as a sacred rite and accomplish a sort of revelation through the self-reflective processes of ceremonial remembrance that are such important constituents of religious cults. Rigorous and profound reflection reveals the transcendent nature of the deity to be ungraspable in whatever concrete, finite terms. The very emptiness of a positive (physical) presence turns commemorative religious rites in the direction of an openness to inspiration – which may even prove to be divine. Reflection exposes an emptiness which then opens a space for the infinite or holy. Particularly medieval pilgrimage rites, which sometimes proceeded paradigmatically to an empty tomb, have been put forward in this sense as a hermeneutical key to the *Vita nuova*.

Julia Bolton Holloway captures Dante's syncretistic juggling with multiple medieval traditions as producing a polyvalent hermeneutics based on two Scriptural paradigms of pilgrimage: Emmaus and Exodus. She discerns in the Emmaus paradigm Dante's "authorial mantle for the self-conscious, self-referential, self-reflective telling of the *Vita nuova*, its pilgrim narration," while the Exodus paradigm, as articulated into forty-two stations in the Book of Numbers (Chapter 33, verses 3–36), furnishes the key to the forty-two chapters of Dante's book as a "cryptography."[23] The book project of Dante's *Vita nuova* results in a self-reflective posture

---

[23] Julia Bolton Holloway, "The *Vita nuova*: Paradigms of Pilgrimmage," *Dante Studies* 103 (1985): 103–12. Holloway acknowledges that she is adapting to the *Vita nuova* John Demaray's method for deciphering the *Divine Comedy* in *The Invention of Dante's Commedia* (New Haven: Yale University Press, 1974). Citations are from her article available online at the Florin website: www.florin.ms/V itanuov.html (accessed June 30, 2020).

"deconstructing his own earlier poetry," while the Promised Land to which the book's pilgrimage is directed remains necessarily occulted.

In the Emmaus paradigm (from the Gospel According to Luke 24: 13–35), reflection reveals to the disciples – and, by their example, to all later readers and interpreters – that they have already been journeying with the risen Lord without realizing it. When Jesus had vanished out of their midst after breaking bread, exactly as in the sacrament of the Eucharist, they reflected on it together, "And they said one to another, Did not our heart burn within us, while he talked with us by the way, and while he opened to us the scriptures?" (24: 32).

The Exodus paradigm, on the other hand, entails journeying into an uncharted desert. Taken together, these scenarios negatively inflect the dialectic between self-reflection and inspiration by an unknown or unrecognized Other. Reflection is thereby oriented to what it cannot encompass. Clinching this argument, an at least covert subversion of self belongs to the movement of going out from and beyond oneself, by the power of reflection, toward an unfathomable Other.

The Intimate Secret of the Subject's Nothingness

In order to further probe this paradoxical conjunction and co-implication of reflection with inspiration, it is worth considering another of the enigmas that mark the *Vita nuova*, that of its constant impulse to a sometimes baffling sort of secretiveness. From early on, Dante could not deny the symptoms that plainly showed his suffering to be of the nature of a love sickness ("Dicea d'Amore, però che io portava nel viso tante de le sue insegne, che questo non si potea ricovrire," IV. 2). But when others asked *for whom* he was being destroyed by love, he would simply "look back at his questioners and, smiling, say nothing" ("E quando mi domandavano 'Per cui t'ha così distrutto questo Amore?', ed io sorridendo li guaradava, e nulla dicea loro," IV. 3).

Dante's concern to conceal the secret of his love – or at least the name of the one whom he loves – seems at times obsessive to such an extent as to pose something of a conundrum. It is not always very clearly motivated by the need to protect his lady and can therefore come across as forced or affected. Even when the identity of his beloved has been revealed as Beatrice because of his uncontainable dismay and coming undone in her presence ("per la vista mia molte persone avessero compreso lo secreto del mio cuore," XVIII. 1), still Dante dreads having to avow her name. This reluctance, not to say paranoia, comes out on another occasion when

Dante is turned into a pathetic semblance of himself just from hearing indirectly about Beatrice's grief at the decease of her father (XXII. 4-6). He covers his eyes with his hands, lest the tears bathing his face be noticed ("alcuna lagrima talora bagnava la mia faccia, onde io mi ricopria con porre le mani spesso a li miei occhi," XXII. 4).

Again, shortly thereafter, muttering her name deliriously in a dream, Dante is terrified that his sickness will be uncovered as due to his fears and worries about Beatrice. Consequently, he is immensely relieved when he discovers that his uncontrolled blurting out of her name in his feverish hallucinations, between sleep and waking, confusing reality and illusion, turned out not to have been intelligible to others because of its being so broken up by his sobbing ("E con tutto che io chiamasse questo nome, la mia voce era sì rotta dal singulto del piangere, che queste donne non mi pottero intendere, secondo il mio parere," XXIII. 13). Moved by Love, he gives those attending him an account of what caused his fear, but he carefully omits mentioning the name of his beloved ("tacendo lo nome di questa gentilissima," XXIII. 15).

Beyond the courtly conventions enjoining secrecy for passions avowed to married women, who were often the consorts of court sovereigns who were themselves the lovers' lords, Dante's obsession with secretiveness is a sign of something supremely important about the process of self-reflection that he is discovering. Introspective psychological reflection can be fastened hold of here in the process of making a historical advance pioneered by Dante. An inner realm of experience is opened up to him by self-reflection. But since, at the same time, it is exposed as a realm precisely of self-reflection – that is, as a purely subjective act – it is unstable and is vulnerable to dissolving into nothing. It turns out to be nothing but a transitory subjective perception having no objective reality beyond its appearance in and to him. When Dante's experiential reality is transformed in this way and reconfigured as consisting entirely in self-reflection, it exists only by virtue of this very act of self-reflection itself.

Self-reflection has to be known inwardly, or not at all. To the extent that it may escape and exist in some form outside of him, his self-reflection is no longer the same reality at all, no longer purely his own. It becomes something public – a piece of the world and thus antithetical to Dante's own intimate secret life in his interior forum. The final consequence, which Dante does not draw but arguably suspects, is that the proximate, real object of his love, after all, is only an ideal projected by his own inner reflection. The immediate reality of Beatrice for him is the Beatrice that he imagines. This realization about self-reflection as mediating all his conscious experience becomes much more explicit and acute in later literature of the modern era, but an inkling of awareness of it is prescient in Dante's closely guarded love for his Beatrice. Who she really is *as known through self-reflection* (not to deny the woman who occasions this reflection nor the revelation of transcendence she communicates to him) can only be a secret buried irretrievably in his own bosom.

Dante must keep his intimate feeling secret because its most authentic being is unveiled by self-reflection as nothing but self-reflection itself – or a product thereof. Exposed as such, self-reflection would no longer have any objective existence at all: once outside of him, it would vanish completely into nothing by the standards of the external world. Reflection makes Dante aware that he has no more substantial a self than reflection itself. Is this, then, the scandal that needs to be kept secret on pain of evacuating the self altogether and showing that the emperor has no clothes? If this secret is divulged, what is being kept close and guarded in secret is itself lost. And yet this secret *must* be divulged, it cannot *but* be divulged as the very condition of its being recognized as secret.[24] A pure interiority is nothing but pure pretense, at least as seen exteriorly and objectively.

This emptiness and nullity of the self purely and merely in itself, by a certain intrinsic necessity, therefore, breaks the self open to others and even makes it susceptible to the absolutely commanding presence of an Other. Corresponding symmetrically to the absolute emptiness of the self purely in itself is an uncanny (w)hol(l)y Other beyond the reach of speaking, an ineffable Other who cannot be said at all without being betrayed: it, too, like the purely inner self, is empty of determinate content. The Other is inevitably betrayed by being said, since to say it is to appropriate otherness into one's own discourse and conceptual framework and thereby to annul or encroach on its absolute otherness. Just like the absolutely inner, essential self, so the absolutely Other cannot be said or expressed any more than God can be grasped or articulated. The lesson of negative theology proves to be valid also for a certain modernity's substitute of the individual self for God as absolute foundation.[25]

---

[24] Jacques Derrida, notably in *Passions* (Paris: Galilée, 1993), subtly contemplates the paradox of the secret as finally being no secret at all, as requiring instead disclosure as the very condition of its being recognized as a secret.

[25] Most instructive here are Mark C. Taylor's books: *Deconstructing Theology* (Chicago: University of Chicago Press, 1982) and *Erring: A Postmodern A/theology* (Chicago: University of Chicago Press, 1984).

Dante's secretiveness about his love can thus be seen as symptomatic of the new, non-objective status of interiority toward which he is feeling his way. This realization moves him away from and beyond his initial, typically medieval position of concretely objectifying "memory" as a book (I. 1). Recognizing this instability and vulnerability of the self-reflective subject proves to be helpful for explaining the often rather exaggerated reactions that Dante displays from scene to scene in guarding his secrecy. Such behavior betrays the extreme precariousness of the subject position that Dante has newly discovered. In the typical *dramatis personae* of the traditional courtly love scenario, there were numerous malignant adversaries out there – Haine, Dangier, Lauzengier (Hate, Danger, Flatterer) – who needed to be evaded, but with the interiorization of this drama in the *dolce stil novo* the motivations for secrecy shift and are no longer evident. Secrecy thenceforth becomes revealing of a previously occulted dimension of purely subjective reality.

As another symptom, in the scene of his delirium in Chapter XXIII, and more broadly in the book, Dante presumes to be able to keep reality and dream, objective facts and subjective experience, clearly distinct from each other and not to confuse them. Yet just such conflation is exactly what happens as a result of the scene's, and the book's, intrinsic propensities to self-reflection. Reflection, which cannot help but be turned eventually also on itself, reveals the inner and the outer alike, and all such settings of boundaries, to be unstable products of self-reflection itself. This is unsettling, as it wipes away stable and statable foundations for the self. Dante understandably tries to cover over this troubling aspect of his own self-discovery.

The elusiveness and vulnerability of the modern subject as purely a product of self-reflection is the legacy that is anticipated here and that will prove to be so essential to the making of the modern novel. Unlike classical epic or the Hellenistic adventure tale or romance, the modern novel by its nature privileges a subjective point of view: it focuses on how events are *lived* and *experienced* by a subject rather than simply on the events themselves for their own sake. This differentiates the modern novel from the ancient epic consisting of *res gestae*, or heroic works in a public domain, as well as from medieval romance, with its serial adventures.

This subjective turn is already much in evidence at the origin of the modern novel with *Don Quixote* (1505–15). A subjective perspective can be felt everywhere in this novel thanks notably to its dialogical constitution as made up largely of ongoing conversations between the knight errant, the titular protagonist, and his squire Sancho Panza: we see the world as filtered through their eyes and through those of other characters. No matter how absurd and preposterous the action becomes in itself, its deadly serious earnestness for Don Quixote makes it really moving for us all. The character's subjective, even if deluded, experience is what counts.

Acute subjective (self-)consciousness in this novel is engendered most directly, however, by Miguel de Cervantes's uncompromising examination and exposure of the fictive construction of his own authorship. Designating himself in the prologue to Part I as "step-father" ("padrastro") rather than as father of the book, Cervantes constructs his own role as simply editing and passing along to the public a "historia" fortuitously found in a marketplace in Toledo. To heighten the scent of scandal, he tells us that he found the story written in an Arabic manuscript by one "Cide Hamete Benengeli," a Moorish (and thus culturally estranged) author.[26]

This "first" modern novel's self-reflection on its own authorship thus carries out a devastating dismantling of any claim to sovereignty over its own characters and contents. It becomes the exposition of a sovereign nothingness – of nothing to be grasped except via relations with a radical alterity at the core of the subject's consciousness of itself. Likewise in an early modern Spanish baroque context, this predicament is searchingly represented and teasingly played out in the parallel medium of painting by Diego Velazquez's *Las Meninas* (1656).[27] This painting specularly represents the painter painting himself and the Spanish king and queen positioned where the viewer would be, but seen only as reflected in a mirror. The vertigo of these self-reflections voids the "subject" of sovereignty in the very act of its creation of itself through self-reflection.

The insubstantiality and nothingness of the subject exposes itself and threatens Dante when he becomes absorbed in self-reproaches, or at least in portraying his own vulnerability and helplessness, for example, vis-à-vis the women who mock and question him in the episodes of the *gabbo* (Chapters XIV–XVIII). In just this liability to annihilation through self-reflection, he is a forerunner also of that other exemplar of modern self-consciousness,

---

[26] Miguel de Cervantes Saavedra, *El Ingenioso Hidalgo Don Quijote de la Mancha*, ed. Salvador Fajardo and James A. Parr (Asheville, NC: Pegasus Press, 1998), Prólogo, p. 4 and Part I, chapter IX, pp. 65–66. Among innumerable discussions of the status of this work as the first and even as the most comprehensive of all modern novels, see Ian Watt, *Myths of Modern Individualism: Faust, Don Quixote, Don Juan, Robinson Caruso* (Cambridge: Cambridge University Press, 1996) and Roberto González Echevarría, "Introduction to *Don Quixote*," in *Miguel de Cervantes*, ed. Harold Bloom (Philadelphia: Chelsea, 2005).

[27] Zdravka Gugleta, "Michel Foucault's (Mis)interpretation of *las Meninas*. Or, *Pure* Representation as the Tautologous Structure of the Sign," *Facta Universitatis, Series Linguistics and Literature* 9/1 (2011): 1–12, pertinently reviews the critical discourse on this most thought-provoking artwork.

Hamlet, who is apt to become absorbed into his own reflections ("To be, or not to be," III. i. 55–89) and self-reproaches for leaving the "dread command" (III. iv. 110) of his father's ghost unexecuted. This risk comes out most pointedly in the dramatic soliloquy at the end of Act II, beginning "O, what a rogue and peasant slave am I!" (II. ii. 515–72).

These epoch-making texts of the modern era are the *Vita nuova*'s heirs in the discovery of the nullity of the self *in itself* – and its consequent breaking open to all possible plenitude in and through relationship with others. In each of these classic texts, the protagonists have to be beaten back, symbolically and literally, to the threshold of death before coming to this saving insight into their own constitutive and founding relation to an absolute (or at least an absolutely shattering) Alterity. Through this relation, they discover that their own egos, as enclosed by self-reflection, are null and void – and this epiphany then frees them to love and act with infinite commitment of their whole existence in relation to others.

Something similar and symmetrical to this discovery concerning the ambiguity of self-reflection and its implication in its own undoing – and therewith in a certain undermining of the self – might be inferred also from the *Vita nuova*'s fascination with clothes and with the paraphernalia of dress. The obsessive investment in these exteriors, through which persons themselves, above all Beatrice, but also Love, are presented,[28] may be read as a symptom of anxiety or embarrassment on the part of the fully reflective self that the object of its veneration may be, at bottom, insofar as it can be presented, nothing else besides these exterior covers themselves. In this case, all the lavishly described attires would serve unwittingly only as veils for a particularly powerful type of void.

The focus and indeed fixation on a merely outward covering such as clothing reads thus as a hint betraying the subliminal suspicion that the idealized object of Dante's love may be generated by reflection itself. Self-reflection, carried to its limit, reveals this lack of any objective foundation outside itself. It is also exposed as void within itself inasmuch as it can comprehend itself only through an inverted (mirror) image of an *absolute* Other – one with no positive content given prior to reflection. This void reveals itself as a prior condition of any revelation of an Absolute that is properly theological – not conditioned by any finite content.

This is the dialectic of *Schein* or "appearing" worked out by Hegel in his *Science of Logic* (see especially Part 1, Book 2, section 1: "Essence as Reflection

---

[28] For Beatrice, this is conspicuous in II. 3; III. 1; XXXIX. 1; and even still in *Purgatorio* XXX. 31–33. For Love, see at least IX. 3 and XII. 3.

into Itself," where "Absolute Essence has no determinate being").[29] Modern philosophy can be inscribed into the wake of the subjectivity that opens up in Dante's "new life" as turned ultimately toward an Other. Fully realizing this orientation turns modern philosophy away from its one-sided assertion of autonomy for the self toward the praise of heteronomy – or of being governed by a grace-giving Other – and thus "makes room" for revelation. This reorientation of philosophy becomes evident from a postmodern perspective that has taken the "hermeneutical turn."[30]

Is something like this anxiety endemic to a subjective yet other-dependent existence, then, the generally dissimulated reason for Dante's pathological secretiveness? Dante's discomfiture is made manifest already in Chapter IV of the *Vita nuova* by what seems his snide refusal to divulge the object of his love passion. He becomes his own impediment ("comminciò lo mio spirito naturale ad essere impedito ne la sua operazione") and makes himself dangerously ill by his determination to keep secret the name of his beloved, which he believes others enviously wish to pry out of him ("molti pieni d'invidia già si procacciavano di sapere di me quello che io volea del tutto celare ad altrui," IV. 1).

In any event, Dante intensifies self-reflection to the point where it mediates the very *existence* of the ego and turns ultimately into a kind of negative theological revelation of self-transcendence. *Not* the self but rather something transcending and enabling it is in command of its own self-exposition. Reflection and revelation become inseparable. This, I submit, is Dante's fundamental bequest to modernity in its radical realization of a secularization of religious revelation.[31] Revelation of the subject to itself by self-reflection seems to give something concrete and graspable to be known, yet, as grounded in the infinite and ungraspable, the real being of the subject escapes its own self-reflection. The subject is torn asunder and opened toward the infinite – what I am calling the theological. Others may prefer to understand this as only a secularized revelation or disclosure. I propose that it, in any case, can be understood as *negatively* theological.

A mesmerizing emblem of this dialectic of immanence and transcendence turns up in the "Veronica." Dante alludes to it in *Vita nuova* XL. 1 in

---

[29] G. F. W. Hegel, *Wissenschaft der Logik* (1812), in *Werke* (Frankfurt a. M.: Suhrkamp, 1979), vol. VI, p. 17: "Das Wesen als Reflexion in ihm selbst."

[30] Merold Westphal, *In Praise of Heteronomy: Making Room for Revelation* (Bloomington: Indiana University Press, 2017), p. 213.

[31] I make this case more generally in the Introduction and in chapters 1 and 9 of *Secular Scriptures: Modern Theological Poetics in the Wake of Dante*, pp. 1–42 and 207–30.

conjunction with pilgrims who are on their way to Rome in order to see the "blessed image" ("imagine benedetta") of the Savior.[32] The article in question is a mere cloth that, because of the myth attached to it, becomes the token of a transcendent reality. Its positive presence as a cloth covers over the infinite absence of the divinity it is supposed to commemorate by having retained the imprint of Christ's face when Veronica wiped it for him along the way of the Cross. This holy relic is treated, according to a perhaps fanciful but widely accepted etymology, as the "true icon" ("vera icona") of Christ. The "Veronica" thus presents a concrete object believed to carry the impress and to communicate the "virtue" of direct contact with divinity. As such, it embodies a typical sort of religious and ritualistic impulse out of which poetry celebrating the theological is also apt to arise.

Such poetry, in fact, is generated by reflection on what is believed to be a kind of real and even absolute presence. Any of its *representations* is *not* it and, therefore, is unstable and subject to being undermined by self-reflection, which comes to realize this fact. Religious rite projects true revelation of a transcendent truth on what is merely an artifact and covers over the necessary, constitutive emptiness of any purported presence. Rationally and reflectively considered, true divinity is infinite and cannot as such be made fully available in any merely finite object. A passion for an absolute that is infinite, yet in finite terms necessarily empty, is transferred onto an iconic token that is concretely present. The self-reflective consciousness of modernity exposes this dialectic at work in the creation of religious myths that, consequently, are inhabited by an inherent insecurity. The contradictions of this dialectic lurk veiled already in Dante's often mystically elusive descriptions. The reflections generated by these contradictions can hardly keep from engaging with theology. Indeed, the contradictions arise from the infinite and unfathomable nature of the Other, which is the ultimate concern of theology.

As revealed after the fact, Dante's education in love and poetry has been, in effect, an induction into theology. The theology in question here arises on the tangible ground of human encounter, which catalyzes self-reflection. Encountering Beatrice is Dante's initiation into his own individual and peculiar experience of the divine. The grounding of theological

---

[32] Alessandro Vettori, "Veronica: Dante's Pilgrimage from Image to Vision," *Dante Studies* 121 (2003): 43–65, underlines continuity and connections, especially through motifs of suffering and hardship, with the explicit reference to "la Veronica nostra" in *Paradiso* XXXI. 104 at the other end of Dante's pilgrimage through life and letters.

revelation in human encounter in Dante's *magnum opus*, his *Divine Comedy*, appears here in its first emergence.[33]

How this appearing or emerging of a revelation of transcendence is to be interpreted and understood – whether as a given phenomenon or as an interpretive construction – is precisely the issue that opens up between the contrasting approaches of phenomenology and hermeneutics taken as methodological paradigms. The next chapter weighs their comparative merits and respective limitations measured specifically as methods capable of illuminating and interpreting the miraculous experience characteristic of religious revelation undergone and realized as an existential phenomenon of personal encounter. The limitations of both methods and of method per se emerge from this comparison, opening a contemplative eye toward the apophatic dimension of the unsayable that engenders infinite figures through interpretation by its witnesses.

---

[33] Vittorio Montemaggi , in *Reading Dante's* Commedia *as Theology: Divinity Realized in Human Encounter* (Oxford: Oxford University Press, 2016), explores this type of humanly embedded theological revelation, delivering a provocative personal witness of his own.

CHAPTER 4

Phenomenology versus Hermeneutics (Debate with Harrison): Revelation as Mediation

> Not the intense moment
> Isolated, with no before and after,
> But a lifetime burning in every moment
> And not the lifetime of one man only
> But of old stones that cannot be deciphered.
>
> (T. S. Eliot, "East Coker," V)

Contrary to my emphasis on the inextricably literary and specifically lyrical mediation of Dante's religious experience of Beatrice, Robert Harrison asserts the absolute priority of Dante's experience of Beatrice as a woman rather than as a beatifier. In its immediacy, stripped of subsequent sublimations and systematizing interpretations, this experience is for Harrison fundamentally erotic and aesthetic rather than a religious experience. It is, above and before all, an immediate and a bodily experience rather than a symbolic elaboration. But from what could this assertion be inferred? What are its grounds as an assertion? Does not the poetic enterprise just as often, or possibly always, co-opt and shape, or even invent, experience that suits it? And is there any experience that is not always already framed by some form of interpretation, without which it would not be able to register and be retained at all? Would Dante's experience of Beatrice be "what it is" apart from the poetry?[1] Harrison admits and insists that Beatrice is accessible to us today only through a "phenomenal veil" and in an "aesthetic order."[2] Yet this does not prevent him from hypothesizing her body as the real thing that overpowered Dante in its immediacy and "transcendent otherness" as an

---

[1] Rainer Warning, "Imitatio und Intertextualität: Zur Geschichte lyrischer Dekonstruktion der Amortheologie: Dante, Petrarca, Baudelaire," in *Ästhetischer Schein*, ed. Willi Oelmüller (Paderborn: Schöningh, 1983), pp. 168–207, argues for the love lyric's own "deconstruction" of any direct apprehension of being, with reference on pp. 172–79 specifically to the *Vita nuova*.
[2] Robert Pogue Harrison, *The Body of Beatrice* (Baltimore: The Johns Hopkins University Press, 1988), p. 28.

epiphany of beauty and gave the initial impulse to his entire itinerary of representation, which covered over this originating experience.

Harrison's realistic way of construing the relation between Dante's poetry and its presumed historical, referential content may be possible, but it is certainly not inevitable. Indeed, whole strains of criticism have been built on precisely the contrary assumption that Beatrice never existed as a real woman at all.[3] Harrison's assumptions represent a decision as to what counts as truly real for him – or perhaps for everyone, in his view. Yet even he stresses that the visionary quality of Dante's experiences and of Dante's descriptive accounts of them blurs the line between the real and the imaginary: "It is difficult to determine the difference in status between Dante's actual 'perceptions' of Beatrice in the *Vita nuova* and his various dreams, visions, and hallucinations" (*Body of Beatrice*, p. 172). Nevertheless, in spite of practical difficulties, Harrison does not, in principle, call the distinction into question. His aim would be, were it only possible, to isolate and recover the original perception, thereby going "back to the things themselves" – according to the familiar procedure of the phenomenological reduction as prescribed by Edmund Husserl's often-quoted slogan ("auf die Sachen selbst zurückgehen").[4] Since the original experience of finite transcendence in the presence of Beatrice's body is no longer accessible, the best we can do is to respect its irrecuperability shrouded in the silence of the book's ellipses and enigmas and protect its inviolability by shielding it from hermeneutic profanations.[5]

In critiquing this approach, I am not claiming that Harrison's hermeneutic biases are necessarily wrong. I only want to identify them as hermeneutic biases so that it will be clear that his conclusions are not yielded simply by "the text on its own terms." I think Harrison's biases are likely to be shared more generally among Dante scholars and literary critics, especially American ones, than my own. Nevertheless, "the hermeneutics of faith" should not be lost sight of in the interpretation of an author for whom religious belief was paramount, as it ostensibly was for Dante – and even if this were only ostensibly so. Much of the truly exceptional experience and insight made accessible by Dante would be lost if we were to

---

[3] Pierre Mandonnet, O. P., *Dante le Théologien: Introduction à l'intelligence de la vie, des œuvres et de l'art de Dante Alighieri* (Paris: Desclée De Brouwer, 1935) is particularly radical in his reduction of Beatrice to pure symbol for the revealed truth of theology. Étienne Gilson examines Mandonnet's assertions with unequalled thoroughness and acumen in *Dante et la philosophie* (Paris: J. Vrin, 1954), in pages on "Les métamorphoses de Béatrice" (pp. 3–81).

[4] The phrase occurs in the introduction to Husserl's *Logical Investigations* (*Logische Untersuchungen*, 1900–1901), vol. II, section 6.

[5] See my critical "Note on Robert Harrison's *The Body of Beatrice*," *Rivista di studi italiani* 6/2 (1988): 78–82.

overlook these hermeneutic practices, which Dante himself initiated with regard to his own works.

An important advantage of a hermeneutic approach – embracing the hermeneutics of existence as well as of the text[6] – is that it makes Dante's faith not an obstacle to, or even an evasion of, his vision of reality but, instead, its very essence. We do not need to discount what was declaredly important to Dante in order to carry out our own reading of the effectual meaning of his perceptions, as if the perception and its meaning were isolable from each other. To try to interpret Dante on the basis of his Catholic faith is an interpretive gamble, but so is any critical methodology, whether declared or implicit.

With regard to Harrison's own approach, we should ask, what is the status of inferences about the genesis of a poem? Admittedly, genesis as such – the origin – is epistemologically beyond our grasp as readers. Still, our engagement with a poem may lead to reconstructions of its hypothetical determining impetus and presumable motivations. And yet, this inevitably entails not a detached scientific analysis or perception of an object but rather personal involvement in a hermeneutic process of entering into relation with the work. Harrison has brought contemporary philosophical methodologies into contact with the thirteenth-century text. He is engaged in philosophical hermeneutics, where questioning a work must involve also questioning one's own being in relation to the work. Harrison would like to get at the work itself, but in actual fact he is dealing with the work only as acted upon by a certain set of instruments. This is ineluctably so, notwithstanding his statement in the preface: "In what follows I try to confront the *Vita nuova* on its own terms and at the same time to avoid the hermeneutic trap of Dantology" (p. ix).

I agree with Harrison that we must understand Dante's representations ontologically, yet this is not because of what they *represent* – purportedly a real woman – but rather because of what they *are*: artifacts produced by and embodying an existential-poetic act. Dante's experience of a real woman, if that is what it was, comes to light in literature. We can agree that it is counterproductive to try to go behind the literary veil. The veil is the enabling condition of the experience such as it exists for us – and for Dante, too, once he becomes the author of his memoires.[7] What if

---

[6] This distinction is rendered perspicuous by David E. Klemm, ed., *Hermeneutical Inquiry* (New York: Oxford University Press, 1986), with its division into volume I (*The Interpretation of Texts*) and volume II (*The Interpretation of Existence*).

[7] Manuele Gragnolati, "Trasformazioni e assenze: la *performance* della *Vita nova* e le figure di Dante e Cavalcanti," *L'Alighieri* 35 (2010): 5–23, analyzes this process as Dante's "performance of authorship." Such an analysis shifts the focus from representing the truth of the past to creating an authentic

historical documents regarding "Beatrice" and even her encounters with "Dante" were to be discovered? Would that add to our understanding of Dante's experience of "Beatrice" otherwise than by contributing to the ensemble of texts surrounding her? It would, in any case, not give us a direct and privileged knowledge of the real significance of the Beatrice of the *Vita nuova*. The same argument can be – and has been – made about the Christ of the Gospels.[8]

In Harrison's view, Beatrice inspires the poems in the sense that "the poem incorporates the animations of her presence into its own new life," and "poetic language becomes in some sense authenticated and substantiated by virtue of its genesis" (p. 30). Genesis as such is hermeneutically indigestible, which may be why Harrison likes it so much. Nonetheless, ironically, in writing the word "genesis," he has at least inadvertently named *inter alia* the Christian mythopoetic interpretation of existence par excellence as elaborated "in the beginning" of the homonymous book of the Bible. What I object to is speaking of the genesis of the poem as a known quantity from which inferences about the poem can be drawn, since such genesis as may be inferred comes to us as readers only filtered through the poem itself – or through the prose glosses, which can hardly be relied on as independent sources.

Moreover, to assert the primacy of perception is to box reality into the experience of a subject – an epistemological, a perceiving subject rather than a subject pragmatically engaged and involved in the world. This subject is an observer whose perceptions are but secondary reflections with regard to the reality that the subject actually lives – and in more ways than can be consciously accounted for in being perceived. Moreover, what is perceived does not in the first instance consist in perceptions. This I affirm together with Maurice Merleau-Ponty, Martin Heidegger, and Aristotle (implicitly), and against the whole epistemological cast of modern philosophy from Descartes to Husserl, not to mention in analytic philosophy. As Heidegger writes, in overturning the general epistemological bias of modern philosophy: "Much closer to us than all sensations are things themselves."[9] Phenomenologically considered, we experience *things*, not "sense impressions." The latter are only abstractions introduced by

---

authorial persona in the present. Gragnolati, however, in the end, valorizes what he takes to be the *Commedia*'s material, corporeal grounding of identity over the *Vita nuova*'s disembodied, linguistically constructed "sense of identity."

[8] Rudolf Bultmann, *Jesus Christ and Mythology* (New York: Charles Scribner's Sons, 1958).
[9] Martin Heidegger, "The Origin of the Work of Art," in *Basic Writings*, ed. D. Krell (New York: Harper & Rowe, 1977), p. 156.

reflection and analysis applied to holistic experience of things as inherently connected and significant. We "hear" not acoustic impressions of grinding and squeaking, but a coach passing below in the street. At least, some such supposition concerning their object is likely to steer and determine what our ears pick up and our brains register and process as experience. Our sensations are always already integrated into our understanding and interpretation of what we are perceiving as whole human beings present among other beings in a world.

Whereas Harrison talks about the primacy of perception in Dante's encounter with Beatrice, Dante insists relentlessly on the symbolic characteristics of each encounter he relates. Dante presents appearances whose meaning is mysterious. Harrison begins with the assumption, informed by the Freudian revolution, that "the true meaning" ("il verace giudicio") of Dante's poetry arises from the body of Beatrice. However, as readers and interpreters, we are in any case dealing with visions written in a book rather than with the vision or perception of a physical body. Dante does make use of the Platonic criterion of an immediate intuitive seeing of truth, yet this is above all a spiritual seeing, and he re-inscribes it within the hermeneutic context of a linguistically reflected and recounted event symbolized from the outset as the "book" of memory.

What you cannot simply see, in the literal sense, about Beatrice (or about Christ, for that matter) is that she is a miracle. This conclusion is reached through hermeneutic methods, for example, through a deciphering of the "nines" that miraculously mark every aspect of her advent. For the *meaning* of existence (even of any given individual existence) is not primarily perceived: it is rather interpreted. It is not given simply as an object to perception, nor can it just be any sort of given at all, not without belying the freedom which is so fundamentally constitutive of human existence. For this reason, the meaning of human experience can never simply be given as a fact: it must rather be decided upon and acted out. Understanding revelation in existential terms need not stop with the primacy of perception, as Harrison would have it. Instead, such understanding leads on to the risk and decision of interpretation such as it has been lived and relived by believers in all ages.

The prose *ragioni* are keys showing how the poems are indeed verbalizations of existential data. Without the *ragioni*, the poems would be contextualized only by a literary and rhetorical tradition rather than by an individual life story. Yet, by virtue of the prose, the poems become the voice of an individual existence. In the *Divine Comedy*, Dante will succeed in making his poetry the story of his personal existence rather than just a rhetorical performance, and he will do so without recourse to a prose complement, but simply by incorporating the story into his lyrical, musically metered, verses. He will thus succeed in making the "I" of his poetry not a conventional lyric subject but a thoroughly individualized, historicized *persona* coinciding (at least by the end) with himself as author.

Seen in this light, the function of the *Vita nuova*'s prose shows up as that of grounding the poems in a personal history. This is quite different from the function attributed to it by Harrison, who construes the prose as an overcoming of the poetry in the direction of a narrative openness. In his view, whereas the static closure of lyric synchrony is left to Petrarch to be played out to its last gasps, Dante's *Vita nuova* opens lyric into a narrative dimension that is unlimited in its linearity. And yet, poetry remains absolutely essential in Dante's life story as he tells it both in the *Vita nuova* and in the *Commedia*. The lyric would seem to be anything but overcome, for example, in Dante's review of his poetic career in *Purgatorio* XXIV, where the *dolce stil novo* is first defined by Dante in his encounter with Bonagiunta da Lucca (verses 49 to 63). It is essentially through poetry that the meaning of Dante's experience is realized and communicated. Although the prose describes the existential circumstances which purportedly gave rise to the visions and, consequently, to the poems recording those visions, in some sense the "original" event must equally be considered to be the poetic writing itself – a sort of incarnation of the Word in Dante's individual existence as writer no less than as lover. This sense of poetry as the lyrical expression of an individual life unfolding in a personal history originates in and with the *Vita nuova* as an autobiographical poetic witness.

The "I" who speaks in the pages of the *Vita nuova* from its opening phrases, as already implied in "la *mia* memoria" ("my memory"), and then as outspoken in "io trovo" ("I find"), sets itself into a self-consciously hermeneutic relation with the story it tells. The "I" finds the words of the story it is going to tell written in the book of its memory. It is perfectly ordinary for the writer of a story, especially an autobiographical story, to stand in such a hermeneutic relation to his or her material. Such an author unavoidably interprets what s/he remembers in telling their story, whether this interpretation is written directly into the re-telling of their memoires or is stated as a commentary delivered from the distance that separates the telling and the interpreting of what is remembered from its actual occurrence.

However, in the case of the *Vita nuova*, Dante treats his own personal memory as a book. The literary mediation of his process of interpretation is itself reified as the object of his interpretation. Thus Dante, as author, interprets not only the past, but also, and more immediately, a linguistically formulated memory of the past – the words written ("scritte le parole") in the book of his memory ("libro de la mia memoria," I. 1). In this sense, *words* are the source of the story the *Vita nuova* tells. In the first instance, those words are the poems Dante transcribes onto the pages of the *Vita nuova*.

Are the poems within the book to be understood as themselves products of hermeneutic endeavor? They are presented as arising out of situations described in the prose. As such, the prose provides a gloss on them. But do the poems perhaps reciprocally, in turn, prior to their being anthologized and set in a narrative frame, interpretively structure the situations out of which they allegedly arise? The poems, on this showing, can function as the origin of Dante's experience and can reveal an underlying truth of his existence that would otherwise remain unperceived.

Interpretation does not necessarily move from the more complex to the more plain and prosaic. More fundamentally, it consists simply in the original verbalization of experience or being.[10] And that is exactly what the poems do. By describing in prose the experiential situations out of which each poem speaks, the scribe of the new life enables us to read and understand the poems as verbalizations of an individual's unique, personal, even intimate, experience. This is perhaps the greatest generic novelty of the *Vita nuova*. The prosimetric form has august precedents, such as Boethius's *De consolatione philosophiae*, but the verse in this work and in other models, such as Martianus Capella's *De nuptiis Phlologiae et Mercurii*, is less the expression of individual experience than a flower of convention-alized rhetoric. The poetry in these models is more philosophical – more impersonal, more about universal truths – than confessional and existen-tial. Dante's poems, in contrast, originate in his individualized experience of love as a revelation of a quality of existence that is uniquely his own.

Hermeneutics of (Theological) Transcendence

Harrison might object that such a reading, by emphasizing the circularity between the poetry and the prose rather than seeing the prose as breaking free from lyric self-enclosure, makes Dante and his work solipsistic and reduces it to writing feeding only on writing itself. We can agree that what is special about Dante, relative to Petrarch and Cavalcanti, is his "access to

---

[10] Aristotle, in *On Interpretation*, formulates the doctrine that any signifying of the real, starting from a significant sound, such as a word, is "interpretation" ("hermeneias").

transcendence." For Harrison, this means that his writing incorporates his experience of an actual woman. Yet, we must ask: Is that what Dante would want to call "access to transcendence"? It is transcendence only of the self-enclosure of the self that is presumed to be typical of Cavalcanti and Petrarch. As such, it still constitutes a form of remaining grounded in the immediacy of the empirically given, which is, from another point of view, a complete denial of transcendence.

From a typically modern perspective, access to otherness in its theological form, or in the form of other worlds, becomes problematic, if not impossible. Only then does the openness to an encounter in mundane space-time with the perceived bodily form of another human being count as the only true and authentic experience of transcendence – "transcendent exteriority," as Harrison terms it (*Body of Beatrice*, p. 96). This perspective, in which only the external world is known by representations, owes more to a starting point in a form of Cartesian subjectivity than to Dante's medieval worldview. This specifically modern form of self-enclosure in a world of representations pertains to the epistemological subject newly constructed in the "classical age" of the seventeenth century.[11] Accordingly, what is transcended here would seem to be only a wholly modern notion of self-enclosure.[12]

In the Middle Ages, transcendence was typically thought to pass rather by an inward channel, and writing, as a tool of inward search and a record of inward contemplative experience, might be a supremely important means of access to it. Writing, as a means of revelation, might even be more important than sighting a beloved person, or more exactly the body of a beloved person, in external space.[13] Harrison's point of view remains circumscribed within an epistemological framework, in which consciousness is hemmed in by its own representations, as indeed his Kantian language about Beatrice's body as a "noumenon" (a non-phenomenal, unknowable, "thing-in-itself") betrays. Through epistemological analysis, everything of which one is immediately conscious turns into a perception

---

[11] Michel Foucault, *Les mots et les choses* (Paris: Gallimard, 1966) can serve as a guidepost to delimit this outlook historically.

[12] For a profound interpretation of theological transcendence as reaching necessarily beyond all human self-transcendence, see Ingolf U. Dalferth, *Transzendenz und säkulare Welt: Lebensorientierung an letzter Gegenwart* (Tübingen: Mohr Siebeck, 2015). Merold Westphal, *Transcendence and Self-Transcendence: On God and the Soul* (Bloomington: Indiana University Press, 2004) treats the distinction lucidly, but in philosophical terms that do not attain to the theological dimension that Dalferth – and Dante – intend.

[13] Jean-Claude Schmitt, *Le corps des images: Essais sur la culture visuelle au Moyen Âge* (Paris: Gallimard, 2002), specifically "Écriture et image," pp. 97–134, demonstrates this in detail.

or representation, and the problem thus becomes that of access to otherness – of reaching beyond merely one's own sensations and perceptions.

The epistemological point of view has become particularly exacerbated in
the West since Descartes and the rise of a scientific worldview. Of course,
there were forms of epistemological entrapment in the Middle Ages, and
Cavalcanti, in Harrison's analysis, certainly proves to be a case in point.
Nevertheless, Dante invents a crucial alternative, and it is hermeneutic in
character. Not knowing the other as an object of perception, but relating
through the word to an otherness that cannot be directly perceived, is the way
of transcendence proper to Dante's Christian medieval culture. This way may
be understood as based, before all else, on a technique developed and practiced
particularly in monasteries, the technique of the *lectio divinis* – the meditative
and interpretive reading of sacred texts, chiefly the Bible, which may evoke the
presence of the holy – the wholly other or transcendent.[14]

Dante's access to transcendence concerns the revelation of a meaning in
his personal experience, experience centered on an absolutely meaningful
event – the extraordinary advent of a woman who is actually much more
than just a woman to him. She is beatitude and salvation for him,
a theological revelation that redefines the whole nature of his experience
and life. He need not strive to know her body, nor to unknow it as
a noumenon, for the body is in any case but a sign to be read – the more
so for being so erotically charged. After all, noumena are only philosophical
fictions. Seen from a religious standpoint, they stand for epistemology's
self-enclosure over against revelation. Revelation of the truly Other can
take place only via relations and their hermeneusis.[15] On the basis of
perception and its alleged primacy, on the other hand, Harrison can only
reach the conclusion that revelation does not take place within the *Vita
nuova* but is rather deferred into the future.

What this approach misses is that, according to Dante's testimony,
revelation actually *has* taken place and, even more importantly, *does* take
place: and it occurs by the instrumentality of the lyric instead of by an
overcoming of the lyrical impulse. Moreover, after the *Vita nuova*, Dante
will continue to witness to the revelation personally conferred on him in
the person of Beatrice, and his witness will be his poetry. I willingly grant

[14] Jean Leclercq, *L'amour des lettres et le désir de Dieu: Initiation aux auteurs monastiques du Moyen-Âge*
(Paris: Cerf, 1957), trans. Catherine Misrahi as *The Love of Learning and the Desire for God: A Study of
Monastic Culture* (New York: Fordham University Press, 1982).

[15] I explore this problematic, distinguishing more exactly a hermeneutic from an epistemological
outlook, in "Hermeneutic Catastrophe in Racine: The Epistemological Predicament of 17th
Century Tragedy," *Romanische Forschungen* 105 (1993): 315–31.

that the finale of the *Vita nuova* announces an interval, a temporary suspension of his activity of writing, in order that Dante may come into more adequate means of poetic expression. But this suspension is not a surrender to an indefinitely hypothetical future. The future in which he will be able to "speak more worthily of her" ("parlare più degnamente di lei") becomes concretely actual in the *Commedia*. A more adequate and abundant fulfillment of the promise tendered at the end of the *Vita nuova* could hardly be hoped for or imagined. But even without looking ahead to Dante's *magnum opus*, there is still no reason to think that the language promised at the end of the *Vita nuova* is likely to be prose rather than a new, more potent – perhaps even an eminently lyrical – type of poetry.[16] And this is just what Dante actually delivers in his *Commedia*.

By removing revelation to a point outside the bounds of inspired lyrical experience and placing it after the end of the *Vita nuova*, thus projecting it into a hypothetical future, Harrison acutely analyzes one dimension, the "not yet," of the eschatological temporality that Dante lives by virtue of his personal revelation. Yet, so far, this is only one aspect of the complete experience of revelation. What Harrison loses is the other aspect of Dante's witness, the "already," the revelation of divinity in Beatrice, enshrined in the *Vita nuova*'s lyrics – just as in the New Testament hymns celebrating Christ as having lived and died and risen to new life.[17] Dante's experience, after all, is simply a particular enactment of the general Christian revelation, which, in turn, is personal for every Christian.

Now this loss (of one aspect of Dante's witness) may be counted as gain by Harrison, for it may be that he does not believe that any such revelation of divinity actually has occurred – or, perhaps, even could occur. And hence the limiting of the revelation to future hypothesis and hyperbole would be a most welcome demystification. But let us be clear that a decision has been made here as to what is or is not susceptible to being revealed to humans by God. Harrison has declined to believe (or at least to

---

[16] Harrison does recognize that the lyric mode comes back in the *Paradiso*, though for him its effect is more the covering over than the revealing of existential truth.

[17] This peculiar, contradictory temporality of "not yet" and, at the same time, "already" defines the eschatological existence of Christians, especially as it is apprehended by Saint Paul in some of the earliest documents making up the New Testament, for example, Philippians 3: 11–14: "Not as though I had already attained, either were already perfect: but I follow after, if that I may apprehend that for which also I am apprehended of Christ Jesus." As developed by Rudolf Bultmann, this "existential" temporality became fundamental to Heidegger's thinking in *Being and Time* and so to what can be called "hermeneutic phenomenology" and its critique of classical (Cartesian) epistemology. Giorgio Agamben applies this Pauline temporality revealingly to the "internal eschatology" of the Troubadour poem in *Il tempo che resta: Un commento alla Lettera ai Romani* (Turin: Bollati Boringhieri, 2000), pp. 77–84.

suspend disbelief) in something that Dante, together with the evangelists, invites us to believe. In "Phenomenology of the *Vita nuova*," Harrison confirms his choice to believe only in what can be directly perceived and not in anything unseen or infinite.[18] He explains his phenomenological approach as "grounded in finitude" (p. 184). He, in effect, literalizes the trope of unmediated vision, which in religious revelation stands for a "seeing" through belief as more immediate and intuitive than chains of reasoning. Harrison ignores, however, that, understood religiously, such "vision" entails perception not just of discrete, finite objects but also, and more significantly, of their infinite "ground" or background.

The different understandings of Dante's literary text that Harrison and I respectively propose are predicated on different decisions, not least decisions of faith or non-faith, that are apt to open certain horizons of possibility. These convictions and decisions are primarily matters of epistemological faith, but they cannot be entirely separated from religious or existential commitments.[19]

Harrison's reading reflects a particular hermeneutic decision vis-à-vis the text; it is not simply confronting the text "on its own terms." What we read in the text of the *Vita nuova* is what we have chosen to believe about the possibilities for ourselves, as for Dante, of really attaining to a new life. This is to suggest not only that the text has been freed by Harrison from Dante's hermeneutic guidelines but that it has, at the same time, been subjected to Harrison's own. We need to recognize that there is no access to the text on its own terms that would be immune to our own personal hermeneutic biases and that the text cannot be understood neutrally. We can decide to believe what the text witnesses to – and thereby risk losing our scholarly objectivity – or we can decide to bracket such religious conviction and decision. But, in either case, our decision will radically determine the text as we encounter it and the possibilities of understanding, and especially of self-understanding, that the work holds out to us.

What makes Dante's story so perennially compelling is surely his very personal re-enactment in his own life of the founding event of the Christian revelation. That transcendent divinity should condescend to reveal itself in incarnate form was the germ and genius of the religion for which Dante became an ideologue and propagandist, but also – in some deeper and more

[18] Robert Pogue Harrison, "Phenomenology of the *Vita nuova*," *Annali d'italianistica* 8 (1990): 180–84.
[19] Aaron Daniels brings out these crucial differences in his extended review of the debate in *Dante and the Other: A Phenomenology of Love*, ed. Aaron B. Daniels (New York: Routledge, 2021), pp. 18–38. Daniels's review serves him for fashioning his own notion of Dante as "proto-phenomenologist" (p. 4).

intriguing ways – a witness and a prophet. Such incarnational revelation was the essence of the Christian religion as conceived throughout the centuries, and Dante realized this essence in arguably the most concrete imaginative form possible. Dante apprehended the event of incarnate revelation of divinity not just through apostolic testimony, as had been the norm for thirteen centuries. He experienced it also in the presence in the flesh of a person who became his life's center, his beatifier and savior. The curious circumstance that this incarnational revelation took the shape of a beloved woman was made possible by the fact that the relation of total loving devotion to a woman had come to represent practically the highest possibility of human existence in the courtly culture to which Dante was heir. This was so at least within the literary conventions of poetry about love, perhaps at least partially as a result of the influence of that very Christianity onto which this courtly love tradition had been grafted.

Under these social and gnoseological conditions, a personal revelation in the flesh, which was the incarnate way of Christian revelation, could be most convincingly realized in the figure of a revered ladylove. We should perhaps add here, following Dante's cue: *or* of a revered "manly love." Dante explicitly includes this possibility in the final line of his sonnet "Amor e 'l cor gentil sono una cosa" in *Vita nuova* XX. He defines "love" as being of a man for a woman, but then adds: "And a man of valor has the same effect on a woman" ("E simil face in donna omo valente," XX. 5). In concluding his poem this way, Dante re-envisions the whole process of beauty inspiring the love passion with the genders reversed.

For whichever gender, this manner of living one's faith in love makes the Incarnation a reality that is, in some sense, an ongoing event in the lives of believers. Incarnation continues to be realized through acts of faith and love by those who integrate themselves into the body of Christ. This type of action can be instigated in many different ways – and even through the inspiration of love for a man or a woman. Yet this type of assimilation, given its mixing of devotion to the holy and divine with a merely human infatuation, is not acceptable to Harrison. Not so unlike certain religious editors since the fourteenth century, who changed Dante's text in order to make it conform to their idea of orthodox belief, Harrison finds that in making "weighty, and somewhat shocking, claims about a mortal woman," the *Vita nuova* "approaches the limits of sacrilege." For Harrison, Dante's little book is "at bottom shocking, even blasphemous."[20]

[20] Robert Pogue Harrison, "Approaching the *Vita nuova*," in *The Cambridge Companion to Dante*, 2nd ed., ed. Rachel Jacoff (Cambridge: Cambridge University Press, [1993] 2007), pp. 35–36.

For Charles Singleton (whom Harrison taxes with being pious), in contrast, the originality of the *Vita nuova* was its proposing that a woman could be a revelation – or, in other words, that the experience of courtly love could lead to God rather than leading inevitably to religiously motivated recantation. The latter result was produced by love that degenerated into some of its more profane expressions. This happened, following closely on Dante's heels, in the famous case of Boccaccio, with his deathbed recantation of the *Decameron* (long thought to have been anticipated by his Epistle XXII to Mainardo Cavalcanti). Something comparable happened again, not long afterwards, in the senescence of Geoffrey Chaucer, with his retraction of the *Canterbury Tales*. At the very end, after the moralistic sermon of the "Parson's Tale," the work concludes with the "retracciouns" of the "makere of this book."

For Singleton, the editors of the *editio princeps* of 1576, who censured the phrase "la gloriosa donna de la mia mente" ("the glorious lady of my mind"), modifying it to the presumably less absolute and idolatrous "la graziosa donna de la mente" ("the gracious lady of my mind"), made a simple error based on a misplaced scruple. Their mistake was "to fail to see that, as the *Vita nuova* has used it, the word [glorious] declares not an identity but an analogy: an analogy which, understood in its proper medieval terms, is no sacrilege at all."[21]

This is a correct and crucial point. Yet it would also be a mistake to take the divinization through Beatrice as *merely* analogy in some purely modern, secular, aseptic sense. As Erich Auerbach brought out, particularly in his archeology of the Christian theory and practice of figural representation and interpretation in "Figura," analogy as understood in the Middle Ages is a way of *participating* in ultimate reality. The Scriptural type or figure "establishes a connection between two events or persons, the first of which signifies not only itself but also the second while the second encompasses or fulfills the first."[22]

The relation here between anticipating or signifying (for the type) and fulfilling (for the antitype) is a real connection and determines to its core the historical being of the individuals or events in question. Dante makes the (presumably) historical woman, Beatrice, work to prefigure her own self as a blessed soul in heaven and even as a kind of figure for Christ. By the grace of God, the absolute gulf between the human and the divine is

[21] Charles S. Singleton, *An Essay on the "Vita nuova"* (Cambridge, MA: Harvard University Press, 1949), p. 4.
[22] Erich Auerbach, "Figura," in *Scenes from the Drama of European Literature* (Minneapolis: University of Minnesota Press, [1944] 1959), pp. 9–71. Quotation, p. 53.

thereby, in significant ways, bridged in Dante's vision. There is thus, certainly for Dante, no choice between human reality and theological figuration. The most real human existence is attained to only through theological symbolization. Perhaps most importantly, this participative ontology carries on in the ongoing historical working of Dante's literary artifact, to the extent that it continues to be incarnated by real readers' re-appropriations throughout subsequent tradition. The next chapter begins to explore in earnest this multifarious progeny and focuses on how we might aim to re-inherit the work's legacy anew today. The dynamism of tradition lives in and from works like Dante's *Vita nuova*, together with the sort of appropriations and incorporations that they inspire down through the ages. Before turning to such afterlives for Dante's new life, and in order to faciliate the transition, a brief note on current criticism will serve to bring us up to date on various demystifying approaches that are, in this respect, akin to Harrison's.

Note on Current Criticism and Its Demythologizing of Theological Transcendence

It is, of course, perfectly possible to read against the intention of Dante's work in its own self-understanding and to demythologize its imaginative construc-tions, exposing their all-too-human anxiousness to impose a meaning on texts and events – and even on the youthful poet's own surely somewhat wayward desires in their initial, spontaneous expression. Certain methods of criticism, which sometimes identify themselves as "de-theologizing" in their general orientation, typically aim to strip the work of the author's own interpretations as often misleading and deceptive idealizations.

This type of approach to reading the *Vita nuova* is adroitly represented in recent criticism, for example, by Manuele Gragnolati and Elena Lombardi in "Autobiografia d'autore."[23] Such critics tend to see this autobiographical work not as Dante's creation of a "true myth," one authenticated by its living interpretations, as I have attempted to demonstrate, but rather as manipula-tive or "tampering" (pp. 153–58). They detect sometimes even a disingenuous effort designed to misrepresent reality in the interest of establishing authorial control over the poems' meaning for all future generations.

Exposing Dante's creation as a human construction of illusion, and perhaps even of deception, if not self-deception, is well attuned to the spirit of our

---

[23]   Manuele Gragnolati and Elena Lombardi, "Autobigrafia d'autore," *Dante Studies* 136 (2018): 143–60.

times – at least in some of its manifestations, given their predilection for a "hermeneutics of suspicion." Such criticism attempts in every possible way, despite the meagerness of the available means, to go behind Dante's own autobiographical construction of his life and to bring to light certain scarcely avowable facts or truths that the author might have preferred to cover over.

I find this approach to be worthwhile and important for opening up certain kinds of lucid, disabused insight into Dante and into our human predicament, but it, too, should not be accepted as *the* true account of what Dante's work boils down to. The contradictions, refusals, and resistances generated by Dante's own self-exegesis and authorial self-fashioning belong to his works' hermeneutic fecundity in the history of interpretations, of which they form an essential *part*. Any surface incoherencies at the textual level should be exposed, but not as if that enabled us, then, simply to discard Dante's own self-interpretations and thereby get to the real truth hidden behind them.

In contrast to certain detheologizing, demythologizing approaches, the next chapter in particular aims to bring out the fabulous fruitfulness of this work's varied afterlives in spite of – and in many instances precisely because of – its highly directive, yet infinitely suggestive mechanisms of self-interpretation. The work's sometimes intrusive gestures and also its subterranean strategies of authorial control can be read simply as part of the witness it bears rather than as obstacles to extracting its truth (as if we could have independent access to the latter).

The fundamental premises and procedures for reading Dante against his own hermeneutic filters and guidelines and constructions are found already subtly developed and ably defended in Harrison's book. My rebuttal, with its reasons for including Dante's theological myth, especially as enveloped in its exalted lyrical expression, as constitutive of the experience conveyed by the book, and even of the truth revealed in it, applies in equal measure to these recent and current critical approaches. Such readings continue to flourish and proliferate at present, which is one of the circumstances that make the book in hand timely and topical, even and especially in its arguing for the *Vita nuova*'s perennial relevance as incarnating a sort of everlasting gospel. In Dante's little book, traditional revealed religion fuses in an unlikely, but highly felicitous, union with an awakening universal, rational humanism. Both of these cultural currents are, of course, vehemently contested today.

A certain deflationary realism, not to say reductionism, has been at least one leading tendency, if not the dominant one, of the renewed and intensified interest among scholars, which has turned of late particularly to the biographical aspects of Dante's legacy. The goal of bringing Dante down to earth has been a powerful driving force in recent research and criticism focusing on his life, whether with the philological rigor of Giorgio Inglese in his "possible biography" of Dante in *Vita di Dante*,[24] or with the novelistic penchant of Marco Santagata in *Dante: Il romanzo della sua vita*.[25] This type of demystifying interpretation is often motivated by the interpreters' own desire to free Dante's texts from their Christian ideology, which the interpreters are likely not to share and may even detest.

In any case, making Dante a common mortal, with as crass motivations as anyone else, has proved to be a very good marketing strategy and has met with considerable popular success. It runs the risk, however, of failing to take account of what makes this sublime poet so exceptional and consequently makes the study of his texts so uncommonly rewarding, as David Wallace effectively points out, with a sane sense of humor, in "Lives of Dante: Why Now?"[26] Wallace's reminder of the quite extraordinary, ongoing revelatory power that Dante's texts have exerted down through the ages makes a fitting conclusion to the recent forum on "Dante and Biography" coordinated by Elisa Brilli in the 2018 issue of *Dante Studies*.[27]

In the end, whether we prefer to see Dante as very much like ourselves, or else as radically different from us, what we reveal in our own interpretive writings, immediately and incontrovertibly, is first and foremost ourselves. Those of us who read Dante's texts primarily, if not excusively, as strategems for imposing his authority might find instructive an examination of their own concern with controlling authority – and the examination might start from our roles within our own profession or field of expertise. More generally, our hermeneutic predispositions disclose the degree to which we are willing to believe – or not to believe – in something such as the possibility of revelation, and in what sense(s). Revelation by its nature originates in, and is referred to, something that is beyond human comprehension. Therefore, what revelation consists in must remain a quintessentially open question, one to which we can choose to be open – or not to be. Even if it generates nothing else of yet greater importance, Dante's work, beginning from the *Vita nouva*, can serve to make us question ourselves openly on this issue.

---

[24] Giorgio Inglese, *Vita di Dante: Una biografia possibile* (Rome: Carocci, 2012).

[25] Marco Santagata, *Dante: Il romanzo della sua vita* (Bologna: Il Mulino, 2011), trans. Richard Dixon as *Dante: The Story of His Life* (Cambridge, MA: Harvard University Press, 2016). The two tendencies of rigorous documentation through historical archives versus literary elaboration of Dante's myth are evident already from the first generation of Dante's biographers, with Giovanni Villani's researches in the chronicles of Florence and Giovanni Boccaccio's *Trattatello in laude di Dante* respectively.

[26] David Wallace, "Lives of Dante: Why Now?" *Dante Studies* 136 (2018): 213–22.

[27] *Dante Studies* 136 (2018): 133–231.

CHAPTER 5

History of Effect and a New Hermeneutics-Oriented Critical Paradigm

A people without history
Is not redeemed from time, for history is a pattern
Of timeless moments. So, while the light fails
On a winter's afternoon, in a secluded chapel
History is now and England.

(T. S. Eliot, "Little Gidding," V)

Concerned to recover an original core of experience, Harrison attempts to separate the real from the "revealed." The latter he spurns as spinning hermeneutic veils that cover over the real nature of the disclosure that Dante experiences in Beatrice. He believes that philological interpretive traditions have immured Dante's work in impenetrable hermeneutical mystifications. He objects that such interpretations center everything on Beatrice's death and have the effect of occulting the animating presence of her body, which he holds to be the true source of Dante's inspiration. What he does not allow for is that the process of interpretation itself, together with its history, can be a necessary – and, in any case, an invaluable – means of revelation and is so particularly of Dante's extraordinary experience. Harrison's approach differentiates sharply between what is revealed, or the thing itself – the body of Beatrice – on the one hand, and its interpretative mediation and appropriation in Dante's reaction and aesthetic response, on the other.

This division of interpretation from its presumed object I hold to be a somewhat false and limiting dichotomy that creates the illusion of a pure positivity of revelation in a moment of absolutely original experience.[1] In a more complete and comprehensive view, the experience is seen to grow along with – and to be discovered in and through – its interpretation, even as

---

[1] Thomas C. Stillinger, *Italica* 67/3 (1990): 403–406, reviewing Harrison's *The Body of Beatrice*, astutely identifies its phenomenological credo as haunted by "a vision of unmediated vision" and reasonably questions the adequacy of such a vision of truth (p. 404).

it is realized ever more fully in the light of other experiences and through ongoing reflection. The interpretations of the original experience belong to that experience as parts or aspects – or at least as developments and extensions – of its own intrinsic self-manifestation. The experience generated by Dante's story and poetic work as it affects others coming later in the "history of effect" (*Wirkungsgeschichte*) can, in this manner, amplify and enrich its meaning.[2] Of course, we can and must distinguish between the original work and what is made of it by others later on, working in other contexts and with other motivations. But we still need to strive to understand what in the original work enables and triggers the appropriations made in later ages. We need, then, to attempt to gain insight into how the later interpretations, too, belong, even if more remotely or indirectly, to the legacy already inherent in the original work. This requires us to envision the original work as already, in some manner, fraught with the full load of potential interpretations – and with the contradictions that inevitably come out more and more in the course of time and continuing interpretation.

Some of the most innovative and interesting work done on the *Vita nuova* in recent years has focused on the history of effect of its myths. The latter include, for instance, the myth of the artist as a young man beset by a contradictory mix of receptiveness and rebelliousness toward reigning cultural authorities, or again, the myth of the beautiful woman as beatifying angel and sacrificial victim transfigured in death. These myths attain to a certain apogee in the nineteenth century during the Victorian Age (1837–1901) and especially with the Pre-Raphaelite Brotherhood (1848–52) and movement (1852–65) as represented and led, in crucial respects, by Dante Gabriel Rossetti (1828–82).

Rossetti's *Beata Beatrix* image (Figure 13) metamorphoses freely in order to become an "intermedial" icon leading to a pervasive "Beatrification" of chief literary protagonists of the age such as Tennyson's Hallam.[3] The Victorians' reception of Dante's Beatrice myth significantly powered their preoccupation with transcending linear time in their hope to escape the finality of corporeal death. In this respect, they stand in partial continuity still with the more radical temporal dislocations of Pound's and Eliot's modernism. The transhistorical and transmedial energies of Dante's myth

---

[2] Hans-Georg Gadamer, *Wahrheit und Methode* (Tübingen: J. C. B. Mohr, 1960), trans. Joel Weinsheimer and Donald G. Marshall as *Truth and Method*, 2nd rev. ed. (London and New York: Continuum, 2004) develops at length this notion of *Wirkungsgeschichte* or "history of effect." See especially pp. 305–11 on "Das Prinzip der Wirkungsgeschichte."

[3] Julia Straub, *A Victorian Muse: The Afterlife of Dante's Beatrice in Nineteenth-Century Literature* (London: Continuum, 2009).

magnify its "influence" (no longer in a strictly historicist sense) as it becomes creatively transformative and reconfigures the Victorian age's entire understanding of itself.[4]

Such reinventions and re-activations are part of the interpretive process that is consciously and programmatically constitutive of the project of the *Vita nuova* from its very inception. This process continues still in the history of the work's reception even long after Dante's own work on his "little book" has been forever concluded. This history of reception has been a focus of much recent study, which bodies forth a fecund growing tip of current research on the *Vita nuova*.

The list of works demonstrating the *Vita nuova*'s history of effect would be endless. Accordingly, a few strategically chosen examples must serve here in order to give some sense of the work's impact along certain major axes organizing the historical production of cultural significations. Ernst Bloch's preface to his epoch-making *The Spirit of Utopia* (*Geist der Utopie*, Munich, 1918) climaxes with the words "incipit Vita nova" as a rallying call for its philosophy of liberation. Drawing out this connection to a liberationist political theology in the Frankfurt school of critical theory, recent research demonstrates that Walter Benjamin recognized Dante as Baudelaire's most significant predecessor specifically with respect to the latter's lyric art as exfoliated in *Les fleurs du mal* (1857), which is very often taken to be the poetic manifesto of modernism.[5] In his notes ("Convolute N") for his *Arcades Project*, Benjamin quotes from Rudolf Borchardt's introduction to the *Vita nuova*. This citation suggests particularly the importance that the pedagogical side ("pädagogische Seite dieses Unternehmens") of Dante's youthful apprenticeship in image-making has for Benjamin's own notion of the dialectical image. This pedagogical emphasis results in Dante's "training the image-making medium in us to stereoscopic and dimensional seeing into the depths of historical shadows" ("das bildschaffende Medium in uns zu dem stereoskopischen und dimensionalen Sehen in die Tiefe der geschichtlichen Schatten zu erziehen").[6]

A related potential for reading Dante's *Vita nuova* in a horizon of political theology is just now beginning to open up a new area of cutting-edge research. The *Vita nuova* can be read as envisioning miraculous possibilities for the redemptive constitution of political community around the sacrificial

---

[4] Alison Milbank, *Dante and the Victorians* (Manchester: Manchester University Press, 1998).
[5] See Marco Maggi, *Walter Benjamin e Dante: Una costellazione nello spazio delle immagini* (Rome: Donzelli, 2017), p.9.
[6] Rudolf Borchardt, *Epilegomena zu Dante; I, Einleitung in die Vita Nuova* (Berlin: E. Rowohlt, 1923), pp. 56–47.

death of a beautiful, young, and perfectly virtuous woman. The collective sorrow engendered by this event as a shared tragedy can function as the means to convert obstinately hard hearts and unite a city torn apart by internecine strife and warfare. Leveraging Benjamin's "Critique of Violence" (*Zur Kritik der Gewalt*, 1921), together with Hanah Arendt's political theories, especially as worked out in *On Humanity in Dark Times: Thoughts about Lessing* (1960), *The Human Condition* (1958), and *On Revolution* (1963), such analysis promises to deliver some scarcely precedented perspectives in the study of Dante's youthful composition on love and poetry as harboring the seeds of an unsuspected revolutionary political vision.[7] Such an incipient vision of "Christian violence," which is a divine, paradoxically non-violent violence that rather absorbs violence, without retaliation, would furnish the kernel of what Dante's later work confirms and unfolds.

The visionary intensity and penetration of Dante's work, which are felt so forcefully in the *Vita nuova*, are certainly key to the work's remaining an inspirational and inaugural text for modern writers. But there is also something less perfectly harmonized and more off-balance, not to say off-key, in Dante's first book. And this makes his apprentice work resonate with much modern literature. Ethan Knapp follows up on the Benjaminian motif by underlining the modernity of Dante's "New Life." He goes so far as to argue that, whereas the *Divine Comedy* embodies a medieval allegory of incarnational transcendence that finds adequate material vehicles, Dante's *Vita nuova* serves as an unsurpassable model for baroque allegory, in which meaning is irreparably broken and lies in ruins. "Like an Egyptian hieroglyph, the text offers us the central figure of Beatrice, hinting that her meaning contains all meaning but also readily admitting that her meaning is now scattered through the wanderings of memory, the disjunctions of lyric representation, and the omnipresent fact of death."[8] As these comments suggest, even if only obliquely, some characteristic motifs of modernity, as a time of crisis and collapse, as well as of new life and new beginnings, are peremptorily announced already in Dante's first book.

The *Vita nuova*'s rich history of effect has served, furthermore, in wide-ranging contexts, as a model for more general theoretical reflection on how

---

[7] This type of interpretation is proposed in an unpublished paper, "La violencia cristiana en la *Vita nuova*: Una reinterpretación de la obra de Dante Alighieri desde la teología política" by Nicolás De Navascués Martínez, that has come to me along its route to publication. A kindred intuition concerning the *Vita nuova*'s political inspiration and motivation is broached by Susan Noakes, "Hermeneutics, Politics, and Civic Ideology in the *Vita nuova*: Thoughts Preliminary to an Interpretation," *Texas Studies in Literature and Language* 32/1 (1990): 40–59.

[8] Ethan Knapp, "Benjamin, Dante, and the Modernity of the Middle Ages, or Allegory as Urban Constellation," *The Chaucer Review* 48/4 (2014): 524–41. Quotation, p. 537.

the history of transmission of a text can reflect back on its original form and determine anew what thenceforth appear to be its decisive characteristics. The *Vita nuova*'s being, by some accounts, the "first book" of Italian literary tradition sets it up to assume this exemplary status.[9] As Martin Eisner emphasizes in concluding his reflections on the future of philology with remarks on the *Vita nuova*, the temporality of this work includes, in an eminent fashion, not only its own unfolding in and through temporal sequence, but also its "diachronic historical existence."[10] In other words, the life of this work in history demonstrates a constitutive narrativity inherent in the philological enterprise itself, and this makes philology a creative invention and endeavor that eludes strict scientific rationalization.

Vast stores of criticism of the *Vita nuova* show the pre-eminent importance of interpretation, even at great historical distances and filtered through very different cultural matrices, in focusing and disclosing the full potential of the event that is brought to birth by Dante's *New Life*. Such birthing by a specific text of a whole cultural history is the premise of the project conducted by Manuele Gragnolati and others in Great Britain under the telling rubric of "Metamorphosing Dante" applied across Dante's entire *oeuvre*: "After almost seven centuries, Dante endures and even seems to haunt the present. His works have been used, rewritten, and appropriated in diverse media and cultural productions. The image of Dante himself has provided many paradigms for performing the poet's role – from civic educator to love poet, from experimenter in language to engaged poet-philosopher, from bard of the 'sublime' *Inferno* to scribe of heavenly rarefaction."[11]

Such critical work of "cultural inquiry" distinguishes itself as an especially fertile branch of contemporary Dante studies – and one that certainly brings to the fore lyric interpretation as constitutive of original meaning. The transmogrifications it traces through history indicate numerous different directions in which the "hermeneutic" approach

---

[9] This recognition can be traced to Domenico De Robertis, *Il libro della "Vita nuova,"* 2nd ed. (Firenze: Sansoni, 1970): "il primo libro de la nostra letteratura" (p. 5). Numerous qualifications might be adduced based on Paolo Cherchi, "Vernacular Literatures," in *Dante in Context*, ed. Zygmunt G. Barański and Lino Pertile (Cambridge: Cambridge University Press, 2015), pp. 371–88.

[10] Martin G. Eisner, "The Return to Philology and the Future of Literary Criticism: Reading the Temporality of Literature in Auerbach, Benjamin, and Dante," *California Italian Studies* 2/1 (2011), particularly the long concluding section on *"Dante's* Vita nuova," http://escholarship.org/uc/item/4gq644zp (accessed February 8, 2017).

[11] *Metamorphosing Dante: Appropriations, Manipulations, and Rewritings in the Twentieth and Twenty-First Centuries*, ed. Manuele Gragnolati, Fabio Camilletti, and Fabian Lampart (Vienna: Turia + Kant, 2011), p. 9. The quotation is from the introduction, "Metamorphosing Dante," signed by all three editors.

that I advocate can lead. Taken together, these directions suggest how interpretation of an artwork throughout subsequent centuries can produce an "increase in being" ("Seinszuwachs"). Hans-Georg Gadamer's philosophical hermeneutics magisterially theorizes this notion, which serves as foundational for a historical ontology of the artwork.[12] Better support and illustration for Gadamer's theory could hardly be hoped for than that which is found exemplarily instantiated in Dante's works and especially in the lyrically crystalized religious revelation of the *Vita nuova* as their generating matrix.

This engendering role of the *Vita nuova* is subtly, albeit implicitly, acknowledged and prophesied by Beatrice's reference to Dante's "new life" ("questi fu tal ne la sua vita nova") in *Purgatorio* XXX. 115. She evokes his exceptional endowments and the unlimited potential displayed in his youth and reproaches him for his erring defection or *traviamento*. His straying from fidelity to her memory figures here as the cause of his subsequently losing his way in a dark wood (the "selva oscura" of *Inferno* 1. 2) and consequently slipping into moral turpitude. By incidentally naming the title of his first book, Beatrice implicitly summons Dante back to this fertile origin of his vocation as both lover and poet.

The fecundity of this text already within Dante's own *oeuvre* has continued augmenting prolifically ever since. Only a handful of select instances from current criticism can be evoked here in order to indicate the theoretical productiveness of this most generative of texts in the long course of its history of effect. When the original text's significance is brought out and enhanced so essentially by later interpretations, this history of effect shows up as revelatory in its own right. Every new age and each distinct culture of interpretation illuminates again, in its own different terms and through its own unique preoccupations, the text's ever still untold truth and never exhausted meaning. The *Vita nuova*'s already unfathomably rich reception history begs and promises still to be filled out further with numerous detailed and intriguing case studies ranging widely across the world and time.[13]

In association with the "Metamorphosing Dante" project, Fabio Camilletti has concentrated on the *Vita nuova*'s reception as pivoting

[12] Specifically Gadamer's *Die Aktualität des Schönen: Kunst als Spiel, Symbol und Fest* (Stuttgart: Reclam, 1977), trans. Nicholas Walker as *The Relevance of the Beautiful* (London: Cambridge University Press, 1986), develops this aspect of his wider hermeneutic philosophy laid out in *Truth and Method*.
[13] Martin Eisner's *Dante's New Life of the Book: A Philology of World Literature* (Oxford: Oxford University Press, 2021), which is still forthcoming as my manuscript goes to press, bears such a promise.

specifically from its vogue in Pre-Raphaelite England.[14] Camilletti's investigation follows up, in some striking ways, on the studies tracing the effects
of the myth of Beatrice among the Victorians. The tendency of this myth
to coagulate into an iconic image is borne out by the rash of pictorial
representations that also flourish particularly in this period, especially in
and around the Pre-Raphaelite circle of artistic activity (see Picture Album
at the end of this chapter). This mythifying and iconizing tendency calls for
a countervailing effort of critical interpretation to pry behind and expose
all that these processes by their nature bury and occult.

As a comparatist, Camilletti reconstructs the *Vita nuova*'s often sub-
merged, and yet pervasive, presence in the late nineteenth and early
twentieth centuries as an archetype of the education of the young artist
in love – for instance, in the French novel, with Balzac, Flaubert, and
Proust. James Joyce, too, is consciously reliving and rewriting the *Vita
nuova* as his essential model and inspiration in *A Portrait of the Artist as
a Young Man*.[15] In this lineage, which leads from realism to symbolism,
sentimental or erotic and aesthetic education proved to be inseparable. The
Vita nuova serves here as a precedent for the objectification of the otherwise
unattainably private and incommunicable subjectivity that is characteristic
of Symbolist poetics. In this line of descent, Dante's love for Beatrice
provides an archetype for the sublimation of an object of sensual desire
projected onto an inner world of ecstatic mystical rapture.

Dante's *Vita nuova* is significantly numbered among the model precursor texts that figure in the Symbolist canon outlined by Jean Moréas in his
manifesto *Le Symbolisme*.[16] Such interpretations are further refracted,
a little later, through the lenses of psychoanalysis. The auto-analysis of
André Gide in his youthful *Les cahiers d'André Walter* (1890), his "psycho-
biography," also turning on the decease of a youthful beloved, finds its
counterpart and precedent in Dante's *libello*, with allusions and echoes that
are picked up on and made evident by Gide's biographer, Jean Delay, in his
monumental *La jeunesse d'André Gide* (1956).

Psychoanalyst Jacques Lacan draws on these and on other sources in
defining the continuity between medieval Romance and nineteenth-

---

[14] Fabio Camilletti, "Human Desire, Deadly Love: The *Vita Nova* in Gide, Delay, Lacan," in
Metamorphosing Dante, pp. 177–200.

[15] James Robinson, *Joyce's Dante: Exile, Memory, and Community* (Cambridge: Cambridge University
Press, 2016), especially pp. 56–66.

[16] *Le Symbolisme-Manifeste* was first published in 1886 in *Le Figaro* (September 18, Supplément
littéraire, pp. 1–2). It was reprinted in Moréas's *Les premières armes du symbolisme* (Paris: Léon
Vanier, 1889), pp. 31–39, with mention of *Vita nuova* on p. 39.

century Romanticism in terms of a certain "angélisme" in which the *lack* of a sexual relationship is turned to creative account by intellectual sublimation.[17] This love, in its courtly character, which entails its being carried out through renunciation and sacrifice, is actually facilitated by the beloved's death as modeled on the story of Dante's Beatrice. As Camilletti wittily suggests, "The relationship between Dante and psychoanalysis is . . . a sort of unconsummated love" (p. 177). In this way, the *libello*'s potential for addressing current concerns with desire and love as mediated by literature is revealed in full through its actual influence on key movements and historic statements.

In a related essay, again employing the tools of psychoanalysis, Camilletti brings out the ontological ambiguity generated by Dante's art of representation of otherworldly phenomena of a religious order.[18] This is particularly pertinent to the question of determining Beatrice's ontological status as a transhistorical figure. Camilletti zeros in on Chapter XXXIV of the *Vita nuova*, with its representations of Dante in the act of drawing. Specifically in question here are the drawn representations of an "angel," while Dante sits in meditative remembrance of Beatrice ("io mi sedea in parte ne la quale, ricordandomi di lei, disegnava uno angelo sopra certe tavolette," XXXIV. 1). However, angels, for Dante, as bodiless, purely intellectual beings, are not in principle susceptible to being depicted.[19] In this chapter, as Camilletti reads it, the problem of representing the unrepresentable surpasses facile assumptions about Beatrice as a real woman. We can see that such assumptions belong to a nineteenth-century positivistic worldview and thus are apt to condition the outlook of Dante Gabriel Rossetti and his contemporaries more than that of Dante Alighieri. The "increase in being" (*Seinszuwachs*) for Dante and his medieval culture comes about, instead, by negation: a higher order of being is indirectly and indistinctly adumbrated by this setting into relief of *what is not and cannot be represented* about Beatrice.

Working from Jacques Lacan and from Georges Didi-Huberman's book on Fra Angelica's painting (*Fra Angelica: Dissemblance et figuration,* 1990), Camilletti shows the representations of the *Vita nuova* to be much more

---

[17] Jacques Lacan, "Jeunesse de Gide ou la lettre et le désir," in *Écrits* (Paris: Seuil, 1966). Lacan's analysis of courtly love in its continuity with Romanticism, passing through Dante, shows up repeatedly throughout *Le Séminaire*, especially in books VII (*L'éthique de la psychanalyse*) and XX (*Encore*).

[18] Fabio Camilletti, "Dante Painting an Angel: Image-Making, Double-Oriented Sonnets and Dissemblance in *Vita nuova XXXIV*," in *Desire and Dante in the Middle Ages*, ed. Manuele Gragnolati, Tristan Kay, Elena Lombardi, and Francesca Southerden (Oxford: Leggenda, 2012), pp. 71–84.

[19] Dino S. Cervigni, "'. . . Ricordandomi di lei, disegnava uno angelo sopra certe tavolette' (VN 34.1): Realtà disegno allegoria nella *Vita Nuova*," *Letture classense* 35–36 (2007): 19–34.

plausibly images of something unrepresentable, something that is "absolutely superessential" in the sense of the early medieval apophatic theologian Dionysius the Areopagite, author of the *Celestial Hierarchy* (*De coelesti hierarchia*). Camilletti's readings of the *Vita nuova*'s history of effect by means of such historical distancing bring out provocatively the problematic of *ineffability*, which actually subtends Dante's *oeuvre* throughout its whole extent.

This at least implicitly theological frame places the question of Beatrice as a "real" woman in a perspective that exposes the hidden hermeneutic assumptions that are operating perhaps inappropriately in our purportedly natural and intuitive reception of Dante's *libello*. Being flesh and blood was not necessarily, nor even normally, deemed to be the highest degree of being in Dante's culture. It was not the "true reality" that it became for a later, empirically minded age ushered in by the advent of modern science and attaining to one of its most rigid and dogmatic instantiations with nineteenth-century positivism and its ideology of "progress," particularly during the Victorian age.

The Beatrice who reaches Dante and redeems him, endowing him with new life in the frame of the *Vita nuova*, is not necessarily, or at least not primarily, the "real woman" he met in the street in Florence. He avows to the honorable "men" paying him a visit during his activity of drawing the angel that she was "present to him." Yet he tellingly (or, rather, *un*tellingly) refers to her simply as "someone," an "Other" who "was just present with me, for which reason I was lost in thought" ("Altri era testé meco, però pensava"). This mysterious "presence" is not evidently physical: it is, primarily, a presence in and for thought. It is destined to take on "flesh" rather through the workings of art, producing in the artwork a palpable embodiment of desire, as epitomized by the Pygmalion myth.

Along these lines, in *The Portrait of Beatrice* Camilletti develops his theory of the Victorian genre of the "imaginative portrait" as envisaging something non-existent except in imaginings striving incessantly, and never quite adequately, after the ineffable.[20] As Camilletti construes it, Rossetti's project is an anachronistic reanimation of what is, in effect, the Lacanian Imaginary – "an externalized simulacrum of the lover's interiority" (p. 8). In this regard, Pre-Raphaelitism proposes a sharp alternative to the reigning paradigm of historicist reconstruction, which characterizes, instead, the approach of "primitivism," with its illusion of a restitution of the past.

---

[20] Fabio Camilletti, *The Portrait of Beatrice: Dante, D. G. Rosetti, and the Imaginary Lady* (Notre Dame: University of Notre Dame Press, 2019), pp. 7–14.

Camilletti underlines the difference, even the distance, between Dante's theological problematic and Rossetti's aesthetic concern with the interiorization of spiritual experience in a secular age (p. 8). This is certainly valid philologically. However, it alienates theology into something from the medieval past rather than appropriating it as possibly a living truth for us and for any time. This move belongs more to a critical consciousness wary of fusions and keen to stake out historical distance and limits rather than eager to fully and sympathetically participate in the experience of creative inspiration that joins authors and artists across epochs transhistorically. Medieval art centered on the theological problematic of representing the unrepresentable and was based on anamorphosis (deformation or evasion of form) rather than on mimesis, in ways that Camilletti himself calls on Didi-Huberman and Agamben to elucidate (pp. 30–34). The transcendent and formless can be approached only through purely interiorized thought or will. Defined form, however perfected, is always inadequate and must eventually be discarded altogether.

Even while living, Beatrice is present to Dante sometimes most intensively through his meditations, or as an imagination of Love ("una imaginazione d'Amore"), or even as "an empty imagination" ("una vana imaginazione"). She is felt by him as an interior "earthquake" in his heart ("tremuoto nel cuore"): "it came to pass one day that, sitting somewhere deep in thought, I felt the beginning of a tremor in my heart, in like manner as if I were in the presence of this lady" ("avvenne uno die che, sedendo io pensoso in alcuna parte, ed io mi sentio comminciare un tremuoto nel cuore, così come se io fosse stato presente a questa donna," XXIV. 1). This imagery lends Beatrice the status (at least for Dante) of an apocalyptic event such as had just been signified in the previous chapter through codified signs including the obscuring of the sun, the falling of birds in mid-flight, and great earthquakes (XXIII. 5). These ominous signs lend prophetic weight to Dante's delirious fantasies, which prove to be premonitory of Beatrice's death. The death of Christ in the Gospels is accompanied by similar apocalyptic signs (Matthew 27: 50–54; Mark 15: 37–39; Luke 24: 44–46). Dante begins to perceive Beatrice in this otherworldly and eschatological perspective already before her death.

This extraordinary presence and perception lead into the episode in which Dante sees the procession of ladies in which Guido Cavalcanti's Giovanna precedes his own Beatrice. Dante interprets this procession as analogous to John the Baptist's preceding Christ in his ministry in Judah and thereby preparing the way for the salvation of humankind. Dante sees all this in his heart, which has become so "happy" or ecstatic that it is, in its new condition, scarcely recognizable to him as his own ("me parea avere lo cuore sì lieto, che me non parea che fosse lo mio cuore, per la sua nuova condizione," XXIV. 2).

These scenes can be read as anticipations of Dante's perceptions of Beatrice *in morte*, which entail a heightening and intensifying directed toward her apotheosis (eventually taking shape in the *Commedia*), as announced in the final chapter of the *Vita nuova* (XLII). In the "anniversary" episode recounted in Chapter XXXIV, with its representations of Dante's inward-directed meditation in a private chamber, the nature of the *libello* as liminal and interlocutory is captured and ingeniously rendered as an oscillation between time and eternity. Dante's contemplation of an "angel" through his activity of painting is interrupted by a visit from the unknown "men," whom he subsequently addresses publicly in a sonnet.

One might even detect here, I would venture to suggest, a faint reminiscence of the "three men" who appear to Abraham at Mamre, as recorded in Genesis 18, given the latter passage's own eerie conflation of routine customs, or the rites of hospitality among humans, with signs pertaining to an extraordinary spiritual visitation. In Christian tradition, the scene is typically taken to be symbolic of a visitation by the three Persons of the Holy Trinity. In the biblical text itself, the "men" seen by Abraham when he "looked up" are declared to be a theophany, since the scene is framed by the statement: "The LORD appeared unto him in the plains of Mamre" (Genesis 18: 1).

Dante's scene commemorating the anniversary of Beatrice's death thus emerges as key to the ontology of the work and its afterlife. It presents, through the intrusion of men upon Dante's meditation, a microcosm of the work's constant oscillation between Dante's interior, private space of phantasmagoria and the exterior, public spaces of street and church, wedding and funeral. The sonnet in which the scene issues, with its two beginnings, furthermore, bifurcates into heavenly and earthly perspectives, the one mourning the lady's death ("piange Amore") and the other glorifying her "value" ("valore") in heaven. These are vestiges, presumably, of the original poem and of its rewriting for insertion in the *Vita nuova* respectively. Dante comments that the original version alone places this event in time ("dico quando," XXXIV. 6). These shifting perspectives tend to cancel each other out so as to become the negative revelation of an unrepresentable reality.

Dante's commemorative thought, his drawing, and his sonnet are not mimetic images but only "vestiges" of what they cannot represent. An iconic embodiment of this unrepresentable reality can be found, Camilletti further suggests, in the text itself consisting of red "rubrics" ("rubrica," 1. 1) on white pages. The book presents itself as a textual simulacrum of the otherworldly reality of angels by oscillating between seraphic white and flaming (cherubic) red in lieu of describing the angel-like lady that it cannot represent except as dissembled by the white and red cloths covering her over. The text offers itself as a material correlate of a purely spiritual, unrepresentable reality. By such metatextual indicators, the work performatively interprets its own meaning, although this requires a further act of reception by a reader in order to be actualized and made manifest. In the interval, readers like Rossetti inevitably introduce their own hermeneutic biases.

The scene, through its one-year distancing, innocently offers an internal illustration of how tracing the history of its reception can break critical ground and shed new light on the meaning of the *Vita nuova* itself, even when it does so only by the negation of misleading assumptions and representations. The principle of such an approach is to take interpretation, even across great historical distances, as productive – rather than only destructive – of *original* meaning. Historical distance, affording us perspective on different epochal understandings of reality, enables us to discern or infer more clearly the original type of being that Beatrice must have had (or not have had) for Dante in order to confer on him a salvific new life. This displacement from presumable plain facts to a focus on the fertility of interpretive mediation through time begins within Dante's text itself – with the testament it deliberately constructs by its witness to a miraculous occurrence. Such an orientation is already implied in Dante's saying at the outset that his source is the "book of my memory" ("il libro de la mia memoria," I. 1), since in memory incidents are not merely stored in their immediacy as events but are rather rearranged into an idealized, or at least ideated, order of sense.

This retrospective arranging is mirrored and becomes further evident in something that critics of the *Vita nuova* have often remarked from their later perspectives: the book is mathematically structured around the three principal *canzoni* occurring in Chapters XIX ("Donne ch' avete intelletto d'amore"), XXIII ("Donna pietosa e di novella etate"), and XXXI ("Li occhi dolenti per pietà del core"). These three major compositions divide its remaining twenty-eight minor poems symmetrically, first into groups of ten before the first and after the last of the *canzoni*, and then into groups of four poems falling between the first and the second and between the second and the third *canzone*. Representing the *canzoni* by roman numerals and totaling up the other poems in bunches yields the following overall pattern:

10 + I + 4 + II + 4 + III + 10. This pattern seems to have been noticed first by Gabriele Rossetti but to have been discovered independently and published first by Charles Eliot Norton.[21]

Building on this work, Charles Singleton reasonably takes the first and last sonnets as preface and epilogue and so produces a pattern peculiarly attuned to Dante's insistence on the number 9. We can represent it algebraically thus: I, 9; I; 4-II-4; III; 9, I. This break-down demands to be added up and rendered also simply (and suggestively) as: I, 9; I; 9; I; 9, I. Or in words: preface poem + nine poems + first canzone + nine poems (four poems – second canzone – four poems) + third canzone + nine poems + epilogue poem. The "minor" poems falling into groups of four or ten between and outside the *canzoni* consist of twenty-five sonnets, a *canzone* fragment, a two-stanza *canzone*, and a ballad. Each full-scale *canzone*, moreover, is indirectly about Beatrice's death – in its foretelling (I), its discerning (II), and its lamenting (III) – as a life-shattering event. A unitary symmetry and orchestration thus emerges as a structuring principle of Dante's memories, which show up as less haphazard and spontaneously recorded than may have seemed to be the case on a first reading – or on any reading that lacks this hermeneutic key to the work's organizational scheme.

Quite apart from this abstract, formal architecture, the core significance or truth of the work is deliberately displaced from fact to interpretation, and to the latter's formal constructions, when the central importance of Beatrice's death is declared to lie not in its drama and pathos as an objective event. Dante writes explicitly that it is not the purpose of his treatise to treat of this event of her death ("non è lo mio intendimento di trattarne qui," XXVIII. 2). Nevertheless, his *own* phantasies and anxieties about her death *are* dealt with, and in painstakingly excruciating detail. His realization that she is a mortal creature and will some day, necessarily, in the ordinary course of nature, die ("'Di necessitade convene che la gentilissima Beatrice alcuna volta si muoia'") provokes delirious visions in him. These visions are studded with apocalyptic signs: the sun blackens, stars weep, birds fall down dead from the skies, and the earth quakes terribly (XXIII. 5). But this apocalyptic revelation, in turn, leads him, in the final analysis, to the realization that the new life that the treatise celebrates is not subject to mortality. It is this new life – the discovery of a new and, in some sense, an eternal life through undying love – that is the purported outcome

[21] Kenneth McKenzie, "The Symmetrical Structure of Dante's *Vita nuova*," *PMLA* 18 (1903): 341–55. Charles Eliot Norton's "On the Structure of the *Vita nuova*," in *The New Life of Dante Alighieri*, 1859, 1867 3rd ed. (Boston: Houghton Mifflin, 1895), pp. 129–34, is available online at: www .elfinspell.com/DanteNewLifeEssay3.html (accessed August 10, 2020).

to which the book bears witness. Dante passes from abject and debilitating fear of the death of a mortal creature to unshakeable love of Beatrice as an eternal ideal. Accession to such an eternal life, or at least afterlife, also turns out to model what happens to the book itself as it becomes an object of enduring love for readers throughout subsequent ages.

This characterization of the book's main point and lasting significance can help to illuminate why it is so upsetting to Dante that his loyalty to his love exclusively for Beatrice should waver through his encounter with the "pitying woman" ("la donna pietosa") after Beatrice's death (XXXV–XXXVI). He reproves his eyes for taking pleasure in another woman and battles with himself ("battaglia che io avea meco") in order to remain unwaveringly true to the memory of Beatrice (XXXVII). "Reason" ("la ragione anima") wins out in the end over "appetite" ("appetito cuore," XXXVIII), and he chooses to delight more in the memory of Beatrice than in the sight of the new gentlewoman ("maggior desiderio era lo mio ancora di ricordarmi de la gentilissima donna mia, che di vedere costei," XXXVIII. 6). The "memory" in question here need not be interpreted as turned toward the past. This "memory" is most vitally to be understood as an interpretive re-actualization in the present and as oriented to a new life in the future. It is precisely the immortality of Dante's love for Beatrice that is at stake here. That love conquers death is the thesis Dante means to prove by his very life – his new life – as he reconstructs and recounts it in the *Vita nuova*.

This affirmation of love above and beyond death, then, might be heard as an echo of the truth asserted in the Bible as a whole, but also, most notably and most poignantly, in the Song of Songs, with its lyrical paean on an erotic and even (in some sense) romantic love. The imagery here communicates across however great cultural and historical, as well as hermeneutical, distances with the figures in Dante's initiatory dream. The dream features Love holding in one hand an object all aflame and solemnly saying that it is Dante's heart ("E ne l'una de le mani mi parea che questi tenesse una cosa la quale ardesse tutta, e pareami che mi dicesse queste parole: 'Vide cor tuum,'" III. 5). These images, and even their intimidating violence, presaging a finally triumphal outcome, read as if they could be remotely derived from the canonical *Canticum canticorum*:

> Set me as a seal upon thine heart,
> as a seal upon thine arm;
> for love is strong as death,
> its jealousy unyielding as the grave.
> It burns like blazing fire, like a mighty flame."
>
> (Song of Songs 8: 6)

The Vulgate of the *Canticum canticorum* formed an important part of Dante's cultural thesaurus (he famously quotes its "Veni, sponsa, de Libano" in *Purgatorio* XXX. 11). In the Vulgate version, these verses, reflecting also on other medieval flaming hearts, read:

> Pone me ut signaculum super cor tuum,
> ut signaculum super brachium tuum,
> quia fortis est ut mors dilectio,
> dura sicut infernus aemulatio:
> lampades ejus lampades ignis atque flammarum.

(8: 6)

Even though such an "echo" first registers distinctly only with subsequent interpretation and particularly in the theoretical construction of the present book – and thus in contexts far removed historically from those in which the text of the *Vita nuova* originated – it can nonetheless contribute significantly to the meaning that this text channels through the passageways of literary history and tradition. Our letting it do so here and now performatively enacts the process of increasing the being and meaning of a text through its appropriation in and by tradition.

Transmedial Transmissions: Dante Gabriel Rossetti and the Cult of the *Vita nuova*

Some well-known illustrations by painters of scenes from the *Vita nuova* are also included here in order to round out this volume as re-envisioning Dante's work not only in its textual but also in its iconic presence throughout subsequent ages of interpretation. According to the central argument and overarching perspective of the critical reassessment proposed here, the history of *reception* of the *Vita nuova* belongs essentially to the life of the work. This goes for the work's reception in artistic, as well as in scholarly, milieus and in pictorial renderings, as well as in literary treatments and re-enactments.

The work's destiny to be renewed ever again by interpretation is coded into its very name as signifying "new life" attained to also by means of ongoing interpretation. This work, even more than others, and in an exemplary manner, is integrally *constituted* by interpretations from its very inception and even internally to the work itself. This is the case already in the diachronic complexity of its own construction as laid bare by the "archeological" investigations that scholars have undertaken in conjunction with the critical examination of the text.[22] The work's layered complexity begins already with Dante's own excavating, incorporating, and repurposing of many of his prior works in the lyric genre into the new genre of the *Vita nuova*.

Recent criticism has contributed greatly to interpreting the visual archives in theoretical perspectives that emphasize the interpretive mediations between cultures, periods, and even art forms, thus embarking on the "intermedial." Scholarship has documented a shift from the dominance, established during the Renaissance, of a severe and grim image of Dante as above all the chastiser of sin in the *Inferno* to quite a different image based on the young Dante of the *Vita nuova* as passionate and in love.[23] The latter iconography gained currency especially from around the middle of the nineteenth century. The Pre-Raphaelites brought about a metamorphosis to a gentler, more debonair portrayal of the poet, exemplarily in paintings by Dante Gabriel Rossetti (1828–82) of scenes mostly from the *Vita nuova*.

Many of the familiar portraitures up to that time were derived from imitating Raphael's painting of Dante in the large mural fresco of the "Dispute of the Blessed Sacrament" ("Disputa del SS. Sacramento") on the wall of the Stanza della Segnatura in the Vatican (Figure 8). The poet seems there to be scowling and to "look daggers," with protruding chin, arched brows, and a harrowingly fixed, piercing gaze. Through the mid-century shift, Dante came to be depicted as less fierce and embattled in temperament, more refined and humane in character, than in the previous renderings. Even portraitures following Raphael's model representing an older Dante seem to have been influenced and softened, as suggested by the mid-century print by Charles Eden Wagstaff after a Stefano Tofanelli etching of Raphael's fresco, with Raphael Morghen acting as intermediary draughtsman (Figure 9). The 1894 engraving of Figure 10 marks an exception.[24]

Dante Gabriel Rossetti's work, which was instrumental in shifting the reigning iconic image of Dante away from the angry prophet of the *Commedia* toward the young poet steeped in love and lyricism, figured Dante especially as he had been newly rediscovered in the entrancing romance

---

[22] In addition to the annotated editions of De Robertis, Pirovano/Grimaldi and Gorni cited above (Prologue, Text and Translation), Gorni's *Dante prima della 'Commedia'* (Florence: Cadmo, 2001), pp. 83–179, in pages on the *Vita nova*, gathers and exhibits elements of this textual archeology. Chapter 3, note 20 details an instance of such examination by Barolini.

[23] Christoph Lehner, *Depicting Dante in Anglo-Italian Literary and Visual Arts: Allegory, Authority and Authenticity* (Newcastle upon Tyne: Cambridge Scholars Publishing, 2017), particularly chapter IV.3: "Rejuvenating Dante: The Historiogram of the Young and Passionate Florentine," pp. 138–49.

[24] Richard Thayer Holbrook, *Portraits of Dante from Giotto to Raffael: A Critical Study, with a Concise Iconography* (Boston: Houghton Mifflin, 1911), pp. 182–85, offers detailed documentation.

of the *Vita nuova*. Accordingly, the Rossetti paintings are given their place of prominence in the collection of images – the Picture Album – that supplements this chapter. The decisive shift is clearly evidenced also in the 1883 Henry Holiday painting reproduced in C. O. Murry's etching (Figure 12) and on the cover of this book.

Rossetti was following tendencies traceable to the German Romantic critic August Wilhelm Schlegel. Schlegel's essay "Dante: Ueber die göttliche Komödie" (1795) assigned a new, thitherto scarcely precedented importance to the *Vita nuova* in portraying Dante's idealistic nature athirst secretly and insatiably for all that is noble and excellent and lovely because of his beautiful and strong soul ("den geheimen unauslöschlichen Durst der schönen und starken Seele").[25] Schlegel himself, moreover, had an important predecessor in the Swiss philologist Johann Jakob Bodmer. In his *Ueber das dreyfache Gedicht des Dante* (1763), Bodmer defended Dante against the denunciations current among Neo-classicist critics during the ascendency of the French Enlightenment. The latter were sometimes prone to decline into outright deprecations of Dante as savage and uncouth.

This German Romantic reassessment was seconded by Madame de Staël and found echoes in William Hazlitt and Percy Bysshe Shelley and other English Romantics, including Walter Savage Landor. The Romantic revisioning remained influential through Victorian times among contemporaries of Rossetti such as Lord Tennyson and especially Robert Browning, although many complexities and contradictions emerge, particularly in the latter's *Sordello*, which ponders Dante in the context of his relations within the society of contemporary fellow poets. Nonetheless, Romantic recastings of Dante's image indelibly shaped the tradition as taken up later even by modernists such as Ezra Pound and T. S. Eliot.[26]

The discovery in 1840, on an interior wall of the Bargello in Florence, in the Saint Mary Magdalene chapel, of a fresco portrait of Dante by Giotto (Figure 6) gave the impetus necessary for the establishment of the new Dante cult focused not on the fulminating accuser of sins of the *Commedia* but on the youthful lover and lyricist. This new image corresponded especially to the Dante who could be found rendered sensitively in the autobiographical musings of the *Vita nuova*. The Bargello portrait of a suave and young-looking

---

[25] August Wilhelm Schlegel, *Sämtliche Werke*, vol. III: *Poetische Uebersetzungen und Nachbildungen nebst Erläuterungen und Abhandlungen*, ed. Eduard Böcking (Hildesheim: Georg Ohms Verlag, 1971), pp. 199–230. Quotation, p. 208. Originally in *Horen: Eine Monatsschrift* 1, vol. III, ed. Friedrich Schiller (Tübingen: Cotta, 1795).

[26] This story is engagingly told by Steve Ellis, *Dante and English Poetry: Shelley to T. S. Eliot* (Cambridge: Cambridge University Press, 1983).

Dante set the poet's features as they were to be reproduced by Dante Gabriel Rossetti over the ensuing decades in his paintings.[27] Its aesthetically pleasing lineaments shaped both the visual and the verbal aspects of the image Rossetti forged of Dante essentially as an awakening, beauty-inspired poet and a high-minded, compassionate lover. The painter Rossetti uses this more graceful portrait consistently in preference also to the gaunt image of the death mask of Dante preserved in the Palazzo Vecchio in Florence (Figure 11). A version of the mask was published in 1842 with Charles Lyell's translations of *Poems of the "Vita nuova" and "Convito,"* the volume that had first introduced Dante's lyric poetry to an English-speaking public.[28]

Dante was identified as the subject of the portrait figuring as a detail among the ranks of the blessed in the Giotto fresco of the Last Judgment in the Bargello, among other reasons, because of his carrying a book, which Rossetti took to be the *Vita nuova*. The fresco was presumed to have been painted around 1293, thus a few years after Beatrice's death in June 1290, according to *Vita nuova* XXIX. 1. A precise reference by Giorgio Vasari in his *Lives of the Artists* (1550) corroborated the identification:

> Onde, ancor oggi dí, si vede ritratto, nella cappella del Palagio del Podestà di Fiorenza, l'effigie di Dante Alighieri, coetaneo et amico di Giotto, et amato da lui per le rare doti che la natura aveva nella bontà del gran pittor impresse; come tratta Messer Giovanni Boccaccio in sua lode, nel prologo della novella di Messere Forese da Rabatta e di Giotto.[29]

> (Whence, still today, is seen portrayed in the chapel of the Palace of the Podestà in Florence, the effigy of Dante Alighieri, contemporary and friend of Giotto and beloved of him for the rare gifts with which nature had endowed the bounty of the great painter; as treated by Messer Giovanni Boccaccio in his praise in the prologue of the novella of Messer Forese da Rabatta and of Giotto.)

At the outset of his chapter on Giotto, Vasari praises the Florentine artist for excelling, by virtue of his natural gifts, in a new and modern manner of imitating nature that banished stiff and awkward Byzantine conventions ("divenne tanto imitatore della natura, che ne' tempi suoi sbandí affatto quella greca goffa maniera, e risuscitò la moderna e buona arte della pittura"). Vasari

[27] J. R. Woodhouse, "Dante Gabriel Rossetti's Translation and Illustration of the *Vita nuova*," in *Britain and Italy from Romanticism to Modernism*, ed. Martin McLaughlin (Oxford: Legenda, 2000), pp. 67–86.
[28] Ellis, "Rossetti and the Cult of the *Vita nuova*," chapter IV of *Dante and English Poetry*, pp. 102–35.
[29] Vasari's *Le Vite de' più eccellenti architetti, pittori et scultori italiani, da Cimabue insino a' tempi nostri* is cited from edition of Lorenzo Torrentino (Florence, 1550). The cited chapter on Giotto is available at: http://bepi1949.altervista.org/vasari/vasari15.htm (accessed June 25, 2020).

credits Giotto with reintroducing into painting the natural portraiture of live persons, which by that time had been neglected for hundreds of years ("introdusse il ritrar di natural le persone vive, che molte centinaia d'anni non s'era usato"). And the leading example Vasari offers for this thesis is Giotto's portrait of Dante in the chapel of the Palace of the Podestà, the building known today as the Bargello. In previous centuries, the chapel was the room where prisoners condemned to death spent the last night of their lives. The presence of Dante's image there is a fact not without a certain power of suggestion regarding Dante's status as guide to another life.

Soon after resurfacing in 1840 and prior to restorations, the Giotto fresco portrait of Dante was copied and sent by British painter Seymour Kirkup to his friend Gabriele Rossetti, Dante Gabriel Rossetti's father, an Italian political refugee and exile who held a position as professor of Italian at King's College in London from 1831 to 1847. Rossetti senior was himself a poet and scholar who contributed especially to the esoteric vein of interpretation of Dante's works.[30] Kirkup sent him a watercolor copy (Figure 7) together with a letter (dated September 12, 1840) that described the portrait image of the roughly 28-year-old medieval poet as "handsome" and as "an Apollo with the features of Dante" ("un Apollo con le fattezze di Dante"). Kirkup saw in it, furthermore, "not the mask of a corpse of 56 – a ruin – but a fine, noble image of the Hero of Campaldino."[31] The decisive impact of this image on the fantasy of the young Dante Gabriel and on his imagining of Dante Alighieri is vouched for by his brother William Michael Rossetti (*Family Letters*, I, p. 65).[32]

Dante Gabriel Rossetti's enthusiastic and fanciful interpretations have been censured as self-indulgent sentimentalizing and as unworthy of the extreme rigors of the Florentine poet's career, given its prodigious artistic production, political engagement, and astonishing intellectual achievement. Steve Ellis emphasizes how Rossetti's reading and depiction of Dante always centers almost exclusively on the *Vita nuova* and remains largely within the confines of the relation to Beatrice presented at the heart of that book. Rossetti's perception of this relation is filtered, moreover, through his own conjugal relation to his beloved wife, of whom he was

---

[30] Gabriele Rossetti, *La Beatrice di Dante* (London, 1842). Eugène Aroux's *Dante hérétique, révolutionnaire et socialiste* (Paris: Renouard, 1854) is based largely on Gabriele Rossetti's direct, personal influence, according to René Guénon, *L'ésoterisme de Dante* (Paris: Bosse, 1925).

[31] Gabriele Rossetti, *A Versified Autobiography*, trans. William Michael Rossetti (London: Sands & Co, 1901), p.146. The letter can be viewed online at: www.gutenberg.org/files/52387/52387-h/52387-h.htm#c144 (accessed December 14, 2020).

[32] *Dante Gabriel Rossetti: His Family Letters*. Memoire by W. M. Rossetti, 2 vols. Cited in Ellis, *Dante and English Poetry*, p. 119.

bereaved in his later years through her death in 1862. Ellis criticizes Rossetti's reduction of the *Commedia* to the relatively restricted terms of the *Vita nuova* and his absolutization of love for a woman. In contrast, "Dante was careful not to allow Beatrice to become an absolute value and to re-set her in the *Commedia* in the context of a Christian belief that allows her a substantial but ultimately secondary role" (Ellis, *Dante and English Poetry*, p. 133). Rossetti's limited focus allegedly induces him to ignore the prodigious development that led to the rich and multifaceted dynamism of the mature Dante, with his earth-shattering historical, cultural, and religious vision.

Ellis is following similarly negative assessments especially by Nicolette Gray, as well by Mario Praz, B. J. Morse, Graham Hough, and Frank Kermode.[33] In various ways, all are reacting against Rossetti's "de-universalizing" (Gray, *Rossetti, Dante and Ourselves*, p. 34) of Beatrice's significance to a private affair of purely personal love, an uxorious idolatry of a type practiced almost compulsively by Rossetti in his own personal life. This sort of devotion belongs rather to Rossetti's realization of his own Victorian ideal of family love, with a certain fulsome sensuality to boot.[34] Such a sensibility, decked out lavishly with heavenly paraphernalia, is on full display in the Pre-Raphaelite poem par excellence, "The Blessed Damozel" – Dante Gabriel Rossetti's signature composition.

Admittedly, Rossetti narrows and perhaps even strays from the wider significance of Dante's work, reproducing only a very limited interpretation of it. Nevertheless, a certain aspect of passionately subjective truth, one that is supported by and suspended on a kind of rapt sentiment to which Dante himself relentlessly attests, has emerged in our analysis as quite an essential component of Dante's own work and testament, one that finds unexcelled and original expression in the *Vita nuova*. Rossetti's continuing to plumb and explore this dimension of existence and its revelatory potential as the peculiar focus of his own work is not without relevance to illuminating and highlighting some crucial aspects of the overall legacy of the *Vita nuova*. At a minimum, Rossetti's interpretations illuminate the *Vita nuova* as it could be received and understood in his

---

[33] Nicolette Gray, *Rossetti, Dante and Ourselves* (London: Faber, 1947); Graham Hough, "Rossetti and Dante," in *The Last Romantics* (London: Dickworth, 1949), pp. 67–82; B. J. Morse, "Dante Gabriel Rossetti and Dante Alighieri," *Englische Studien* 68 (1933–34): 227–48; Mario Praz, "T. S. Eliot and Dante," in *The Flaming Heart* (New York: Doubleday, 1958), pp. 365–66, originally in *Southern Review* 2/3 (1937); Frank Kermode, *Romantic Image* (London: Fontana, 1971), pp. 56–57, 71.

[34] Such, at least, was the charge of Robert Buchanan in *The Fleshly School of Poetry* (London: Strahan, 1872). This charge, although later retracted, deeply hurt Rossetti and damaged his reputation.

own day and age, with its more materialist and less vitally metaphysical outlook on reality. We may grant that Rossetti's painting, like his poetry, is revealing, first, about Rossetti himself.[35] Yet, even so, it thereby demonstrates one fateful destination of the type of self-reflexive mode inaugurated by Dante's earliest and most narcissistic book.

Several of Rossetti's paintings are highly suggestive of how an intensely personal interpretation of the medieval poet can be revealing of something vital to Dante's tradition and central even to its original life and inspiration. When Rossetti pictures Giotto painting Dante, with Cimabue looking over the painter's shoulder and Guido Cavalcanti leaning on the poet's own shoulder and holding an open book of Guido Guinizelli's poetry, while a procession with Beatrice passes by in the foreground, we are stimulated to revisit and contemplate the possible connections between apparently disparate elements of Dante's legend. "Giotto Painting the Portrait of Dante" (Figure 3) is an invention and a slightly anachronistic one, but it, too, delivers a provocative witness to how Dante's *oeuvre* can operate in an interart and intermedial dimension, and to how it has been creatively received in a later age. A sketch for this painting held by the Tate Gallery in London (Figure 4) bears a quotation from *Purgatorio* XI that refers to both Cimabue and Giotto and to "one" and "another Guido," bringing together in imagination the personages that Rossetti depicts as present in a single, shared space:

> Credette Cimabue ne la pittura
> tener lo campo, e ora ha Giotto il grido,
> sì che la fama di colui è scura.
> Così ha tolto l'uno a l'altro Guido
> la gloria de la lingua; e forse è nato
> chi l'uno e l'altro caccerà del nido.
>
> (*Purgatorio* XI. 94–99)

> (In painting Cimabue believed
> that he held the field, but now the cry goes to Giotto
> so that the fame of the first named is obscured.
> Likewise, one Guido has wrested from the other
> the glory of the language; and perhaps one is born
> who will banish both from the nest.)

While depicting a scene that never actually took place, nor one that is described as such in the poet's texts, the painting is nevertheless very much in the spirit of Dante's own syntheses and suggestively represents certain

---

[35] This is confirmed by Joan Rees, *The Poetry of Dante Gabriel Rossetti: Modes of Self-Expression* (Cambridge: Cambridge University Press, 1981).

lines of influence and succession indicated by the Florentine poet himself – transposing all from a written text to a pictorial medium. Neither does the painting conceal its intent to resurrect Dante in the light of a new, contemporary context. Rossetti recognizably projects his own facial features onto the portrait of the painter Giotto in the final painting of 1852 (Figure 3). In the same vein, the features of Rossetti's wife, Elizabeth Siddal, easily recognizable from numerous sketches serving as studies for his *Beata Beatrix* (Figure 13), have been discerned in the face of Beatrice in this painting.[36]

Rossetti's painting "Dante Drawing an Angel on the Anniversary of Beatrice's Death" (Figure 1) likewise embroiders on the givens of the Dantean text, going beyond the actual contents of Chapter XXXIV of the *Vita nuova*, which it illustrates. But, again, the misprisions involved are not without a certain fecundity in revealing what was going to be made of Dante's experience and his description of it in its historical existence as continued in further interpretation through application to new situations. And these interpretive angulations can reflect surprising light back onto the original handling of his experience by Dante himself.

Alighieri's text mentions only "men" in this scene, ones worthy of honor ("uomini a li quali si convenia di fare onore, XXXIV. 1). However, a female figure shows up in the painting. Rossetti seems to be taking liberties with his source and to be interjecting an idea of his own. Yet Dante's being told later ("secondo che me fu detto poi") that the men were there a while before he noticed them indicates that someone else must have been present. As revealed by a note in Rossetti's translation of the *Vita nuova*, the female figure in this painting is intended to represent Gemma Donati, Dante's wife, whom Dante Gabriel speculates might have been the pitying lady in the window of *Vita nuova* XXXV. 2.[37] Drawing on information from Boccaccio, Rossetti places Dante's marriage with Gemma at exactly one year after Beatrice's death – and thus at the same time as the anniversary scene. Rossetti thereby produces a synthesis that again endeavors to connect Dante's story together in ways that correspond to his own experience and testify to the story's searing contemporary relevance for him personally.

Rossetti's painting of his own wife a year after her decease (Woodhouse, "Dante Gabriel Rossetti," p. 76), like Dante's painting of the angel on the anniversary of Beatrice's death, constitutes yet another poignant hint of his

---

[36] Woodhouse, "Dante Gabriel Rossetti's Translation and Illustration of the *Vita nuova*," p. 74.
[37] Dante Gabriel Rossetti, *The Early Italian Poets*, ed. Sally Purcell (Southampton: The Anvil Press, 1981), p.205, n. 1.

intimate sense of identification with Dante Alighieri's own autobiographical love story as recorded in the *Vita nuova*. Rossetti's work proposes an
impassioned interpretation or *mediation* via his own preoccupations with
conjugal love, and this certainly remains an intriguing area of mystery in
the biography of the Florentine poet. Students are often curious about how
Dante's marital status and relationship are to be fit into the idealized story
he narrates – or, if not, then at least on what grounds they can be excluded.
Surely, these circumstances must somehow have conditioned the life and
existence which give rise to the story, even if they remain outside of its
express terms and statements. There is a silence here that, not surprisingly,
raises questions and invites speculation.[38]

In the notes to his translation of the *Vita nuova*, Rossetti offers another
intriguing speculation in this regard, one bearing on Dante's traumatic
symptoms, starting with the "mirabile tremore" (strange tremor or throb-
bing) in the left side of his breast ("nel mio petto da la sinistra parte" –
anatomically, where the heart is) and quickly spreading throughout his
body. In Chapter XIV, Dante recounts that he had been led by a friend to
a gathering of beautiful ladies without his knowing where he was going or
why. This gathering turns out to be for a wedding at which Beatrice is
present, although almost everything else about it is left vague and mysterious. Reference is made to a certain gentle lady ("gentil donna") who had
been married that day ("che era disposata quel giorno"), and the friend
informs Dante that they are there to attend upon the noble ladies, literally
"to ensure that they are worthily served" ("Per fare sì ch'elle siano degnamente servite," XIV. 3). His own lady's presence, unbeknownst to him,
accounts for Dante's reactions, with their typical love pathology. But
Rossetti goes further and sees Dante's extreme indisposition here as an
allegorical displacement of his chagrin over the marriage of Bice Portinari
at twenty-one years of age with the banker Simone de' Bardi. The scene in
Vita nuova XIV may have been used obliquely to dissemble this event,
which might well be imagined to have been devastating for Dante.

Rossetti comments in *The Early Italian Poets*: "It is difficult not to
connect Dante's agony at this wedding-feast with our knowledge that in
her twenty-first year Beatrice was wedded to Simone de' Bardi. That she
herself was the bride on this occasion might seem out of the question from
the fact of its not being in any way so stated; but, on the other hand,
Dante's silence through the *Vita nuova* as regards her marriage (which

---

[38] The role of Gemma has been re-evaluated as actually a secret key to the life and work of Dante by
Kolja Micevic in his French edition of *Enfer* (Paris: J'Agis Seul Avec Toi, 1996), p. 152.

must have brought deep sorrow even to his ideal love) is so startling, that we might almost be led to conceive in this passage the only intimation of it which he thought fit to give" (p. 167).

It is a challenging hypothesis, and there is a palpable lack of specificity in Dante's descriptions in *Vita nuova* XIV that lends some plausibility, or at least some playing room, to Rossetti's inferences. Certain latent possibilities lurking in Dante's text can be discovered in a rather different and surprising new light thanks to Rossetti's engaging with it so intensively through his mixing in the most heartfelt concerns of his own wrenching existence and affectivity. He thereby gives an intelligible account as to what Dante does with what might reasonably be expected to have been overpowering emotions that he seems nowhere else to work through or express, or even acknowledge. Might he have covertly coded his reactions into his work at this point in order to objectify and evacuate them? Rossetti's reading effectively motivates what otherwise seems to be a rather uncharacteristic evasiveness on Dante's part. Rossetti's interpolation here enables him to give a more concretely vivid reading of this passage in Dante's original writing than seems to be otherwise readily available.

In his watercolor painting "Beatrice at a Marriage Feast Denying her Salutation to Dante," first exhibited in 1852 and acquired in a second version in 1855 by John Ruskin (Figure 2), Rossetti extrapolates from these heartfelt hunches in imagining a scene of his own invention. Yet Rossetti's working through another medium, painting, as well as through personal appropriation into his own existence, proves to be fruitful for suggesting potential new angles of investigation. He thereby furnishes some striking illustrations of hermeneutic productivity – of "value added" through interpretation.

The last-mentioned Rossetti painting conflates the scene of Dante's reactions at the wedding, in Chapter XIV, with the scene in which Beatrice denies him her greeting. The latter incident takes place in Chapter X. This montage suggests that there may be a connection between Beatrice's displeasure with Dante's feigning to love screen ladies, which had sullied his reputation, and her marriage to another. For Rossetti – and for a certain Romantic logic (ignoring the Florentine customs of betrothal of children by their families) – the first event could even be felt to have caused the second, or at least to have some measure of responsibility for bringing it about. Dante's apparent betrayal of his and Beatrice's ideal love might be imagined to have motivated her acceptance of a worldly marriage to a banker. Verisimilarly, she might have consented to it because of her disillusionment with Dante. We need not share or be persuaded by these conjectures, but we can discern a certain kind of emotional coherence at work in their construction. They, at any rate, make manifest Rossetti's intensely lived and self-transforming relation to Dante's text and legend.

Rossetti's "Salutation of Beatrice on Earth and in Eden" (Figure 5), which exists in many sketches and reproductions again creates its own synthesis by bringing together images representing two different encounters, one in the streets of Florence, as presented in *Vita nuova* II, and one in the Earthly Paradise or Eden, as related in *Purgatorio* XXX. This is certainly one of Rossetti's most audacious tropings of Dante's texts, one that almost contradicts them by leaving out all the severity of Beatrice's appearing to Dante "like an admiral" ("quasi amiraglio") and putting him to shame in the Earthly Paradise (*Purgatorio* XXX. 58–145). Still, it is not an uninteresting or an unmotivated appropriation, and it is not devoid of a certain power of illumination of important aspects of these two texts' afterlives. Rossetti captures the fascination of Dante's rapturous gaze on the beauty of his beloved, which the original texts never cease to emphasize and exalt. We might neglect to imagine this rapture, given the scolding that Dante receives. It is hard not to see a scowl on Beatrice's face as she delivers her reproaches excoriating Dante for his infidelities, when he meets her in Purgatory. Rossetti's transfigured vision raises the question of whether the tender, loving gaze does not need to be given some kind of precedence even in the latter encounter in the Earthly Paradise at the top of Mount Purgatory. The constraints of being able to depict only one moment of time per image – unlike the dynamic process of unfolding that can be recorded and represented in the poetic text – force these considerations into the foreground.

Rossetti's depictions are steered by a drive to synthesis – to imagining Dante's story as a whole. Imagining the tradition in his own terms, Rossetti illustrates some of the liabilities and also some potentialities and difficult-to-foresee possibilities of disclosure that are latent in the original works and destined to emerge through the process of accumulating historical effect. Access to the works' full and ultimately ineffable sense can be gained only through the efforts of individuals struggling to make Dante's works make sense in terms of their own personal and cultural existences. Such interpretive mediation is to be received, and even deserves to be celebrated, for its richness of suggestion. Of course, it also invites and requires a sharpening of critical discernment – even if without the pretension of being able to define one absolute, original meaning as a basis for apodictic judgments. What can be concluded from this?

Picture Album

Figure 1 Dante Gabriel Rossetti, "Dante Drawing an Angel on the Anniversary of Beatrice's Death" (1853), Ashmolean Museum, University of Oxford

Figure 2 Dante Gabriel Rossetti, "Beatrice at a Marriage Feast Denying Her Salutation to Dante" (1851–55), Ashmolean Museum, Oxford University

Figure 3 Dante Gabriel Rossetti, "Giotto Painting the Portrait of Dante" (1852),
Andrew Lloyd Webber collection photograph © akg-images

Figure 4 Dante Gabriel Rossetti, Study for "Giotto Painting the Portrait of Dante" (1852), © Tate Gallery, London

Figure 5 Dante Gabriel Rossetti, "Salutation of Beatrice on Earth and in Eden" (1859–63), Harvard Art Museums/Fogg Museum, Bequest of Grenville L. Winthrop, Photo © President and Fellows of Harvard College

Figure 6 Giotto, Dante Portrait in Fresco of Paradise, Saint Mary Magdalene chapel, Bargello, Photo © Getty Images

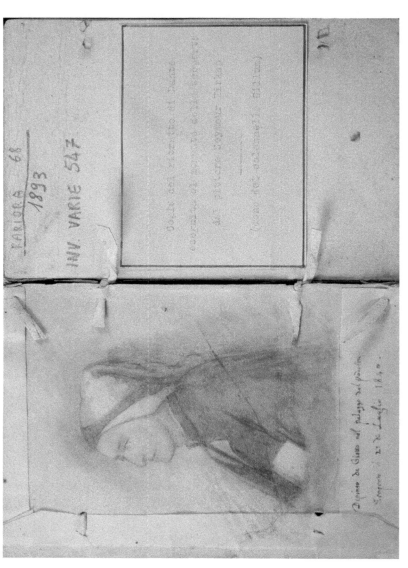

Figure 7a Seymour Kirkup, "Dante Alighieri." Tracing of portrait by Giotto discovered in 1840 in the Bargello. © Gallerie degli Uffizi, Florence

Figure 7b Seymour Kirkup, "Dante Alighieri." Color lithograph (Arundel print),
1859, after Kirkup's tracing. Wellcome Collection. Attribution 4
.0 International (CC BY 4.0)

Figure 8 Raphael, portrait of Dante, detail in the "Disputation of the Holy Sacrament" (1510–11), Stanza della Segnatura, Vatican City, Vatican State, Photo © Governatorato SCV – Direzione dei Musei

Figure 9 Dante Portrait, 1840–60. Print by Charles Eden Wagstaff, after Raphael
Morghen and Stefano Tofanelli, Prints and Drawings, © The Trustees
of the British Museum

Figure 10 Dante Portrait, 1894. Engraving after Raphael. Photo © Getty Images

Figure 11 Death Mask of Dante, ca. 1879, Palazzo Vecchio, Florence, Photo ©
Sebastien Beaucourt/Bridgeman Images

Figure 12 Henry Holiday Painting of Dante and Beatrice. Etching by C. O. Murry after Holiday painting. Photo © Getty Images

Figure 13 Dante Gabriel Rossetti, *Beata Beatrix* (1871), Harvard Art Museums/Fogg
Museum, Bequest of Grenville L. Winthrop, Photo © President and Fellows of
Harvard College

CHAPTER 6

Conclusion: The Existential Grounding of Revelation in Lyric

> We shall not cease from exploration
> And the end of all our exploring
> Will be to arrive where we started
> And know the place for the first time.
> Through the unknown, remembered gate
> When the last of earth left to discover
> Is that which was the beginning . . .
>
> (T. S. Eliot, "Little Gidding," V)

It might be objected to my argument for poetry as the generative source of Dante's narrative that Dante himself explicitly asserts, or at least implies, the contrary. In Chapter XXV of the *Vita nuova*, he declares that poetic figuration is justified only on the basis of an independently demonstrable prose "sense" ("intendimento"), of which the rhetorical figure is merely the "garment" ("vesta"). He holds authors responsible for being able to state in prose the plain sense of their less than transparent, figurative utterances, "since it would be very shameful for anyone who made rhymes with poetic figures if, later, when asked, he did not know how to strip his words of their figurative dress or rhetorical color, so that they would have their true meaning" ("però che grande vergogna sarebbe a colui che rimasse cose sotto vesta di figura o di colore rettorico, e poscia, domandato, non sapesse denudare le sue parole da cotale vesta, in guisa che avessero verace intendimento," XXV. 10).

The true meaning of poetic figures is equated here with their prose sense. Nevertheless, it is crucial to observe in this passage that Dante actually conceives of the poetic figure as being offered first. Only "later" ("poscia"), if asked, must the poet be able to deliver the true meaning of the figure in terms which Dante presumes would be non-figurative, but which a more modern literary theory might well consider to be necessarily figurative as well. After Vico, Herder, and Nietzsche, we no longer necessarily assume that language can be anything other than figurative.[1]

On Dante's own account, the prose version of originally poetic (or figural) meaning comes after the fact, even though he seems here to assert its priority in meaning and conception. His own rhetoric, nevertheless, assumes that the poetry actually comes first and that its sense is then drawn out later in the prose. This same order of events was implied already in the slightly earlier pronouncement: "worthy is the [vernacular] rhymer to do the same [i.e. to use personification, like the Latin poets], yet not without a reason, but only with some reason that *afterwards* it is possible to open up in prose" ("degno è lo dicitore per rima di fare lo somigliante [i.e. "li poete hanno parlato a cose inanimate"], ma non sanza ragione alcuna, ma con ragione la quale *poi* sia possibile d'aprire per prosa," XXV. 8, italics added). Dante is clearly concerned to align his theory about literature with a certain Scholastic rationalism, since this discourse enjoyed a very high degree of prestige in his day. And yet, with his poetic intuition, he is already evidently feeling his way toward the doctrine of the priority ("primatum") of poetry over prose that he asserts some years later programmatically at the outset of Book II of his *De vulgari eloquentia*. In that groundbreaking work, as we already had occasion to observe, prose writers are said to receive most of their language from poets ("prosaycantes ab avientibus magis accipiunt," II. i), who remain their model, as is central to the argument of Book II of that work.

Dante's statement in *Vita nuova* XXV already implicitly acknowledges that poetry and figural language are originary articulations of reality and direct expressions of experience, even while conceding that it must be possible to interpret them subsequently in prose.[2] Verisimilarly, Dante's idea of providing a prose explanation of poetic meaning would be something like what he has done in Chapter III of the *Vita nuova* by contextualizing his dream vision with a narrative account of its engendering circumstances. As described in the sonnet that Dante circulated on its own to the *fedeli d'Amore*, the dream vision at the time had been

---

[1] I outline some far-reaching speculative implications of this extended understanding of figurative language in terms of hermeneutic theory in "Metaphor and the Making of Sense: The Contemporary Metaphor Renaissance," *Philosophy and Rhetoric* 33/2 (2000): 137–54, and in "Symbol and Allegory," in *The Routledge Companion to Hermeneutics*, ed. Jeff Malpas and Hans-Helmuth Gander (New York: Routledge, 2014), pp. 367–77.

[2] Ernesto Grassi persuasively links the more modern, hermeneutic theories of language as essentially metaphor with Dante and his humanist heritage in *La metafora inaudita* (Palermo: Aesthetica, 1990). Along similar lines, and most succinct, is his essay "The Claim of the Word and the Religious Significance of Poetry: A Humanistic Problem," *Dionysius* 8 (1984): 131–55.

understood by no one ("Lo verace giudicio del detto sogno non fue veduto allora per alcuno," III. 15). In light of its prose context in the *Vita nuova*, however, the "marvelous vision" ("maravigliosa visione") becomes perfectly intelligible. Filling in these surrounding circumstances leads Dante to the express conclusion that the vision's meaning is now plainly manifest even to the simplest of readers ("ora è manifestissimo a li più semplici," III. 15). The prose narrative would, by this logic, be even more fundamental than the *divisioni* through which Dante explicitly anatomizes the meanings of his verses. Of course, the narrative itself remains far from univocal in meaning: it furnishes a ground for radically multivalent significance.

Dante's "divisioni" are modeled on the Troubadour *razos*, which explain the conditions giving rise to a poem and thus complement and supplement the *vidas* in placing the poems in a biographical context. Indeed, the *ragioni* that Dante offers in order to "denude" ("denudare") the sense of his poems hardly make the figures in the poems into a superfluous adornment or "vestment" ("vesta"). In practice, his poetry remains inextricably entrenched in figural modes of expression that defy exhaustive, definitive prose translation because they indicate uncanny, ineffable, or even otherworldly realities. Dante ignores this intrinsic untranslatability of poetic figures in formulating his demand for the possibility of prose equivalents. In this regard, his literary theory in Chapter XXV of the *Vita nuova* proves to be rather constricted with respect to his manifest creation as a poet. One can see in certain strands of this early, composite work the somewhat rigid rationalism of a Scholastic philosophy striving clumsily and in vain to account for the prodigious creations of a lively and sublime poetic imagination.[3]

Elsewhere in the *Vita nuova*, Dante gives another account of the ground of poetic figuration, and it is one that is more profound than this Scholastic analysis based on the classical rhetorical notion of figures being the dress or "vestment" of a literal meaning. He suggests that figuration has an existential ground, when he notes that the figure of Love was absorbed into him, Dante, the speaking poet: "Then I took so great a part in him / that he disappeared, and I could not tell how" ("Allora presi di lui sì gran parte, / ch'elli disparve, e non m'accorsi come," IX. 12). Or, if the less suspect prose version should be preferred in the context of answering this objection, so as to avoid the *petitio principi* of arguing for poetry's originariness from the

[3] Robert Hollander, in "*Vita nuova*: Dante's Perceptions of Beatrice," *Dante Studies* XCII (1974), cogently suggests that, at the stage of the prose redaction of the *Vita nuova*, Dante is embarrassed by the personifications of Love as a full-fledged, independent character in the poems written at an earlier stage. For the prose writer, Love has become rather "an internalized agency of Dante's being" (p. 5).

poetry itself, we have: "this imagination of mine suddenly disappeared completely due to the very great portion of himself that Love seemed to give me" ("disparve questa mia imaginazione tutta subitamente per la grandissima parte che mi parve che Amore mi desse di sé," IX. 7).[4]

Dante implicitly acknowledges here that the figure of Love, under whose sign he labors as a love-poet, in fact derives from his own existential reality and so "disappears" back into Dante himself. But this (new) existence of Dante depends itself, in turn, on that of Beatrice, and accordingly on Love, who comes to be incorporated also into her. Following this same assimilative logic, Beatrice is later called "Love" by the god himself on account of her "great similarity" with him ("E chi volesse sottilmente considerare, quella Beatrice chiamerebbe Amore per molta somiglianza che ha meco," XXIV. 5). Similarity or analogy, pushed to the extreme in this way, turns into ontological identity or dependence (presumably on the Platonic model of "participation") and even wholesale absorption and subsumption.

Clearly, then, poetic figuration derives directly from existential reality instead of being strictly just a function of a prose sense. Dante embraces this view of language as direct manifestation of reality rather than just a sign that is meaningless apart from a convention that would assign it its "true meaning" ("verace intendimento") also in his espousal of the principle: "Nomina sunt consequentia rerum" (XIII. 4). That "Names are consequences of things" is turned from a conventional juridical dictum into a theory of ontological revelation through language in Dante's appropriation of it in his work. The *nomen* (name) is taken to encapsulate a kind of omen or revelation (according to the Latin motto: *Nomen est omen*). The key example of this is Beatrice's name. We learn in the very first statement concerning her, as was noted already at the outset of Chapter 1, that this name is a consequence of the effect of her presence upon others, namely, that she blesses them and is called "Beatrice" even by many who did not know her name ("fu chiamata da molti Beatrice li quali non sapeano che si chiamare," II. 1). If names and language follow from things ("li nomi seguitino le nominate cose," XIII. 4), then they are not just arbitrary signs. The mental intention that their user could be held liable to make explicit, in this case, would be nothing other than an existential testimony of the ontological experience of being blessed by the mere sight of this woman.

---

[4] A. S. Kline, in *La Vita nuova / The New Life* (Delaware: CreateSpace Independent Publishing Platform, 2001), reasonably translates this incorporation of love into Dante by "Amor merged himself with me."

This motif of "blessed is the one who sees you" ("beato chi te vede") recurs, for example, in XXIII. 10 and 28, and continues all the way through to the antepenultimate chapter of Dante's little book. Dante imagines himself mentioning to passing pilgrims that, with Beatrice's death, the city of Florence has lost its beatifier ("Ell'a perduta la sua Beatrice," XL. 10). At this final stage, Beatrice's beatifying powers seem to have expanded to become civic in scope. Dante sees them as taking on a public function. He is now evangelically intent on universalizing this saintly woman's peculiar powers by appealing to passing pilgrims who come from far away ("venite voi da sì lontana gente") as if to acknowledge and glorify his own personal redeemer, namely, Beatrice. Dante can now be characterized as "almost like one of the evangelists" in his desire to communicate his experience of the miracle of Beatrice.[5]

The inherent logic of Dante's whole *libello* is to ground poetry in existence and, finally, in a redeemed existence. Having supplied an account of the life situation out of which the poems arise, Dante has already disclosed their true meaning. This is why he can declare, as we have just seen, at the end of Chapter III, that the "verace giudicio" or true meaning of his dream is now manifest to even the most simple-minded or naïve, despite the fact that it was not discerned by anyone at the time when Dante circulated his sonnet about it separately ("Lo verace giudicio del detto sogno non fue veduto allora per alcuno, ma ora è manifestissimo a li più semplici"). Even though the dream's enigmatic symbolism remains notoriously obscure still to some interpreters today, he has indeed made manifest the circumstances in his personal life that gave rise to the dream, and these circumstances elucidate the dream's meaning, making clear at least the presumable facts standing behind and occasioning, or at least contextualizing, it.

Dante ends Chapter XIV in similar terms, again evoking what is now plainly manifest to all. The sonnet of the "gabbo" or mocking of Dante is said to require no explanatory divisions because the verbally narrated or "reasoned cause" ("ragionata cagione") for the incident as given in the prose account makes its meaning manifest ("per la sua ragionata cagione assai sia manifesto, non ha mestiere di divisione," XIV. 13). Similarly, in Chapter XXXV. 4, Dante says that all that is narrated in his prose discourse ("tutto ciò che narrato è in questa ragione") about the gentle lady who pities him in his grief makes the meaning of his sonnet manifest so that he

---

[5] Donato Pirovano, "*Vita nuova*: A Novel Book," *Studi romanzi* 14, n.s. (2018): 149–63. Quotation, p. 162.

does not have to divide it ("E però che per questa ragione è assai manifesto, sì nollo dividerò"). Also ccncerning "Tanto gentile e tanto onesta pare," he writes that, "This sonnet is so clear to understand from what has been previously narrated that it requires no division" ("Questo sonetto è sì piano ad intendere, per quello che narrato è dinanzi, che non abbisogna d'alcuna divisione," XXVI. 8). Again, in XXXVI, he esteems that the sonnet is clear enough from its narrative context so as not to require divisions ("Ed è piano sanza dividerlo, per la sua precedente ragione").

This default to the narrative for explanation amounts, in effect, to placing the evidence of an *existential reality* above any specific interpretations in the form of glosses assigning and formulating meaning. The real-life event as such is thus the limit case that can be seen as the end and the surpassing of hermeneutics.[6] The lived fact of what actually happened is the definitive explanation of the figurative representations of the poem. Nevertheless, hermeneutics still serves – and is in fact indispensable – in order to lead us to precisely this limit, which is an "end" in two senses, both that of the goal and that of a denouement. Hermeneutics, in the end, opens toward and issues in the incarnate mystery of actual life and history.

The great breakthrough of the *Vita nuova*, then, I submit, is not so much breaking out of the lyric circle into narrative linearity but rather the grounding of revelation in the lyric and, in turn, of lyric in life. By contextualizing his lyric poems with prose descriptions of the circumstances that led up to their being written, Dante makes us understand his poems as personal expressions and revelations of his real-life experience. This sort of revelatory expression is more existentially dynamic than the figurative mode of the Troubadour *canso*, at least as the latter is typically conceived. The formal, archetypal character of the speaking "I" in the Troubadour poem is tellingly exposed in Paul Zumthor's description of the latter. The Troubadour poem is "a mode of saying that is entirely and exclusively referred to an I who, on account of often having no other than a grammatical existence, nonetheless fixes the plan and modalities of discourse, outside of all narration."[7] Precisely the *Vita nuova*'s narration unfixes the coordinates of the "I" and opens the lyric "I" to being informed by present re-membering of actual existence. The "I" of Dante's *Vita*

---

[6] This is what Hans Ulrich Gumbrecht calls "the power of presence" and exalts over any and all determinations of meaning, and thus over hermeneutics, in *The Production of Presence: What Meaning Cannot Convey* (Stanford: Stanford University Press, 2004).

[7] Paul Zumthor, "De la circularité du chant," *Poétique* 2 (1970): "un mode de dire entièrement et exclusivement référé à un je qui, pour n'avoir souvent d'autre existence que grammaticale, n'en fixe pas moins le plan et les modalités du discours, hors de toute narration" (p. 129).

nuova, thanks especially to the prose narrative, is no longer just the impersonal voice of song, as in Troubadour lyric, but an individual subject capable of personal, existential commitment in love – and in faith.

The "new life" is thus indeed – as Italian interpreters including Sanguineti and De Robertis are wont to suggest – a new life for the lyric.[8] The foregoing reflections have shown this to be the case in certain philosophical and religious senses reaching perhaps beyond what these critics intend. This new life is best characterized, furthermore, as a *redeemed* life. Dante will remain true to his commitment to love and its lyric expression all the way through to the end of the *Commedia*, in which epic-prophetic narrative and lyric effusion are wedded together inextricably. Just this integrative type of vision, fusing lyric and narrative (especially autobiographical narrative), lyric and life, discourse and existence, poetry and love, turns up at the center of Tristan Kay's analysis of Dante's entire poetic production from the *Vita nuova* to the *Commedia* as directed toward "lyric redemption":

> While other poets, such as Guittone and Folco, previously espoused religious, political, and didactic content, Dante's poetry in the *Commedia* retains an indissoluble connection to love, and forges a new, middle way between erotic and spiritual commitment, an unlikely redemption of – and indeed through – love poetry. Dante's epic poem is simultaneously a radically reimagined lyric poem, defined by lyric desire as well as by epic narration.[9]

Crucial is that the lyric, as it occurs already in the *Vita nuova*, is inscribed into the life story of Dante, and its newness is a participation in the total renewal of Dante's life. Thus, the lyric is renovated within the movement of an existential transformation or rebirth in the sense of a personal renaissance, an experience of being spiritually reborn. The prosaic account of the transformation that the lyrics embody and express does not supersede but rather serves the lyrics hermeneutically, providing them with an existential interpretation that grounds them in Dante's life as he imagines and reinvents it. The prose makes explicit the interpretation of existence that the poems already inscribe in the more elusive, musical, and revelatory notes and rhetorical colors of lyric.[10] Even if the prose embellishes and

---

[8]   Edoardo Sanguineti, "Per una lettura della *Vita nuova*," in *Vita nuova* (Milan: Garzanti, 1977). The *Vita nuova* remains centered in lyric also for Vincent Moleta, "The *Vita nuova* as a Lyric Narrative," *Forum italicum* 12/3 (1978): 369–90.

[9]   Tristan Kay, *Dante's Lyric Redemption: Eros, Salvation, Vernacular Tradition* (Oxford: Oxford University Press, 2016), p. 247.

[10] The way in which the prose narrative validates the poems' affective expression as authentic witness is subtly analyzed by Sara Sturm-Maddox, "The Pattern of Witness: Narrative Design in the *Vita nuova*," *Forum italicum* 12/3 (1978): 216–32.

enhances, and sometimes twists, the poems' meaning, this, too, in retrospect, belongs to the full disclosure of their originary hermeneutic potential *as incarnate revelation*, revelation that is ongoing – not a history closed within words as merely verbal structures, but the opening to a new and embodied life along an unconfined, uncircumscribed historical trajectory.

While the meaning of the poems is explained or illuminated by the prose, this does not mean that the poems are replaced or superseded. On the contrary, the meaning in question belongs primarily to the poems, and the prose *ragioni* are only a heuristic device helping to open to understanding and make transparent the otherwise unsoundable, mysterious depths of meaning in the poems. Meaning originates with the poems, but it is illuminated and explicated by the prose. Ultimately, more than their prose meaning, what counts is the inspirational presence that is realized in the poems. Finally, the meaning in question is not exactly anything that can be stated as such. It transpires *in* what happens as recounted in the narrative and in its meditative re-actualization in reading and in re-telling. Hence the silence of the poet in the book's concluding chapter (XLII) in the face of a predicament that will be developed finally in the *Paradiso* in terms of the ineffability of his vision.

This is what I take to be the fundamental innovation of Dante's *Vita nuova*. As a religiously revelatory text, it integrates the lived existence of its individual author fully into the revelation it confers. To the extent that revelation is realized concretely in the world and in the actual existence of an historical individual, we can call this a "secularization" of revelation. Moreover, Dante also writes this innovation into the existing literary genres of his time, transforming them and inaugurating new possibilities for specifically poetic literature to work as religious revelation. Boldly original, Dante's *Vita nuova* combines and adapts all the genres of the *cansos*, *vidas*, and *razos*, as well as of the grammars (whence the *divisioni*), to produce his own unique amalgam, the genre of which has proved to be such a puzzle. Yet, however intractable, this puzzle has proved also to be generative.

From Dante's "Little Book" to the Book of – and as – Revelation

The originality of the *Vita nuova* begins with its sui generis form as a literary hybrid of poetry and prose, specifically of courtly song and personal autobiography, a kind of grafting of song onto an individual existence. The book thereby also amalgamates, in unprecedented ways, these and other genres inherited from ancient and medieval literatures. These innovations make clear that this youthful work already evinces

Dante's penchant (consummated in the *Comedy*) to create a *summa* of all genres available to him in the cultural fields from which he chooses his materials.

Michelangelo Picone, in "Traditional Genres and Poetic Innovation in Thirteenth-Century Italian Lyric Poetry," discusses the effacing of distinct lyric genres due to their amalgamation into a system and the creation of a macro-genre – the *canzoniere* – through narrativization of the poet's life as lover, in early Italian lyric.[11] This development, is already underway in the *Vita nuova* as an anthology of lyric poems. The work reads as a first seeding anticipating a process that will eventually grow into the modern novel as the genre of all genres – or as a non-genre erasing the generic distinctions of traditional rhetoric between lyric, epic, and drama.

Jacques Rancière, in *La parole muette: Essai sur les contradictions de la littérature*, in a broad philosophical interpretation of the phenomenon of literature, propounds just such an idea of the novel as a non-genre that, instead of being just a genre, functions as the genre of genres.[12] Consideration specifically of the novel as an omnibus genre gravitates especially to debates around *Don Quixote* as the first modern novel.[13] While not obviously in a direct line of genealogical descent from Dante, this later blossoming of the novel serves to intimate the wide reach of the *Vita nuova*'s relevance to the entire phenomenon of literature developing in its wake as the "first book" in one of the earliest and most pathbreaking modern vernaculars to produce a flourishing imaginative literature. All the genres distinguished and enumerated above, and several more besides, can be reconceptualized as modes that blend together in producing a generically fluid form of literature that serves, fundamentally, as a vehicle or mode of revealing the deeper reality of things to human reflection and interpretation. In this strain of tradition, literature discovers its prophetic vocation.[14] Destined to be realized monumentally

---

[11] Michelangelo Picone, "Traditional Genres and Poetic Innovation in Thirteenth-Century Italian Lyric Poetry," in *Medieval Lyric: Genres in Historical Context*, ed. William Paden (Urbana: University of Illinois Press, 2000), pp. 146–57. In its current state, the question extends even to the individual lyrics gathered in Dante's *Rime*, hypothesized as forming a book. Fifteen of them have been viewed as a *canzoniere* originally structured by Dante, based on Boccaccio's copies of what he calls the "canzoni distesi." Raffaele Pinto, *Le rime di Dante: Libro di canzoni o rime sparse?* (London: Receptio Academic Press, 2020) relaunches this inquiry.

[12] Jacques Rancière, *La parole muette: Essai sur les contradictions de la littérature* (Paris: Hachette, 1998).

[13] I attempt to address this subject in another related project: "Meta-Theological Meditations on *Don Quixote*."

[14] I extend this reflection in "Poetry as Prophecy: From Anthropological Origins to Postmodern Apocalypses," in *Prophetic Witness and the Reimagining of the World: Poetry, Theology and Philosophy in Dialogue*, ed. Mark S. Burrows, Hilary Davies, and Josephine von Zitzewitz (London: Routledge, 2021), pp. 9–30.

with the *Commedia*, this synthesizing work of cultural and existential imagination is already an integral part of the revelation propounded by Dante's "little book" ("libello") or "booklet."

This term "libello" reads as a kind of litotes, an understatement, hence a gesture of humility, in spite of the author's rather grand ambitions, which already begin to make themselves felt from the opening chapter of the *Vita nuova*, in which this diminutive first appears (I. 1). It recurs in XII. 17; XXV. 9; and XXVIII. 2, each time insinuating a kind of completeness, even if in a minor key. The very last chapter (XLII) finally opens out beyond the book itself by registering another "miraculous vision" ("mirabile visione," corresponding to Chapter III's "maravigliosa visione") that makes Dante suspend his writing until such time as he shall come into possession of means more worthy of his exalted subject, his forever blessed lady. This resolution and implicit promise point in the direction of what will eventually take shape as the *Commedia*. Indeed, the "revelation" conferred, or at least claimed, reaches beyond the historical-cultural realm altogether to the properly transcendent dimension of an otherworldly gift – a divine grace granting beatitude.[15]

Despite these prodigious surpassings of every form and of everything finite, the idea of the book, with its connotation of completeness, remains key to this purportedly divine revelation. The book as such is a figure, and a crucial one, in Dante's narrative. The book is made up by the prose narratives constructed around the lyrics, but it, too, in a more fundamental, existential sense, we have seen, is generated by the inspiration of the lyrics. Dante's autobiographical narratives are pieced together around the lyrics in such a way as to constitute a book. The book is to be understood as filling in the context of a life-world (*Lebenswelt*) that orients the meaning of the revelation conveyed most directly in and through the lyrics. Dante's *libello* is very much a *little* book in comparison to *the* book par excellence, the Bible (τὰ βιβλία, literally "the books," connoting plurality and openness). Yet, as a revelatory text, it participates in the same revelatory genre of literature and demands to be understood in light of the Bible, particularly the New Testament, as its enabling paradigm.

The book as revelation emerges, in this light, as a major theme of Dante's little book, the premier book of Italian vernacular tradition. In his careful construction of and manifest fascination with the book and its

---

[15] Alberto Casadei, "La 'mirabile visione' nel finale della *Vita nova*," *Italianistica* 44/2 (2015): 15–20, illuminates Dante's gesture as at once mystical and rhetorical, adducing precedents in Hildegard of Bingen (among others), who likewise labors long years to become capable of expressing her *mirabilem uisionem*.

revelatory potential and mystique, Dante is building, with whatever degree of consciousness, on medieval sources such as Hugh of St. Cher, whose gloss on "the book of life" in Apocalypse 20: 12, identifies the book as the presence of God (*Dei praesentia*).[16] Rabanus Maurus likewise, in his *Allegoriae in universam sacram scripturam,* significantly writes of the book in the same terms as the actual "presence of God" ("Liber est praesentia Dei").[17] God's presence in and as the book turns the latter into a theological revelation in the strongest sense.

Dante's word "libello," although presumably intended modestly as a diminutive form, nonetheless re-echoes and re-deploys the term *libellum* in the Latin Vulgate (translating the Greek Septuagint: βιβλαρίδιον) from no less a text than the Book of Revelation (10: 2ff.) – a book that, surely, for Dante, given his Christian culture and convictions, counted as *the* canonical text for religious revelation in general. The Book of Revelation, Chapter 10, stages the initiation of the apostle John on Patmos as Christian prophet in a scene featuring a "little book" ("libellum"). An angel clothed with cloud and with a rainbow on its head, but with a face like the sun ("amictum nube, et iris in capite ejus, et facies ejus erat ut sol"), has descended from heaven with a "little book" ("libellum") open in its hand ("habebat in manu sua libellum apertum," 10: 2). The angel, standing astride the earth and sea, cries with a great voice like a lion's roar ("et clamavit voce magna, quemadmodum cum leo rugit") in which seven thunders uttered their voices ("Et cum clamasset, locuta sunt septem tonitrua voces suas").

Following the orders of the voice that speaks to him from heaven ("et audivit vocem de caelo iterum loquentem mecum"), John takes the book and eats it, replaying a scene from Ezekiel 2: 9–3: 3. The book is promised to be bitter in his stomach, but to become sweet like honey in his mouth. It is, indeed, sweet in his mouth, when he eats it, but it becomes bitter in his stomach. He is then told that he is to go forth and prophesy to many peoples and nations and tongues and kings. The passage stands out for its own solemnly visionary rhetoric – of a kind which Dante, in his own inimitable way, was to echo:

> [9] And I went unto the angel, and said unto him, Give me the little book. And he said unto me, Take it, and eat it up; and it shall make thy belly bitter, but it shall be in thy mouth sweet as honey.

---

[16] See Jesse Gellrich, *The Idea of the Book in the Middle Ages: Language, Theory, Mythology and Fiction* (Ithaca: Cornell University Press, 1985), p. 161.
[17] *Patrologia Latina,* ed. J.-P. Migne 112, 987c.

¹⁰ And I took the little book out of the angel's hand, and ate it up; and it was in my mouth sweet as honey: and as soon as I had eaten it, my belly was bitter.

¹¹ And he said unto me, Thou must prophesy again before many peoples, and nations, and tongues, and kings. (Revelation 10: 9–11)

⁹ Et abii ad angelum, dicens ei, ut daret mihi librum. Et dixit mihi: Accipe librum, et devora illum: et faciet amaricari ventrem tuum, sed in ore tuo erit dulce tamquam mel.

¹⁰ Et accepi librum de manu angeli, et devoravi illum: et erat in ore meo tamquam mel dulce, et cum devorassem eum, amaricatus est venter meus:

¹¹ et dixit mihi: Oportet te iterum prophetare gentibus, et populis, et linguis, et regibus multis.

This scene plays in the background of Dante's own commissioning as a prophet – his being commanded to write his major book, the *Commedia* – by Cacciaguida in *Paradiso* XVII. 124–42. He is told by Cacciaguida to "make your whole vision manifest" ("tutta tua vision fa manifesta"), holding nothing back, since even though the prophetic voice which delivers this vision will be harsh or bitter to the taste at first, nevertheless it will prove to be vital nourishment when digested:

Ché se la voce tua sarà molesta
    nel primo gusto, vital nodrimento
    lascerà poi, quando sarà digesta.   (*Paradiso* XVII. 130–32)

(For if your voice proves noisome
    in its first taste, it will deliver vital nourishment
    thereafter, when it is digested.)

Dante is still savoring the sweet with the bitter of this revelation at the outset of the following canto, Canto XVIII, where he remains in silent meditation and "tastes" ("gustavo") his inner word, "tempering the bitter with the sweet" ("temprando col dolce l'acerbo," XVIII. 1–3). The bitter sweetness of his prophetic word suggests the alignment of Dante's prophetic project with the model of prophetic revelation in the New Testament. Replayed thus in a sort of delayed echo spanning Dante's whole *oeuvre*, the far-reaching resonances of the *Vita nuova*'s diminutive "libello" first become fully audible in the context of this New Testament tradition.

In retrospect, we can see even more clearly than Dante could at the time of writing it how the *Vita nuova* was destined to place his poetic prophecy into continuity with the New Testament's prophetic revelation of a new life. Especially in light of its further interpretation in the *Commedia*, specifically the "libellum" of the Apocalypse of John (10: 2) shows up as already mirrored in Dante's first complete and programmatic work, designated internally and with insistence as his "libello" (I. 1; XII. 17; XXV. 9; XXVIII. 2). Here Dante, in effect, introduces and integrates into his work the image of the "little book" that, once ingested, speaks and will eventually expand into a great voice of prophecy for the salvation of the world. The people of Florence, those who knew, or at least knew of, Beatrice, are among the first to be able to experience the potential of this prophecy for being bitter-sweetly beatifying. Alongside them are, finally, also the pilgrims who transit through the city at the time of Beatrice's death (*Vita nuova* XL. 1–10). These pilgrims are also among the first who are able to witness to this tragic event's being good news and even salvation for all.

There is already some hint here that the pilgrims passing through Florence might be carriers of this message abroad, bearing it on a universal mission. Whether they embark on such a mission or not, their simply being there signifies, even without saying so, the potential of this sacrificial death of a beautiful, virtuous, and saintly young woman to become the bearer of a universal message of reconciliation. Like the pilgrims, the book's gospel of new life through undying love travels from within a city torn by internecine strife to a world outside likewise in dire need of geopolitical pacification. Nor does Beatrice's sacrificial and redemptive death emerge here as just an afterthought. It is alluded to already in the dream vision in Chapter III, with which the drama of this Passion story for Dante begins. Particularly the figure of the blessed, redemptive Lamb who is sacrificed, and in whose blood the garments of the martyrs are washed in Apocalypse 22: 14 (cf. 5: 6–14), furnishes precise images and stylemes for Dante's dream vision of his beatifier under a crimson, blood-colored ("sanguigno") sheet or veil in a scene involving sacrificial nourishment – the eating of a flaming heart.[18] This sacrificial coloring bleeds all the way through to Beatrice's reappearing in the Earthly Paradise "dressed in the color of living flame" ("vestita di color di fiamma viva," *Purgatorio* XXX. 33). She is hailed there with the blessing – "*Benedictus qui venis*" (XXX. 19) – that is of a piece liturgically with the prayer to the Lamb of God (*Agnus Dei*) whose sacrifice takes away the sins of the world ("qui tollis peccata mundi") in the Canon of the Mass. In retrospect, from this initial premonitory dream vision, Beatrice's untimely

---

[18] Igor Candido , in "Per una rilettura della *Vita Nova*: La prima *visio in somniis*," *Lettere italiane* 71 (2019): 21–50, examines the wide range of proposed interpretations and shows the New Testament apocalyptic tradition to be most pertinent for elucidating this dream.

death and Dante's all-consuming love passion show up as (re)enacting the Christic sacrificial Passion that is the means of universal redemption and salvation.

At least immediately after Beatrice's death, Dante's message is harsh, indeed devastating, in its first impact as news of a great loss eliciting bitter lamentations that echo yet another biblical model. The Lamentations of Jeremiah are explicitly cited and resound plangently ("*Quomodo sedet sola civitas*" / "How doth the city sit solitary," *Lam.* 1: 1) in *Vita nuova*, Chapter XXX. 1. This mournful note has already been struck early on in *Vita nuova*, Chapter VII. 7 ("*O vos omnes qui transitis per viam, attendite et videte si est dolor sicut meus*" / "O all ye who pass by this way, behold and see, if there is any sorrow like unto my sorrow," *Lam.* 1: 12) on the occasion of the death of a companion of Beatrice. The *incipit* of Lamentations is recalled with deliberate flourish in XXVIII. 1, following the "departure" ("partita") of Beatrice, before being evoked again in Chapter XXX, where the tone of lament is sounded in the aftermath (revolving around the number 9) of the untimely death of Beatrice. This rending sorrow, too, plays its part in transforming Dante's existence by wrenching it away from itself and thereby making it "new." He is effectively converted by this agonizing mourning to another life and into another, or a new, person. The consequences, in their universalizing propensity, become civic and even cosmic – opening the dimension in which we are all "pilgrims and strangers on the earth" ("peregrine et hospites sunt super terram") and in quest of another home or "patria," according to Hebrews 11: 13–14.[19]

Dante's work, early and late, delivers an incomparable demonstration of how revelation takes place through interpretive synthesis by the work of the imagination grounded in personal existence and witness. Revelation is not simply given as a purely positive fact. Instead, in full accord with the Christian Gospel – most specifically, with the Gospel According to John 1: 1: "In the beginning was the Word, and the Word was with God" – it is a revelation that originates in and with the word. Dante's incarnate revelation is emphatically a revelation in and through the word, especially the lyrically elaborated and poetically enhanced word. This poetic word proclaims the advent of Beatrice into Dante's life as a salvific revelation of truth through the experience of beauty and grace – thereby paralleling and,

---

[19] Ronald L. Martinez, "Mourning Beatrice: The Rhetoric of Threnody in the *Vita nuova*," *Modern Language Notes* 113 (1998): 1–29 shows that the rites of mourning in the medieval tradition of the Threni (Book of Lamentations) tended to be directed beyond the private to the public sphere and to encompass the entire "widowed" city of the deceased individual. Dante quotes Lamentations tellingly in his letter to public authorities, the "princes of the earth," after Beatrice's death (XXX. 1).

in a sense, further propagating the Gospel of John's proclamation that "the Word was made flesh and dwelt among us, full of grace and truth" (1: 14).

Dante's little, but hardly lightweight, book superlatively illustrates and enacts, by focusing on the case of a single individual, how the miracle of divine revelation in the vast literature of the Bible actually comes to take up residence in a world of words and thence to live in the flesh. It is constructed by poetic inspiration grounded in passionate, affective life and in existence aspiring to intellectual vision. The *Vita nuova* brilliantly illuminates the poetic work of revelation underway in the New Testament and is, in turn, illuminated by it. Dante's book elucidates how this work of revelatory myth-making in Scripture can be extended further into the unlimited field of creative, imaginative literature. It remains at work throughout the perambulations of subsequent poetic tradition even down to our own time. This little book thereby confers abundant new life reaching all the way to our own otherwise often tragically disenchanted present.

Coda

I have counterpointed this defense of the permanent centrality of the lyric mode in Dante's project as a poet with verses from T. S. Eliot's *Four Quartets* (1941–42). This procedure stands in deliberate contrast to Harrison's frequent evocation of Ezra Pound's *Cantos* (1922–62) as offering leitmotifs for his readings of early Italian lyrics by Dante and Cavalcanti. I choose this procedure because, from its very title, which turns on a musical metaphor, Eliot's poem programmatically signals the inherently musical or lyrical nature of poetic and religious vision as it survives still in modern literature.

Just the title "Four Quartets" already offers multiple figures of sameness, which I have contended is constitutive of the lyrical. One is phonic: "four" rhymes with "quar" in "quar-tets." Others are arithmetic and semantic: the concept of the number four is embedded in the meanings of both words in this title heard in the etymological registers of English and Latin. The four is embodied concretely – iconically and icastically – in the letters of each of these words taken in groups of four. Such figures make this title an epitome of the symmetrically closed, self-reflexive structure of lyric in general.

Such figural closure, however, does not exist merely unto itself. The quartet is by definition a composition for four instruments or voices. Nevertheless, included in the definition of this musical genre, at least generally in its classic form, is its being made up of five movements. Thus, in the actual deployment of its contents, the form of the "quartet" already breaks out beyond the figure of four. The quartet materially contains more than is formally figured by its generic name. Indeed, each of Eliot's four component poems is divided into five parts or movements, and their intensively meditative, self-reflexive structure serves as a basis for dynamically stepping out beyond their conceptually regulated form into an infinite repertoire of material expanding as an open reservoir waiting to be explored ("We shall not cease from exploration," etc.).

Significantly homologous in this respect to the four Gospels, this fourfold form adopted by Eliot articulates and makes available for application to existence a self-reflective structure of significance that can multiply its applications indefinitely. Such self-reflective figuration provides a paradigm through which existence can be given a measure of intelligibility and be consciously appropriated by an individual subject for the purpose of opening it up without limit to further, new experience. Self-reflexivity embodied in figures of repetition thus enables literary representation originating in lyrical expression to become the hermeneutic vehicle of a revelation of transcendent meaning made immanent in the existence of an incarnate individual.[1] And that is exactly what the *Vita nuova* claims to be and do.

---

[1] I pursue the lyrical origins of the logic of self-reflexivity in Dante's *oeuvre* further in *Dante's* Paradiso *and the Theological Origins of Modern Thought: Toward a Speculative Philosophy of Self-Reflection* (New York: Routledge, 2021), Routledge Interdisciplinary Perspectives on Literature Series.

Epilogue: Dream Epistemology and Religious Revelation in Dante's Vita nuova

The dream as revelation is a topic that proves to be particularly germane to the concerns of the foregoing chapters. Dreams can themselves be construed as first-order interpretations (even if unconscious ones) of inner and/or outer reality presented as immediate experience. They embody an intimate and internalized type of knowing. However, dreams also reveal more than they can know or say about a reality that they only indirectly refract: they present a plethora of manifestly significant, yet non-transparent, symptoms and indices. They invite us to interpret their enigmatic representations as encodings of the mysteries of our existence.

For all their teasing ambiguity and indirectness, dreams can be uncannily powerful means of disclosure, whether of our repressed psychic depths or of universal and timeless archetypes. Accordingly, a focus specifically on the dream is taken up here as a fitting denouement and supplement in order to push further these reflections on the hermeneutics of revelation in the *Vita nuova*. These concluding reflections project the speculatively philosophical and theological considerations developed in the foregoing chapters beyond into wider psychological and anthropological contexts.

Dante himself sees in dreams a revelation of the immortality of the human soul as a fundamental condition of our existence. He argues explicitly for this thesis in Book II of his *Convivio*:

> Again, we see continual experience of our immortality in the divinations of our dreams, which we could not have unless there were some immortal part in us; the reason is that the revealer, whether corporeal or incorporeal, must necessarily be immortal, if we consider carefully. I say corporeal or incorporeal because of the diverse opinions I find on this subject. That which is moved or informed directly by an informing agent must bear a proportion to the informing agent, and there is no proportion between the mortal and the immortal. (*Convivio* II. viii. 13)

(Ancora: vedemo continua esperienza de la nostra immortalitade nelle divinazioni de' nostri sogni, le quali essere non potrebbono se in noi alcuna parte immortale non fosse; con ciò sia cosa che immortale convegna essere lo rivelante, o corporeo o incorporeo che sia, se bene si pensa sottilmente – ed dico o corporeo o incorporeo, per le diverse oppinioni che io truovo di ciò –, e quello ch'è mosso o vero informato da informatore immediato debbia proporzione avere allo informatore, e dallo mortale allo immortale nulla sia proporzione.)

In something like an ontological argument applied to dreaming, Dante reasons that you must actually *be* immortal in order to be able to conceive of and so reveal something immortal. And just such conceiving, he maintains, takes place when we dream, since we are able to divine immortal things.

Whatever we may think of Dante's reasoning about this, with his inference from our capability of conceiving immortality to its actual existence in our souls, the fact that the *Vita nuova* is, in many respects, a revelatory dream text has been well recognized all along in the critical tradition. Consideration of the pervasive role played in the *Vita nuova* by dreaming and dream visions, furthermore, brings to light a key aspect of the book's hermeneutics – and inseparably its poetics – of revelation. The literary work in general, with its symbolic and metaphorical modes of expression, participates in certain mechanisms of phenomenological disclosure that can be apprehended as operating exemplarily in the dream. This is even more evident in the work specifically of lyric poetry. It is not surprising, then, that dreaming turns out to be a chief concern not only of Dante's "little book" (*libello*, I. 1), but also of his greatest work, the *Divine Comedy*, where it remains a structuring principle, even if in a somewhat more veiled manner. The trope of dreaming, by this account, emerges as a supporting axis running throughout Dante's entire creative production.

Taken in terms of its own framing metaphors, indeed the whole of the *Divine Comedy* is a dream text and recounts a dream experience. The action is set between references to dreaming at its opening and close: both subtly hint at its status as a dream sequence. At the outset of the *Inferno*, in its prologue (Canto I), Dante indicates that he was so full of *sleep* ("sonno") at the point where he abandoned the true way that he no longer knows how to re-tell by what way he entered there ("Io non so ben ridir com'i' v'intrai, / tant'era pien di sonno a quel punto / che la verace via abandonnai," I. 10–11). And upon actually entering into the Inferno or Hell at the end of Canto III, he falls like a man seized by sleep ("e caddi, come l'uom cui sonno piglia," 136; cf. also IV. 1: "Ruppemi l'alto sonno").

At the other end of the journey, at the conclusion of the penultimate canto of the *Paradiso*, as the poem winds up for its final vision of God in Canto XXXIII, Saint Bernard remarks that the time in which Dante sleeps, or that "makes him sleep," is "fleeing," or coming to an end ("Ma perché 'l tempo fugge che t'assonna," XXXII. 139). And in the concluding canto itself, Dante employs the simile of a man awaking from sleep and its visions, which immediately vanish, leaving behind only the "passion" or the feeling impressed on him, a sweetness born in his heart ("Qual è colui che somniando vede / che dopo 'l sogno la passione impressa / rimane, e l'altro a la mente non riede // cotal son io ché quasi tutta cessa / mia visione, e ancor mi distilla / nel core il dolce che nacque da essa," XXXIII. 58–60).

These are all hints that Dante's greatest and most revelatory poem as a whole, from beginning to end, is at some level to be understood as a dream vision. This parabola remains indispensable to grasping the whole arc of Dante's project as tracing out a subtly nuanced figure of dream thinking. Most to our purpose, however, a precedent for Dante's use of the dream as a vehicle and a frame for his ultimate revelatory visions is already set by the *Vita nuova*.[1]

The *Vita nuova*'s Initiatory Dream in Its Cultural Contexts

Revelation through the dream is, of course, a commonplace in medieval culture, one that is transmitted most influentially by Macrobius in his early fifth-century CE *Commentary on the Dream of Scipio* (*Commentarium in Ciceronis Somnium Scipionis*). This work expands into an encyclopedic treatise on the subject of dreams and much else besides, all articulated from the perspective and in the vocabulary of Neo-Platonic philosophy. Macrobius's treatise is cast as a commentary on Cicero's *De somnium Scipionis* (54–52 BCE), which itself unfolds as a vision of the entire cosmos and of the protagonist's destiny within it. This last-named work of classical antiquity emerges expressly as a primary model for the dream as revelation of universal knowledge in the *Divine Comedy*. It is alluded to in relation to Dante's dream in *Purgatorio* IX. 63 and backgrounds Dante's look back down on the earth from the sphere of the fixed stars in *Paradiso* XXII. 128–29, as well as his hearing the music of the spheres in *Paradiso* I. 78, to mention only a few of the numerous telling traces. Leaving these allusions

---

[1] This is thoroughly demonstrated by Nicolò Mineo in "Visionismo iniziatico nella *Vita nuova*," chapter II of his *Profetismo e apocalittica in Dante: Strutture e temi dalla* Vita Nuova *alla* Divina Commedia, pp. 103–42.

aside, we concentrate here specifically on how the *Somnium Scipionis* and its medieval interpretations can cast some illumination in relation already to the *Vita nuova*.

Roman general Scipio Aemilianus dreams that he is guided by his adoptive grandfather Scipio Africanus into the sky above Carthage among the stars in view of the Milky Way ("orbem lacteum"). The dream and its narration are set two years before the destruction of Carthage by Rome in 146 BCE under the leadership of Scipio Aemilianus. The dreamer, in his visions, sees the ninefold structure of the celestial spheres, all of which are connected and folded into the supreme god, who encompasses and holds them all together ("Novem tibi orbibus vel potius globis conexa sunt omnia, quorum unus est caelestis, extimus, qui reliquos omnes complectitur, summus ipse deus arcens et continens ceteros").[2] With directives and explanations again from his ancestral guide, Scipio hears how the turning of the spheres produces the music of the universe (*musica universalis*). Cicero's detailed descriptions of Scipio's dream give rise, moreover, to numerous speculative considerations on the part of Macrobius concerning the various manifest forms and presumable hidden causes of dreams. Macrobius organizes them into a comprehensive typology.

Dante's dreams as a youthful lover similarly resonate with a kind of cosmic and prophetic-allegorical significance; they, too, are treated as revelations of mysterious universal arcana. They are chronicled as occurring enigmatically at the ninth hour of the day (*Vita nuova* XII. 9) or in the first of nine remaining hours of the night (II. 8). These and other oblique signs are taken, following Arabian and Syrian, as well as Christian calendars, as conforming to and confirming the sovereign rule of the number nine over each crucially significant episode of Dante's love story. The theme of the dream as revelation in the *Vita nuova* is implicitly informed by this broad field of classical and medieval tradition about dreams, which serves as a background for his little book's meaning as a whole. That no specific mention is made of this particular classical pagan text (*De somnium Scipionis*) as precedent helps to keep the focus on Christian revelation in the Bible as Dante's primary cultural frame and on the New Testament in particular as his cardinal point of reference. Nevertheless, cumulatively, the sense of the dream vision as a religious revelation, with its imperious truth claims, is strongly reinforced by its being viewed from the perspectives of all these traditions.[3]

---

[2] M. Tulli Ciceronis, *De Republica liber sextus*, paragraph 17, available at: www.thelatinlibrary.com /cicero/repub6.shtml (accessed September 11, 2019).

[3] Cicero's *De divinatione* is another important source on dreams that has a proven influence on Dante, especially via Albert the Great and his *De somno et vigilia*. Albert himself has unavowed debts to Arab

Nonetheless, despite this weighty patrimony of cultural tradition, the dream vision's function as revelation in the *Vita nuova* is asserted with a certain evident immediacy. The dream's role as revelatory is presented there naked, or at least as only thinly veiled. Even in the popular culture of the Middle Ages, dreams were associated especially with revelations from the other world and were often understood as affording the dreamer providential opportunities to prepare in advance for death. This needs to be said particularly of the genre of the *autobiographical* dream, of which Dante's *Vita nuova* offers several exemplary instances. The genre is surveyed and its contents are made available in the form of an extensive anthology of medieval texts collected by Gisèle Besson and Jean-Claude Schmitt.[4] Schmitt's work, furthermore, on Dante as a medieval dreamer in the tradition of autobiographical dream narrative and funerary rememoration, reads the dreams specifically of Dante's *Vita nuova* as revolving consistently around Beatrice's death and its memorialization.[5] Reconfiguring it as an autobiographical dream text in light of this now well-discerned and extensively documented genre devoted to a widespread, even if not exactly common, medieval phenomenon gives a sharp focus and emphasis to the *Vita nuova*. For Schmitt, Dante's little book in its entirety addresses itself to the deceased Beatrice ("Tout le livre, je le répète, s'addresse à Béatrice morte"), as if seen in a dream vision (p. 191).[6]

Beatrice's long speech at the conclusion of *Purgatorio* XXX (103–45), addressed to the angels and alluding expressly to Dante's "vita nova" (115), mentions her attempts (all in vain) to win him back through inspirations *in dream* and by other means ("Né l'impetrare ispirazion mi valse, / con le quali e *in sogno* e altrimenti / lo rivocai," 133–35). The *Vita nuova* itself, notably in Chapter XXXIX, alludes to certain revisitations in dream and in vision of the deceased Beatrice. Schmitt reads the *canzone* "Li occhi dolenti" as recounting the apparition of Beatrice as a "revenant" (p. 189) appearing to Dante mourning for his beloved. The pain he experiences

---

sources, particularly Avicenna and Al-Ghazali. See Bruno Nardi, "Dante e Pietro d'Abano," in *Saggi di filosofia dantesca* (Florence: La nuova Italia, [1930] 1967), pp. 40–62.

4 Gisèle Besson and Jean-Claude Schmitt, eds., *Rêve de soi: Les songes autobiographiques au Moyen Age* (Toulouse: Anacharsis, 2017).

5 Jean-Claude Schmitt, "Dante en rêveur médiéval: 'Memoria' funéraire et récit autobiographique," *Dante Studies* 136 (2018): 187–200.

6 Schmitt develops at length his analysis of dreams in the Middle Ages as the privileged means of communicating with the dead, as well as with divinity, also in other books including *Le corps, les rites, les rêves, le temps: Essais d'anthropologie médiévale* (Paris: Gallimard, 2001) and *Le corps des images: Essais sur la culture visuelle au Moyen Âge* (Paris: Gallimard, 2002), p. 29 and Part III: "Rêves, Visions, Fantasmes."

wakes him from sleep ("Ch'io mi riscuoto per dolor ch'i' sento," XXXI. 14),
at least as Schmitt translates it ("la douleur que j'éprouve me réveille,"
p. 189). Most conspicuously of all, however, the "forte imaginazione"
("strong imagining," XXXIX. 1), in which Beatrice appears to Dante in
the original crimson-colored clothing ("nobilissimo colore, umile e onesto,
sanguigno," II. 3) and youth of his first seeing of her, has all the typical
markings of a (waking) dream vision. It recalls, by the same token, his first
dream of her draped with a crimson cloth ("drappo sanguigno," III. 4).

The same term "imaginazione" is used also in XXIII. 6–10 for Dante's
delirious, dream-like premonition of Beatrice's death and again for his
vision of Giovanna preceding Beatrice when the two ladies appear in
procession before him, as recorded in Chapter XXIV. All of this is apt to
suggest that dreaming continues to function as a framing device for
Dante's visionary experience of Beatrice throughout the *Vita nuova* and
even well beyond it.

"Visio, -onis," in the Middle Ages, was a word also for "dream,"[7] and it
is used in this sense in the *Vita nuova* by Dante, whose entire *oeuvre*,
starting from this first book, is nothing if not visionary. The text of the *Vita
nuova* as a whole is dreamy in texture and in atmosphere. But, even more
basically and literally, its plot structure is dream-driven right from the
dream vision described very near its opening in Chapter III. 3–7. This
dream-frame is extended thereafter in the many detailed reminiscences
throughout the work that are drenched in dream imagery. There are
numerous waking dreams in the *Vita nuova*, and there are also perfectly
literal dreams, all serving, in very different ways, to open or allude to
a visionary dimension of reality.[8] All this allusiveness calls out for examination in greater detail of the premier instance that the book specifically and
unequivocally presents as a dream vision – indeed as an oneiric revelation at
its generative source.

A highly charged and mysterious tone is set from the third paragraph of
Chapter III with the book's initial "marvelous vision" ("maravigliosa
visione"), which comes to its autobiographical protagonist in a "sweet
sleep" ("soave sonno"). The marvelous vision is thereby marked as given
to Dante in the guise of a revelatory dream ("mi sopragiunse uno soave
sonno, ne lo quale m'apparve una maravigliosa visione," III. 3). The sleep

---

[7] Valerio Cappozzo, *Dizionario dei sogni nel Medioevo: Il Somniale Danielis in manoscritti letterari*
(Florence: Olschki, 2018) amply substantiates and illustrates this usage.
[8] Ernesto Livorni, "Dream and Vision in Dante's *Vita Nova*," in *"Accessus ad Auctores": Studies in
Honor of Christopher Kleinhenz*, ed. Fabian Alfie and Andrea Dini (Tempe, AZ: ACMRS, 2011), pp.
93–114.

itself comes upon or "*over*comes" Dante ("mi *sopra*giunse"), as if from beyond or above him. This dream presents the dreamer with the vision of "a person" who is recognizable as "the lady of the greeting" from the preceding day ("conobbi ch'era la donna de la salute, la quale m'avea lo giorno dinanzi degnato di salutare," III. 4). She herself is sleeping in the arms of Love and is naked, except for being lightly wrapped in a crimson cloth ("Ne le sue braccia mi parea vedere una persona dormire nuda, salvo che involta mi parea in uno drappo sanguigno leggermente," III. 4).

Appropriate to its status as a dream and in sleep, this marvelous vision takes place in Dante's bedchamber ("camera"). But what first appears to him in this setting is "a cloud the color of fire" ("che me parea vedere ne la mia camera una nebula di colore di fuoco," III. 3) in which he discerns the figure of "a lord" ("dentro a la quale io discernea una figura d'uno segnore"), who will turn out to be the god Love. The woman who is the object of Dante's passionate meditation and desire is seen only through these narrative frames and veils bringing with them their enormous freight of mythical and mystic connotations.

The "cloud of the color of fire" in the chamber, with which the whole dream begins and which serves it as a general frame, is an apt image for the dream specifically as a revelation, since it both radiates light and remains shrouded in mystery. It borrows its light from biblical images of apocalypse in the prophetic visions of Amos, Ezekiel, Isaiah, and John on Patmos, to name just the principal sources. Ezekiel, for example, in his revelatory "visions of God" by the river of Chebar, famously sees a whirlwind coming out of the north. It appears as "a great cloud, and a fire infolding itself, and a brightness was about it, and out of the midst thereof as the colour of amber, out of the midst of the fire" ("nubes magna et ignes involvens et splendor in circuiti eius et de medio eius quasi species electri id est de medio ignis," 1: 4).

Such imagery of cloud mixed with fire runs pervasively throughout biblical prophecy and apocalyptic. It lights up vividly as refracting the theophantic pillars of cloud and fire that accompany and guide the Hebrews by day and by night on their journey through the desert in the Exodus (13: 21–22, etc.). This imagery extends to the New Testament and reaches its final destination in the Book of Revelation. Already, near the end of the last chapter, we noted how the angel of the Apocalypse (10: 1) descends "wrapped in a cloud" ("amictum nube") and with a face like the sun, having "feet (or legs) like a column of fire" ("et pedes eius tamquam columnis igni").

In this sometimes rather frightening visionary register, the "lord" who appears in Dante's marvelous vision or dream, and who will be identified, just a little later, as the god Love, is of fearful aspect to one who looks at him ("di pauroso aspetto a chi la guardasse"). Yet he appears *in himself* ("quanto a sé") to be remarkably, wondrously joyful ("e pareami con tanta letizia, quanto a sé, che mirabile cosa era," III. 3). With his words, he is saying many things, most of which Dante cannot understand ("ne le sue parole dicea molte cose, le quali io non intendea se non poche"), but among the things that Dante does understand, he hears Love say: "I am your lord" ("Ego dominus tuus"). Love speaks here with the added authority of Latin rather than in the normally vernacular idiom of Dante's little book.

The dream thus reveals a superior, mastering power as a source of joy in itself, yet one inducing fear in the dreamer, fear which turns out, in the sequel, to be not without cause. For when Dante looks with great intensity ("la quale io riguardando molto intentivamente," III. 4), he recognizes that what Love is holding in his arms is the woman who on the preceding day had bestowed on him her blessed greeting. With this startling recognition, then, the provocative and eerily macabre action of the dream begins to unfold. Love apparently wakes the sleeping lady ("pareami che disvegliasse questa che dormia," III. 6) and uses his art or ingenuity ("suo ingegno") to prevail upon her to eat the dreamer's flaming heart ("tanto si sforzava per suo ingegno, che le facea mangiare questa cosa che in mano li ardea"). After she does so timorously or, more literally, "doubtfully" ("ella mangiava dubitosamente"), Love's previously noted great joy turns to most bitter weeping ("la sua letizia si convertia in amarissimo pianto," III. 7). Grieving and shedding tears in this manner, Love gathers the lady back into his arms and disappears with her toward the heaven ("e così piangendo, si ricogliea questa donna ne le sue braccia, e con essa mi parea che si ne gisse verso lo cielo," III. 7).

At the conclusion of his dream, and in reaction to its disturbing contents, Dante suffers such anguish that his fragile sleep is broken ("io sostenea sì grande angoscia, che lo mio deboletto sonno non poteo sostenere, anzi si ruppe e fui disvegliato," III. 7). Following this rude awaking, the manifestly revelatory intensity of this apocalyptic imagery fades from focus, along with the dream itself. Dante, at this juncture, enters into the more hermeneutically distanced mode of reflecting on and questioning what has been revealed to him. However, while he was dreaming, this revelation was in the immediacy of the present. In practice, the interpretive act itself becomes a re-actualizing in the immediacy of the present of the originally revelatory experience and in this sense a revelation in its own right. Only in this way can interpretation approach and proffer an adequate comprehension of the dream. This much, I submit, has been made evident through the foregoing analyses and elucidations that I have offered in this book.

As recounted in Chapter III. 9–15, immediately subsequent to the description of the dream, Dante initiates a collective endeavor to interpret his dream by circulating a poem recounting it. Not the prose version itself, but only the poem recounting the dream tells us straight out that the figure of the "lord" whom Dante discerns is Love. The prose reports that Dante writes a sonnet in which he greets all of Love's faithful subjects ("fedeli d'Amore"), and the fourth line of the sonnet specifies that this greeting is in the name (or in consideration or in respect) of "their lord, that is, Love" ("salute in lor segnor, cioè Amore," III. 10). The prose is less explicit and does not serve, finally, to disambiguate the dream, making it more plain and manifest, but aims rather to safeguard its mystery.

Dante's poem about his dream provokes a flurry of poetic exchanges among the poets of his circle in Tuscany. A significant link is thereby forged, making for a strong and productive complicity between dreaming and poetry. Dante sets up the category of the dream as essential to his whole experience and poetic enterprise in the *Vita nuova*. The dream turns out, furthermore, to be, in telling ways, an indispensable model for understanding the very nature of knowledge, including especially poetic knowledge, as it is revealed in the *Vita nuova*. These considerations show forth the more general, epistemological stakes that motivate the present wide-ranging investigation of the role of dreaming as revelatory and even as quasi-religious revelation in Dante's work.

De-limiting Knowledge through Poetry and through Dream

The *libello*'s model of knowing, with its debts to and derivation from dreaming and revelation, reflects on knowledge in general, especially in the eminent sense in which knowledge can be approached and explored in humanities studies and particularly through literature and poetry. In the *Convivio*, looking back on the *Vita nuova* ("sì come nella Vita Nuova si può vedere," II. xii. 4), Dante describes how his intellect or "genius" ("mio ingegno") was able to "see" already intuitively "*as in a dream*" ("quasi come sognando") many things about which he subsequently read in learned authors such as Boethius and Cicero. He had already essentially understood, or at least glimpsed, in this prescient, dream-like manner, the things that he then came across externally and found fully expounded in the "words of authors and of sciences and of books" ("vocabuli d'autori e di scienze e di libri," II. xii. 5). The dream serves here as a metaphor for some sort of intuitive, pre-articulate, visionary knowledge of – potentially – whatever is knowable.

The dream, accordingly, can be a revelation of a kind of consciousness in which direct, first-person knowing, or at least first-person experience, is boundless and becomes capable of attaining to somehow unlimited forms of knowing or awareness. Dante's literary creation of the dream experience makes it shine forth in its limitless potential for meaning. Dreaming, of course, is a highly subjective form of consciousness, one about which we are accustomed to say that the dreamer is out of touch with reality. It can even be diagnosed clinically as a kind of psychosis that is permissible and tolerable only because it is strictly circumscribed by a fantasy world that remains separate from waking life and that is habitually experienced by perfectly "normal" people on a quotidian (or, more commonly, a nocturnal) basis.[9]

Dreams are based on, and flow forth from, a kind of suspension of reality as it ordinarily impinges on us. However, this subjective dream consciousness can also become the revelation of a higher order of reality. This sort of expanded dream consciousness is a widespread cross-cultural phenomenon, if not an anthropological constant. Such a motif is found, for example, in Australian aboriginal "dream time." Carl Gustave Jung's autobiography provides a provocative and influential introduction to dreams studied in a clinical key, but also on a broadly cross-cultural basis that particularly highlights their status as revelations of the mysteries of the otherworldly.[10]

Dreams have provided a medium for shamanic voyages through the spiritual universe as conceived in cultures from around the world, often emanating, in this respect, from origins in Siberia, or sometimes in Mongolia or Mexico. In the dream-state (*swapna*) of Indian myth and philosophy, the dreamer's body becomes identical with the god (Shiva) and expands to encompass the entire universe; the dreamer thereby attains to cosmic consciousness.[11] Shamanism has repeatedly been evoked in relation to Dante's initiatory journey in the *Divine Comedy* and has been explored

---

[9] For orientation in this field of research, I have consulted Silvio Scarone et al. "The Dream as a Model for Psychosis: An Experimental Approach Using Bizarreness as a Cognitive Marker," *Schizophrenia Bulletin* 34/3 (2008): 515–22.

[10] C. G. Jung, *Erinnerungen, Träume, Gedanken*, ed. Anelia Jaffé (New York: Pantheon Books, 1961), trans. Richard and Clara Winston as *Memories, Dreams, Reflections* (New York: Vintage, 1965). Jungian analyst Claudio Widmann develops a "distant reading" of Dante on this Jungian basis in his monumental three-volume *La Divina Commedia come percorso di vita* (Roma: Magi, 2021).

[11] Marc Ballenfat, *Introduction aux philosophies de l'Inde* (Paris: Broché, 2002).

specifically in relation to Dante's "pilgrim spirit" ("spirito peregrino") in the *Vita nuova*.[12]

Especially this context of primordial cultures points us to the threshold where dreaming touches on and arguably coincides with religious experience. Mythologies of primordial peoples often lend themselves to being understood as collective dreams and may even understand themselves that way. In more modern and highly individualized phases of society, dreaming takes on undeniably also an ineffaceable *subjective aspect*, a quality of direct personal experience that can even become religious witness. This latter quality is very marked and programmatic notably in the Gospels. Precisely this aspect is clearly evidenced by Dante's experience, both awake and in dream, of Beatrice in the *Vita nuova*. But the individualism and idiosyncrasy of one's own dream world can also make it liable sometimes to take even a pathological turn.

Dreams and poetry are very often assessed as near to madness in popular culture – and even in media and milieus that normally count as scientific, or at least clinical. Dante himself is, at times, by his own admission, at the edge of madness in his delirious dreaming – for example, in *Vita nuova*, Chapter XXIII. 3–5. Yet he manages to turn his dreams into means of a higher knowledge of the inner self and of the secrets of the heart. They even become revelatory of a metaphysical order of reality. Thanks especially to this access to a higher wisdom gained through dreaming, his "little book" can be read as furnishing some basic elements for adumbrating a general theory, or an epistemology, of dreaming. Dreaming emerges as a form of knowledge akin to theological revelation to the extent that it exceeds the normal, if not the natural, perceptions and the customary capacities of mortals.

In the dream state, everything is possible. Dreaming is commonly and proverbially taken as a medium of wish fulfillment. This connotation registers most familiarly, for instance, in the cliché: "it was a dream come true." Likewise, religious revelation can induce or allude to a state in which everything is possible. As Jesus puts it with regard to the difficulty for the rich man of entering into the kingdom of God, or of anyone's being saved, for that matter, "With men this is impossible; but with God all things are possible" (Gospel According to Matthew, 19: 26). The world is thus revealed as open to being made over anew and as wholly without

---

[12] Robert Klein, "Spirito Peregrino," chapter 4 of *La forme et l'intelligibile* (Paris: Gallimard, 1970), pp. 31–57, especially pp. 32–44. Wider-ranging implications of the "spiritual pilgrim" figure for Dante's *oeuvre* and overall project of self-transformation are taken up by Didier Ottaviani, *Dante: L'esprit pèlerin* (Paris: Seuil, 2016).

restrictions as to what may or may not be possible. This requires us to conceive of revelation simply as endlessly open manifestation and announcement. The German word for "revelation" – *Offenbarung* – in its literal meaning, says that what is revealed is made "open" (*offen*). Ongoing, open-ended interpretation of texts such as the *Vita nuova* (as explored especially in Chapter 5 above on the work's "history of effect") occasions and even embodies revelation in this extended sense. Revelation, in this wide acceptation, reaches to infinity – at least, to the infinity of interpretations that always invite further interpretations and are never final or definitive.

A dream or a vision's having a given, determinate content does not fix its meaning once and for all. Its content remains plastic and expandable and rather opens it to all imaginable forms of enrichment or revision, according to the various contexts into which it is interpreted. A particular content comes to communicate with others without limit in the mode of a "concrete universal." The latter term was used especially by Hegel to indicate that everything is internally related to everything else – everything mirrors and shows forth some aspect of any and every other thing.[13]

Dreaming and literature are closely related precisely by virtue of their being both such wide-open, revelatory media based on ongoing, potentially inexhaustible experiences of disclosure. Literature and dreaming alike become revelation – even, in a certain sense, "theological" revelation – in Dante and in prophetic poets like Milton and Blake, or, earlier, in the dream visions of Chaucer or the Pearl poet, or in William Langland's *Piers Plowman* (1370–90).

Even visionary satirists like Rabelais (in particular in chapters XIII and XIV of the *Tiers Livre* on the Dream of Panurge – "Le songe de Panurge") or James Joyce, in *Finnegans Wake*, exploit the capacities of dreaming to produce an astonishing host of otherwise impossible scenes of preposterous fantasy. These scenes are apt to open up unexpected, penetrating insights into reality, often by virtue of their being so topsy-turvy. Their wild implausibility stretches our assumptions about reality past their usually accepted limits to include what we normally exclude. This normally excluded material or potential must be included, or at least allowed for, in order for our conception to reach out toward the real in every form without limit. Without this unrestricted inclusiveness or openness, our conception could never be fully or totally true.

---

[13] Richard Rorty, "Relations, Internal and External," in *Encyclopedia of Philosophy*, 2nd ed., ed. D. M. Borchert (Detroit: Thomson Gale, 2006), vol. VIII, pp. 335–45.

"Theology," as I conceive it, is likewise a discourse about the alpha and the omega, the beginning and the end of All, albeit an All that exceeds our comprehension and remains veiled in mystery, a mystery of "transcendence." Theological revelation embraces, or at least envisages, the Whole in its infinity. But, as such, it reaches beyond our comprehension and even beyond our conception.

The logic of the dream, consequently, is in certain outstanding respects a logic of revelation. This logic does not obey the law of non-contradiction because in dreaming everything turns into a form of *self*-reflection and thus into some sort of version of the same. A dream is a presentation, in whatever form, of the world of an "I." The self of the dreamer is immediately present in everything appearing in dreams and is, in a strict sense, always at the origin of everything that is dreamed – whether in the mode of wish fulfillment or of phantasms of horror. Dreams can be filled with contents in any emotional register. In all cases, self-reflection and mirror imaging dominate this type of experience, which in one way or another doubles the self back upon itself in mirror-like representations – no matter how alien and fraught with alterity these forms of manifestation may appear to be.

These observations enable us to discern some remarkable ways in which Dante's literary construction of prophetic revelation, beginning with the *Vita nuova*, is comparable to "dream work" as this concept was forged and given currency by Freud.[14] Dreaming is governed by a logic that can freely shape things according to desire, but also according to vision, insight, hope, and even love. This desire is not arbitrary. Such desire is in search of an alternative coherence and meaning – alternative to the apparently "real" world, with its harsh, unbendable, ineluctable laws. The dream, in contrast, employs a fluid and holistic logic. This logic does not simply shape things arbitrarily. It adheres to conditions of another type that require striving after the ideal, or longing after something emotionally compelling or even, sometimes, seeking after what is felt to be absolutely loving or capable of fostering the strongest possible attachment to others. While remaining an isolated operation of the self, dreaming unfolds also with the exigency of an opening to the Other – or to a world of mystery beyond the ken and conscious control of the dreamer.

Nevertheless, this orientation to an Other, or at least to a weird strangeness, does not preclude, but rather accentuates, the innerness of knowledge in dream and in revelation. The outer world that is set against this inner

[14] Sigmund Freud, *Die Traumdeutung* (1899), trans. as *The Interpretation of Dreams*.

world fades to untruth or to merely external contingency within the logic of the dream. Things in dream and revelation have a higher grade of necessity, an inner necessity, in their *raison d'être*. Yet this inwardness opens itself into an abyss of infinite alterity with respect to the familiar world and its laws and norms. In dreaming, if one explores it radically, despite the greatest felt intimacy, everything is apt nevertheless to show itself in the alienating guise of the strangely other or even the surreal. These contradictory propensities are often seen to be simultaneously at work, and this produces the peculiar sense of heightened reality *and* unreality so typical of many dreams.

Dreaming discloses exemplarily how "merely" subjective and inward experience can metamorphose into revelation of a higher reality.[15] This can be made evident simply by our asking, Who dreams? When we dream, we come into contact with a higher or deeper or more universal "I." The dream's own thinking is not mastered by an "I." Instead, the "I" is revealed to itself by the "thinking" that takes place in the dream. Emblematic for this mysterious alterity of the dreaming subject to itself is Arthur Rimbaud's exclamation: "*I is an other*" ("*Je est un autre*").[16] Just as implicated in an ambience of dreams, and potentially of hallucinations and madness, Gérard de Nerval (who completely identified with Dante) declared "Je suis l'autre" ("I am the other"), which holds almost necessarily for the suspended consciousness and identity of the dreaming "I."[17] We are ourselves what we dream. What we dream is what we ourselves are as projected by fantasy in desire or in apprehension.

On the basis of its holistic, all-comprehending, amorphous logic, the dream can even lay claim to being the foundation of all our experience and of all our discourses. It has this status, for example, in Australian aboriginal and in Native American cultures, especially the Anishinaabe, Sioux, Cheyenne, and Blackfoot, for whom the dream was an essential part of the individual's "vision quest." This personal revelation, at the same time, linked individuals with their peoples and with the great All. The dream conveys a wholeness of sense or meaning, in which all articulations are already contained in anticipation. In the dream, nothing excludes its opposite. We see in surrealist paintings, for instance, those of Marcel Duchamp and Giorgio Di Chirico, how absurd and shocking dreams can be. However, in their madness, dreams may well be truer than the

---

[15] Dino S. Cervigni , *Dante's Poetry of Dreams* (Florence: Olschki, 1986), p. 195.
[16] In a letter to Paul Demeny, May 15, 1871.
[17] Nerval wrote this phrase underneath a photographic portrait of himself.

everyday world that we usually take for reality because they are based on the hanging together of all things and on their being astonishingly folded or woven into one another beyond our ability to understand and rationally account for how or why. Only the dream can be true to this all-encompassing wholeness, with all its inherent contradictions and absurd-ities, in which everything possible may become simultaneously actual.[18]

In the dream, contradictions are suspended. According to Leibniz's *Théodicée* (1710), possible worlds are defined as being free of contradiction. Precisely the exclusion of contradiction for Leibniz is what distinguishes reality (even if only *possible* reality) from dream. In dream, by contrast, the principle of non-contradiction, like that of the excluded middle, no longer applies. But perhaps such so-called logical "laws" are only our own human abstractions and narrowings – delimitations that set restrictions on the full range of possibilities harboring within the real, or at least within what we can experience as real. In this case, reality might well be revealed better by the dream than by waking consciousness.

In dreaming, boundaries are suspended and supposedly fixed or factual reality is set in flux. Yet the dream remains, nevertheless, within the parameters of an experiential reality – the experience of an "I." This is the reality of the always endlessly malleable, further shapeable, molten material of the real, but it is given a direction and coherence by the desire – or alternatively by the nightmarish fear – of an "I." Dreaming can grasp this *intimate* aspect, this subjective side of the real – or else can fail to "grasp" it but rather simply follow it out and adhere to and convey it. Such a paradoxically intimate transcendence is key to the general phenomen-ology of the dream that I theorize here in such a way as to make it communicate with religious revelation. In the present context, I hasten to underscore, furthermore, the specifically and properly hermeneutic premises of such revelatory dreaming.

Dream Hermeneutics

In conjunction with the overall interpretation of the *Vita nuova* proposed here, I emphasize that dreaming is essentially a form of interpretation. This interpretive essence of the dreams that we have when asleep at night

---

[18] Purveying kindred insight drawn from some other sources, Elliot R. Wolfson, in *A Dream Interpreted within A Dream: Oneiropoiesis and the Prism of Imagination* (New York: Zone Books, 2011), treats dreams as positing "the identity of opposites" – dream and reality – on the basis of biblical, rabbinic, and Kabbalistic traditions, as well as of psychoanalytic, phenomenological, and neuroscientific frameworks.

becomes only more explicit in the consciously constructed narratives and lyrical compositions of poetry that elaborate and extend into daytime consciousness the mysteriously imaginative modes and darkly felt emotions of dreaming. Along these lines, my thesis about the *Vita nuova* as a dream-text expands into a hermeneutic thesis about dreaming in general.

Dreaming manifests a structure of meaning. Perhaps it structures our world according to wishes and unconscious desires, as Freud maintained. But not necessarily and, in any case, not only. Crucial is that the dream reaches beyond our consciousness and its control. Dreaming is a form of interpreting that reveals something transcending all that we can logically account for and consciously produce. Whence dreams come is not fully explicable. Dreaming declares itself with an immediate authority that cannot be grounded on something else or be seized from behind – as if it could be explained by a perfectly plain-text reality that could be accessed independently of it. A dream has its own kind of manifest evidence, even in all its enigmatic ungraspability. Everything in dreams is intimate and self-reflective, but it also all originates in and is steered from somewhere mysteriously beyond the control of the conscious mind.

As a phenomenal reality referring to a "beyond" and an Other, the dream discloses a higher level of the real than is perceptible on the basis of mere empiricism. The dream effects a kind of transcendental (un)grounding of reality: it opens a perspective that parallels and invites endless interpretation by modes of symbolic representation such as literature and art. Dream meaning remains inexhaustible equally for conceptual investigation such as psychoanalysis or philosophical speculation and even for empirical study through comparative religions and cultural criticism. The existential dimension of meaning in the dream opens to the unending and eternal. The dream does not abide within any determinable limits. Time does not restrict or contain the meaning of an incarnate (embodied, encultured, historical) existence as it is refracted in the dream. Instead, time becomes a revelation of its own other – of Eternity, we might say.

Dream time is peculiarly unbound from worldly time and can actualize the past and the future simultaneously within the present. This opening to eternity and revelation can take place in and through the dream and through the hermeneutic process that is illuminated by dream consciousness. Dreaming allows what is "repeated" in existential enactment to make the phenomenon that is interpreted into an absolute reality: it is not just a representation or conception *of* something else. It is a real presence in an actually lived moment. This hermeneutic praxis enables discovering the real in its absoluteness and in its transcendence of our webs of conceptualization, including the objective, purely pragmatic, workaday world that results from a scientific worldview and especially from its degeneration into a technical, managerial apparatus of universal rationalization and control.

At stake in hermeneutics is our access to the real, and most fundamentally to the very nature and constitution of reality itself, at least to the extent that we can know and experience it. Reality, viewed hermeneutically, is understood as relational and participatory. It is, then, also infinitely open and inexhaustible. It is impossible for this all-comprehending real to be encompassed and articulated in its entirety: everything within it is always related to other things. Dreaming, in fact, needs a language of unsayability, one that remains open to an Other but that is dependent on, or at least co-determined by, a self. Dante invents just such a symbolic language in the *Vita nuova*.

The existential grounding of Dante's poetry is, in many ways, the fundamental issue of the *Vita nuova*, as is brought out in the final chapter (6) of the foregoing critical interpretation: existence itself can disclose the poetry's unconscious meaning as more than what is expressly said and intended. This anchoring in real life (whatever that is) affords an access to understanding that reaches behind all our own conscious awareness. The prose that surrounds the poetry contextualizes it within life experience. Existence, and particularly Dante's own existential situation, provides the hermeneutic key to the meaning of the dream in *Vita nuova*, Chapter III. Of course, the inverse holds true as well: the dream also proves to be key to the interpretation of Dante's existence.

Like a number of other readers such as Gregory Stone, Robert Harrison finds that Dante's inaugural dream in the *Vita nuova* is not at all explained but is left, instead, completely enigmatic by the prose text that claims to make it clear to all. Yet the meaning is left open and infinite only because it is integrated into Dante's existence itself – just as the god of love is incorporated into Dante's own being or person (IX. 7 and 12). Something approximately equivalent, or at least parallel, occurs, as we saw above, when the god is incorporated into Beatrice in turn, with the consequence that she can be called simply "Love" ("Amore," XXIV. 5). This existential meaning of love cannot be defined in words because it is infinite and inexhaustible: the words that are actually used open metaphorically into endless transformations of meaning. Through existential hermeneutics, we discover reality anew in its wholeness – as a revelation of a higher, truer, more unified whole than what we ordinarily are able to think and perceive.

As such, hermeneutics is not just an instrument or a method. The activity of interpretation enfolds, and is enfolded into, a reality that is more integrated and unified than ordinary empirical reality. Hermeneutics, as a practice not only of textual interpretation but also of existential engagement, mediates reality to us as revelation and as an interconnected Whole in which everything bears potentially on everything else. It is worth trying to recover this visionary outlook on reality, even from within, if not beyond, the modern worldview and its objectivizing epistemologies. Dreams can have a higher degree of truth than the ordinary empirical reality that presents us simply with one thing after another because the dream reveals more openly and directly the deeper desires and shaping drives that infiltrate our actual experience of the real. The dream makes apparently separate things coalesce together and exposes the otherwise unapparent connectedness of them all. All become part of a unified meaning that the dream conveys.

Literary interpretation, or criticism in the tradition of philosophical hermeneutics, can itself become a form of revelation that opens reality per se rather than only discerning the relevant codes for deciphering a specific literary genre or work. The historical and prehistorical paradigms of hermeneutics actually participate in and transform the real as a whole rather than just schematizing or mirroring it. This is clearly the case for hermeneutic interpretation in its primordial avatars, which prevailed before the more scientific, positivistic development of the techniques of textual interpretation, with their codification and canonization, for example, in Scholasticism, with its fourfold method of Scriptural exegesis.[19] The primordial forms of interpretation employed, paradigmatically, in hunting or seafaring, as well as in oracle reading and mantic divination, embody the truth and full potential of the hermeneutical art embryonically and yet still in its wholeness.[20] They illuminate what constitutes criticism, in its original and deeper nature before it narrows its own self-awareness and reduces to an often merely analytic exercise based on schematic classification.

The New Testament, with its apparently realistic narrative entailing even a certain pretense to historicity, would seem prima facie to be situated at the antipodes with respect to a dream narrative. But, more exactly considered, the revelation of existence through the filter of subjective

---

[19] Henri de Lubac, *L'éxégèse médiévale: Les quatre sens de l'écriture* (Paris: Aubier, 1959), trans. E. M. Macierowski as *Medieval Exegesis*, 4 vols. (Grand Rapids, MI: Erdmans, 1998).

[20] Among the many outstanding works of research disclosing this potential, I have learned especially from Wolfram Hogrebe, *Metaphysik und Mantik. Die Deutungsnatur des Menschen*, 2nd rev. ed. (Berlin: Akademie Verlag, 2013) and Carlo Ginzburg, "Spie: Radici di un paradigma indiziario," in *Miti, emblemi, spie: Morfologia e storia* (Turin: Einaudi, 1986), trans. John and Anne C. Tedeschi as "Clues: Roots of an Evidential Paradigm," in *Clues, Myths, and the Historical Method* (Baltimore: The Johns Hopkins University Press, 1989), pp. 96–125.

experience is common to both the Gospel narrative and to dream texts. Dante's *Vita nuova* helps us to see this more clearly by the way it combines these apparently incommensurable modes of dreaming and personal history or witness. Both prove to be bound up with the revelation of an intimately personal type of truth.

The juxtaposition of Dante's *Vita nuova* with the New Testament in this literary-critical reflection and philosophico-religious meditation has brought into a more intelligible light the supra-historical (or infra-historical) dimension of both works. The role of the dream in the *Vita nuova* shows itself to be highly instructive for elucidating the preternatural type of knowing realized in religious revelation. Although often uncanny, this type of knowing is no stranger to humanities texts. To the extent that such poetic texts, by their very nature, engage the endlessly open mystery of being human, they too harbor and model the unpredictable and inexplicable type of revelation that is characteristic of dreams. The revelatory power of the dream has served here for adumbrating the far-reaching potency of poetically inspired knowledge to afford a kind of religious revelation. This book of speculative criticism has shown this potential to be realized in the mutual light shed by the marvelously – not to say, miraculously – revelatory texts of the *Vita nuova* and the New Testament in their scintillating reciprocal illumination.

Italian Text and English Translation of the Vita nuova

Contents of *The New Life*

La Vita nuova	*The New Life*

Chapter I: Incipit *of Book of Memory*

(1) In quella parte del libro de la mia memoria dinanzi a la quale poco si potrebbe leggere, si trova una rubrica la quale dice: *Incipit vita nova*. Sotto la quale rubrica io trovo scritte le parole le quali è mio intendimento d'assemplare	(1) In that part of the book of my memory before which little could be read, a rubric is found which says: "*Incipit vita nova* Here begins the new life." Under that rubric, I find written the words which it is my intention to copy into this little book; and

Chapter I: (*cont.*)

| in questo libello; e se non tutte, almeno la loro sentenzia. | if not all of them, at least their essential purport. |

Chapter II: *Dante's First Meeting with Beatrice*

(1) Nove fiate già appresso lo mio nascimento era tornato lo cielo de la luce quasi a uno medesimo punto, quanto a la sua propria girazione, quando a li miei occhi apparve prima la gloriosa donna de la mia mente, la quale fu chiamata da molti Beatrice li quali non sapeano che si chiamare.	(1) Nine times already since my birth, the heaven of light had returned to almost the same point in its own proper gyration, when there appeared to my eyes the glorious lady of my mind, who was called Beatrice by many who did not know by what name she was called.
(2) Ella era in questa vita già stata tanto, che ne lo suo tempo lo cielo stellato era mosso verso la parte d'oriente de le dodici parti l'una d'un grado, sì che quasi dal principio del suo anno nono apparve a me, ed io la vidi quasi da la fine del mio nono.	(2) She had already been in this life so long that the starred heaven had moved toward the East by the twelfth of a degree, so that she appeared to me almost at the beginning of her ninth year, and I saw her almost at the end of my ninth year.
(3) Apparve vestita di nobilissimo colore, umile e onesto, sanguigno, cinta e ornata a la guisa che a la sua giovanissima etade si convenia.	(3) She appeared to me dressed in the most noble color of crimson, humble and modest, girded and adorned in the style that most suited her very young age.
(4) In quello punto dico veracemente che lo spirito de la vita, lo quale dimora ne la secretissima camera de lo cuore, cominciò a tremare sì fortemente, che apparia ne li menimi polsi orribilmente; e tremando disse queste parole: «Ecce deus fortior me, qui veniens dominabitur michi».	(4) At that point I say truly that the vital spirit that dwells in the most secret chamber of the heart began to tremble so violently that I felt it terribly, even in the most minimal pulsations; and, trembling, it uttered these words: "*Ecce deus fortior me, qui veniens dominabitur michi*: Behold a god stronger than I, who in coming will dominate me."
(5) In quello punto lo spirito animale, lo quale dimora ne l'alta camera ne la quale tutti li spiriti sensitivi portano le loro percezioni, si cominciò a maravigliare molto, e parlando spezialmente a li spiriti del viso, sì disse queste parole: «Apparuit iam beatitudo vestra».	(5) At that point the animal spirit, which dwells in the high chamber to which all the spirits of the senses bear their perceptions, began to marvel greatly, and speaking particularly to the spirits of sight, said these words: "*Apparuit iam beatitudo vestra*: Now your blessedness has appeared."
(6) In quello punto lo spirito naturale, lo quale dimora in quella parte ove si ministra	(6) At that point the natural spirit, which dwells in that part where our

Chapter II: (*cont.*)

lo nutrimento nostro, cominciò a piangere, e piangendo disse queste parole: «Heu miser, quia frequenter impeditus ero deinceps!».

(7) D'allora innanzi dico che Amore segnoreggiò la mia anima, la quale fu sì tosto a lui disponsata, e cominciò a prendere sopra me tanta sicurtade e tanta signoria per la vertù che li dava la mia imaginazione, che me convenia fare tutti li suoi piaceri compiutamente.

(8) Elli mi comandava molte volte che io cercasse per vedere questa angiola giovanissima; onde io ne la mia puerizia molte volte l'andai cercando, e vedeala di sì nobili e laudabili portamenti, che certo di lei si potea dire quella parola del poeta Omero: «Ella non parea figliuola d'uomo mortale, ma di deo».

(9) E avvegna che la sua imagine, la quale continuatamente meco stava, fosse baldanza d'Amore a segnoreggiare me, tuttavia era di sì nobilissima vertù, che nulla volta sofferse che Amore mi reggesse sanza lo fedele consiglio de la ragione in quelle cose là ove cotale consiglio fosse utile a udire.

(10) E però che soprastare a le passioni e atti di tanta gioventudine para alcuno parlare fabuloso, mi partirò da esse; e trapassando molte cose le quali si potrebbero trarre de l'essemplo onde nascono queste, verrò a quelle parole le quali sono scritte ne la mia memoria sotto maggiori paragrafi.

nourishment is digested, began to weep and, weeping, said these words: "*Heu miser, quia frequenter impeditus ero deinceps!*: O misery, how frequently I will be impeded from now on!"

(7) From that time forward, I say, Love governed my soul, which was at once wedded to him, and he began to reign over me with such assurance and lordship, due to the power given him by my imagination, that I could not but do all his pleasure to the full.

(8) Often he commanded me to go and try to see this most youthful angel, so that in my boyhood I went looking for her many times, and I saw in her such a noble and praiseworthy bearing that certainly one could say of her the words by the poet Homer: "She seemed to be the daughter not of mortal man, but of god."

(9) And although her image, which was continually with me, was an audacity used by Love to lord it over me, nevertheless it was of such superlatively noble virtue in its power, that it never suffered Love to reign over me without the faithful counsel of reason in those things in which such counsel is usefully heeded.

(10) However, since to dwell on passions and actions of such youthful years might seem to some vain fantasizing, I will leave this, and passing over many things that might be drawn from the sample from which these were taken, I will come to those words that are written in my memory under larger paragraphs.

Chapter III: *Greeting and Dream*

(1) Poi che furono passati tanti die, che appunto erano compiuti li nove anni appresso l'apparimento soprascritto di

(1) When so many days had passed that exactly nine years were completed since the appearance described above of this most

Chapter III: (*cont.*)

questa gentilissima, ne l'ultimo di questi die avvenne che questa mirabile donna apparve a me vestita di colore bianchissimo, in mezzo a due gentili donne, le quali erano di più lunga etade; e passando per una via, volse li occhi verso quella parte ov'io era molto pauroso, e per la sua ineffabile cortesia, la quale è oggi meritata nel grande secolo, mi salutoe molto virtuosamente, tanto che me parve allora vedere tutti li termini de la beatitudine.

(2) L'ora che lo suo dolcissimo salutare mi giunse, era fermamente nona di quello giorno; e però che quella fu la prima volta che le sue parole si mossero per venire a li miei orecchi, presi tanta dolcezza, che come inebriato mi partio da le genti, e ricorsi a lo solingo luogo d'una mia camera, e puosimi a pensare di questa cortesissima.

(3) E pensando di lei, mi sopragiunse uno soave sonno, ne lo quale m'apparve una maravigliosa visione: che me parea vedere ne la mia camera una nebula di colore di fuoco, dentro a la quale io discernea una figura d'uno segnore di pauroso aspetto a chi la guardasse; e pareami con tanta letizia, quanto a sé, che mirabile cosa era; e ne le sue parole dicea molte cose, le quali io non intendea se non poche; tra le quali intendea queste: «Ego dominus tuus».

(4) Ne le sue braccia mi parea vedere una persona dormire nuda, salvo che involta mi parea in uno drappo sanguigno leggermente; la quale io riguardando molto intentivamente, conobbi ch'era la donna de la salute, la quale m'avea lo giorno dinanzi degnato di salutare.

(5) E ne l'una de le mani mi parea che questi tenesse una cosa la quale ardesse tutta, e pareami che mi dicesse queste parole: «Vide cor tuum».

gentle one, on the last of these days it happened that this marvelous lady appeared to me dressed in whitest white between two gentle ladies who were of greater age than she; and passing through a street she turned her eyes toward where I was abiding in great fear, and in her ineffable courtesy, which today is rewarded in the life everlasting, she greeted me so virtuously that I seemed then to see the furthest limits of beatitude.

(2) The hour at which this sweetest greeting reached me was firmly the ninth of that day; and since that was the first time that her words had stirred in order to come to my ears, I was so smitten by sweetness that like one inebriated I parted from all company and repaired to the solitary site of a chamber of mine and set myself to thinking about this most courteous one.

(3) And thinking of her, I was overcome by a sweet sleep, in which a marvelous vision appeared to me: I seemed to see in my chamber a cloud the color of fire, within which I discerned a figure of a lord of frightful aspect to whoever looked at him; and he appeared to me to be so joyful in himself that it was a wonder; and with his words he said many things, of which I could understand only a few; among them I understood these: "*Ego dominus tuus*: I am your lord."

(4) And in his arms I seemed to see a sleeping person, naked except for being wrapped lightly in a crimson cloth; looking intently, I recognized that it was the lady of the greeting, she who had deigned to greet me earlier that day.

(5) And in one of his hands it seemed to me that he held a thing that was all aflame, and it seemed to me that he said these words: "*Vide cor tuum*: Behold your heart."

Chapter III: (*cont.*)

(6) E quando elli era stato alquanto, pareami che disvegliasse questa che dormia; e tanto si sforzava per suo ingegno, che le facea mangiare questa cosa che in mano li ardea, la quale ella mangiava dubitosamente.

(6) And after a little while, it seemed to me that he awakened her who slept; and he so insisted with his ingenuity that he had her eat the thing that was burning in his hand, which she ate hesitatingly.

(7) Appresso ciò poco dimorava che la sua letizia si convertia in amarissimo pianto; e così piangendo, si ricogliea questa donna ne le sue braccia, e con essa mi parea che si ne gisse verso lo cielo; onde io sostenea sì grande angoscia, che lo mio deboletto sonno non poteo sostenere, anzi si ruppe e fui disvegliato.

(7) A short while after this, his joy turned into most bitter weeping; and weeping thus, he gathered this lady into his arms, and with her he seemed to me to go toward heaven; at this point, I sustained such great anguish that my feeble sleep could not bear it but broke, and I woke up.

(8) E mantenente cominciai a pensare, e trovai che l'ora ne la quale m'era questa visione apparita, era la quarta de la notte stata; sì che appare manifestamente ch'ella fue la prima ora de le nove ultime ore de la notte.

(8) And immediately I began to reflect, and I found that the hour in which this vision had appeared to me had been the fourth of the night; so that it appeared manifest that it was the first hour of the last nine hours of the night.

(9) Pensando io a ciò che m'era apparuto, propuosi di farlo sentire a molti li quali erano famosi trovatori in quello tempo: e con ciò fosse cosa che io avesse già veduto per me medesimo l'arte del dire parole per rima, propuosi di fare uno sonetto, ne lo quale io salutasse tutti li fedeli d'Amore; e pregandoli che giudicassero la mia visione, scrissi a loro ciò che io avea nel mio sonno veduto. E cominciai allora questo sonetto, lo quale comincia: *A ciascun'alma presa.*

(9) Thinking on that which had appeared to me, I proposed to make it known to many who were famous troubadours at that time: and since I had already acquired on my own the art of speaking words in rhyme, I proposed to make a sonnet in which I greeted all the faithful subjects of Love; and bidding them to interpret my vision, I wrote to them what I had seen in my sleep. I then began this sonnet, which begins: "*A ciascun'alma presa*: To every captive soul."

(10)
A ciascun'alma presa e gentil core
nel cui cospetto ven lo dir presente,
in ciò che mi rescrivan suo parvente,
salute in lor segnor, cioè Amore.

(10)
To every captive soul and gentle heart
into whose view the present speech comes,
that they may write back with their opinion,
greetings in their lord, who is Love.

(11)
Già eran quasi che atterzate l'ore
del tempo che onne stella n'è lucente,
quando m'apparve Amor subitamente,
cui essenza membrar mi dà orrore.

(11)
Already nearly three hours had passed
of the time that every star is shining,
when Love suddenly appeared to me,
the memory of whose essence horrifies me.

Chapter III: (*cont.*)

(12)
Allegro mi sembrava Amor tenendo
meo core in mano, e ne le braccia avea
madonna involta in un drappo dormendo.
Poi la svegliava, e d'esto core ardendo
lei paventosa umilmente pascea:
appresso gir lo ne vedea piangendo.

(13) Questo sonetto si divide in due
parti; che ne la prima parte saluto e
domando risponsione, ne la seconda
significo a che si dee rispondere. La
seconda parte comincia quivi: *Già eran.*

(14) A questo sonetto fue risposto da
molti e di diverse sentenzie; tra li quali
fue risponditore quelli cui io chiamo
primo de li miei amici, e disse allora uno
sonetto, lo quale comincia: *Vedeste, al
mio parere, onne valore.* E questo fue
quasi lo principio de l'amistà tra lui e
me, quando elli seppe che io era quelli
che li avea ciò mandato.

(15) Lo verace giudicio del detto sogno
non fue veduto allora per alcuno, ma ora
è manifestissimo a li più semplici.

(12)
Joyfully Love seemed to me to hold
my heart in hand, and in his arms he held
my lady wrapped in a cloth sleeping.
Then he woke her, and this burning heart
he humbly fed her in her fear: After
that, I saw him go away weeping.

(13) This sonnet is divided into two parts: in
the first, I greet and ask for a response; in the
second, I signify that to which a response is
asked. The second part begins here: "*Già
eran*: Already nearly."

(14) To this sonnet many replied and with
diverse interpretations; among the
respondents was he whom I call the foremost
of my friends, who at the time wrote a sonnet
which begins: "*Vedeste, al mio parere, onne
valore*: You saw, in my opinion, all worth."
And this was the beginning of the friendship
between him and me, once he knew that
I was the one who had sent him
the poem.

(15) The true meaning of said dream was not
seen by any one at the time, but now it is fully
manifest even to the most simple.

Chapter IV: *Dante Sick and Secretive in Love*

(1) Da questa visione innanzi cominciò lo
mio spirito naturale ad essere impedito ne
la sua operazione, però che l'anima era tutta
data nel pensare di questa gentilissima;
onde io divenni in picciolo tempo poi di sì
fraile e debole condizione, che a molti
amici pesava de la mia vista; e molti pieni
d'invidia già si procacciavano di sapere di
me quello che io volea del tutto celare ad
altrui.

(1) From the time of this vision, my
natural spirit began to be impeded in its
operation because my soul was completely
given to the thought of that most gentle
one; as a result, I became in a short time so
weak and frail that the sight of me
worried many friends; and many people
full of envy undertook to learn from me
that which I wanted to conceal from
others.

Chapter IV: (*cont.*)

(2) Ed io, accorgendomi del malvagio domandare che mi faceano, per la volontade d'Amore, lo quale mi comandava secondo lo consiglio de la ragione, rispondea loro che Amore era quelli che così m'avea governato. Dicea d'Amore, però che io portava nel viso tante de le sue insegne, che questo non si potea ricovrire.

(3) E quando mi domandavano «Per cui t'ha così distrutto questo Amore?», ed io sorridendo li guardava, e nulla dicea loro.

(2) And realizing the maliciousness of the prying with which they pressed me, through the will of Love, who commanded me according to the counsel of reason, I answered them that Love was he who so governed me. I said "Love" because I bore so many of his signs on my face that it could not be covered over.

(3) And when they asked me "For whom has Love so destroyed you," I looked at them smiling and told them nothing.

Chapter V: *A Screen Lady*

(1) Uno giorno avvenne che questa gentilissima sedea in parte ove s'udiano parole de la regina de la gloria, ed io era in luogo dal quale vedea la mia beatitudine; e nel mezzo di lei e di me per la retta linea sedea una gentile donna di molto piacevole aspetto, la quale mi mirava spesse volte, maravigliandosi del mio sguardare, che parea che sopra lei terminasse.

(2) Onde molti s'accorsero de lo suo mirare; e in tanto vi fue posto mente, che, partendomi da questo luogo, mi sentio dicere appresso di me: «Vedi come cotale donna distrugge la persona di costui»; e nominandola, io intesi che dicea di colei che mezzo era stata ne la linea retta che movea da la gentilissima Beatrice e terminava ne li occhi miei.

(3) Allora mi confortai molto, assicurandomi che lo mio secreto non era comunicato lo giorno altrui per mia vista. E mantenente pensai di fare di questa gentile donna schermo de la veritate; e tanto ne mostrai in poco tempo, che lo mio secreto fue creduto sapere da le più persone che di me ragionavano.

(1) It happened one day that this most gentle lady sat in a place where words about the queen of glory were being heard, and I was in a place where I could see my beatitude; and in between her and me along a straight line sat a gentle lady of very pleasing aspect, who often looked at me, marveling that my gazing seemed to come to rest on her.

(2) Whence many people became aware of her looking; and attention was paid to it, so that in leaving that place I heard them talking behind me: "See how that lady destroys the person of that man," naming her; and I understood that they said this of her who had been in the middle along the line that proceeded from the most gentle Beatrice and terminated in my eyes.

(3) Then I was much comforted, reassured that my secret had not been divulged that day to others because of my gaze. And I immediately thought of making this gentle lady into a screen for the truth; and I made a show of it, so much so that in little time my secret was believed to be known by most of the people who had been speaking about me.

Chapter V: (*cont.*)

(4) Con questa donna mi celai alquanti anni e mesi; e per più fare credente altrui, feci per lei certe cosette per rima, le quali non è mio intendimento di scrivere qui, se non in quanto facesse a trattare di quella gentilissima Beatrice; e però le lascerò tutte, salvo che alcuna cosa ne scriverò che pare che sia loda di lei.

(4) I hid myself through this lady for some years and months; and to reinforce the belief of others, I made certain trifles for her in rhyme, which it is not my intention to write down here, unless it should serve to treat of that most gentle Beatrice; and thus I leave them all aside, except for something I will write that is evidently in praise of her.

Chapter VI: *A Serventese for Sixty Ladies, Beatrice the Ninth*

(1) Dico che in questo tempo che questa donna era schermo di tanto amore, quanto da la mia parte, sì mi venne una volontade di volere ricordare lo nome di quella gentilissima ed accompagnarlo di molti nomi di donne, e spezialmente del nome di questa gentile donna.

(1) I say that in the time that this lady was the screen for such great love on my part, a will rose up in me to record the name of my most gentle lady and accompany it by many names of women, especially with that of this gentle lady.

(2) E presi li nomi di sessanta le più belle donne de la cittade ove la mia donna fue posta da l'altissimo sire, e compuosi una pistola sotto forma di serventese, la quale io non scriverò: e non n'avrei fatto menzione, se non per dire quello che, componendola, maravigliosamente addivenne, cioè che in alcuno altro numero non sofferse lo nome de la mia donna stare se non in su lo nove, tra li nomi di queste donne.

(2) And I took the names of sixty of the most beautiful ladies of the city where my lady had been placed by the highest lord, and I composed an epistle in the form of a *serventese*, which I will not write here: I would not have mentioned it except to say that, in composing it, miraculously it came about that the name of my lady suffered to stay in no other position except the ninth among the names of these ladies.

Chapter VII: *The Screen Lady Departs Outside Florence*

(1) La donna co la quale io avea tanto tempo celata la mia volontade, convenne che si partisse de la sopradetta cittade e andasse in paese molto lontano; per che io, quasi sbigottito de la bella difesa che m'era

(1) The lady through whom I had for so long hidden my will found it necessary to leave the above-mentioned city and go to a very distant place; and I, upset by the loss of my beautiful defense was

venuta meno, assai me ne disconfortai,
più che io medesimo non avrei creduto
dinanzi.

(2) E pensando che se de la sua partita io
non parlasse alquanto dolorosamente, le
persone sarebbero accorte più tosto de lo
mio nascondere, proposi di farne
alcuna lamentanza in uno sonetto; lo
quale io scriverò, acciò che la mia donna
fue immediata cagione di certe parole
che ne lo sonetto sono, sì come appare a
chi lo intende. E allora dissi questo
sonetto, che comincia: *O voi che per
la via*.

(3)
O voi che per la via d'Amor passate,
attendete e guardate
s'elli è dolore alcun, quanto 'l mio, grave;
e prego sol ch'audir mi sofferiate,
e poi imaginate
s'io son d'ogni tormento ostale e chiave.

(4)
Amor, non già per mia poca bontate,
ma per sua nobiltate,
mi pose in vita sì dolce e soave,
ch'io mi sentia dir dietro spesse fiate:
«Deo, per qual dignitate
così leggiadro questi lo core have?»

(5)
Or ho perduta tutta mia baldanza,
che si movea d'amoroso tesoro;
ond'io pover dimoro,
in guisa che di dir mi ven dottanza.

(6)
Sì che volendo far come coloro
che per vergogna celan lor mancanza,
di fuor mostro allegranza,
e dentro da lo core struggo e ploro.

(7) Questo sonetto ha due parti
principali; che ne la prima intendo
chiamare li fedeli d'Amore per quelle
parole di Geremia profeta che dicono:
«O vos omnes qui transitis per viam,
attendite et videte si est dolor sicut

considerably put out, more than I myself
would have believed previously.

(2) And thinking that unless I spoke
dolorously of her departure, people
would become aware of my subterfuge, I
resolved to make lamentation in a
sonnet, which I will write here, since my
lady was the immediate cause of certain
words in the sonnet, as is apparent to
whoever understands it. And then I
composed this sonnet, which begins: "*O
voi che per la via*: O you who pass along
the way."

(3)
O you who pass along the way of Love,
stop and look to see
if any sorrow is as heavy as mine;
and I beseech you only to suffer to hear,
and then to imagine,
whether I am hostel and key of every
        torment.

(4)
Love, surely not for my little worth
but for its nobility,
placed me in a life so sweet and suave,
that I heard it said behind me often:
"God, for what merit
does this man have so light a heart?"

(5)
Now I have lost all my audacity,
which flowed from an amorous treasure;
therefore I remain in poverty,
in such manner as I shrink from saying.

(6)
So that willing to do as those
who hide their insufficiency out of shame,
I show cheerfulness on the outside
and inside my heart I am wasted and weep.

(7) This sonnet has two principal parts;
in the first, I intend to call Love's faithful
ones by the words of Jeremiah the
prophet, which say: "*O vos omnes qui
transitis per viam, attendite et videte si est
dolor sicut dolor meus*: O all you who pass

Chapter VII: (*cont.*)

dolor meus», e pregare che mi sofferino d'audire; ne la seconda narro là ove Amore m'avea posto, con altro intendimento che l'estreme parti del sonetto non mostrano, e dico che io hoe ciò perduto. La seconda parte comincia quivi: *Amor, non già.*

along the way, listen and see if there is any sorrow like unto my sorrow," and I beseech them to suffer to hear me; in the second, I tell where Love had placed me, with another intent, which the last parts of the sonnet do not show, and I say that I have lost that. The second part begins here: "*Amor, non già*: Love, surely not."

Chapter VIII: *Poem on the Death of Beatrice's Companion*

(1) Appresso lo partire di questa gentile donna fue piacere del segnore de li angeli di chiamare a la sua gloria una donna giovane e di gentile aspetto molto, la quale fue assai graziosa in questa sopradetta cittade; lo cui corpo io vidi giacere sanza l'anima in mezzo di molte donne, le quali piangeano assai pietosamente.

(1) After the departure of that gentle lady, it pleased the lord of the angels to call to her glory a young lady of very gentle aspect, who was a considerable grace to the above-mentioned city; whose body I saw lying lifeless in the midst of many ladies, who were weeping most piteously.

(2) Allora, ricordandomi che già l'avea veduta fare compagnia a quella gentilissima, non poteo sostenere alquante lagrime; anzi piangendo mi propuosi di dicere alquante parole de la sua morte, in guiderdone di ciò che alcuna fiata l'avea veduta con la mia donna.

(2) Then, remembering that I had seen her in the company of that most gentle lady, I could not hold back some tears; weeping, I resolved to say some words about her death as a recompense for my having seen her sometimes with my lady.

(3) E di ciò toccai alcuna cosa ne l'ultima parte de le parole che io ne dissi, sì come appare manifestamente a chi lo intende. E dissi allora questi due sonetti, li quali comincia lo primo: *Piangete, amanti*, e lo secondo: *Morte villana.*

(3) And I touched on something of this in the last part of the words I wrote on it, as appears evident to whoever understands it. And then I composed two sonnets, which begin first: "*Piangete, amanti*: Weep, you lovers," and second: "*Morte villana*: Villainous Death."

(4)
Piangete, amanti, poi che piange Amore,
udendo qual cagion lui fa plorare.

(4)
Weep, you lovers, since Love weeps,
hearing what causes him to pour down
    tears.

(5)
Amor sente a Pietà donne chiamare,
mostrando amaro duol per li occhi fore,
perché villana Morte in gentil core

(5)
Love hears ladies calling on Pity,
showing forth bitter sorrow from
    their eyes,

ha miso il suo crudele adoperare,
guastando ciò che al mondo è da laudare
in gentil donna sovra de l'onore.

because villainous Death in a gentle heart
has performed his cruel operation,
ruining all which in the world is worth praise
in a gentle lady except for her honor.

(6)
Audite quanto Amor le fece orranza,
ch'io 'l vidi lamentare in forma vera
sovra la morta imagine avvenente;
e riguardava ver lo ciel sovente,
ove l'alma gentil già locata era,
che donna fu di sì gaia sembianza.

(6)
Hear how Love paid her honor,
whom I saw lament in his true form
over the comely lifeless image;
and he looked often to heaven,
where the gentle soul was already placed,
who had been a lady of such grace.

(7) Questo primo sonetto si divide in tre
parti: ne la prima chiamo e sollicito li fedeli
d'Amore a piangere e dico che lo segnore
loro piange, e dico 'udendo la cagione per
che piange', acciò che s'acconcino più ad
ascoltarmi; ne la seconda narro la cagione;
ne la terza parlo d'alcuno onore che Amore
fece a questa donna. La seconda parte
comincia quivi: *Amor sente*; la terza quivi:
Audite.

(7) This first sonnet is divided into three
parts: in the first, I call and solicit Love's
faithful to weep and say that their lord
weeps, and I say "hearing the reason for
which he weeps" in order to dispose them
more to hear me; in the second, I narrate
the reason; in the third, I speak of some
honor that Love paid to this lady. The
second part begins here: "*Amor sente*: Love
hears"; the third here: "*Audite*: Hear."

(8)
Morte villana, di pietà nemica,
di dolor madre antica,
giudicio incontastabile gravoso,
poi che hai data matera al cor doglioso
ond'io vado pensoso,
di te blasmar la lingua s'affatica.

(8)
Villainous Death, pity's enemy,
ancient mother of sorrow,
incontestable grave judgment,
since you have given the heart matter for
    grief, with which I am burdened,
the tongue tires itself blaming you.

(9)
E s'io di grazia ti voi far mendica,
convenesi ch'eo dica
lo tuo fallar d'onni torto tortoso,
non però ch'a la gente sia nascoso,
ma per farne cruccioso
chi d'amor per innanzi si notrica.

(9)
And if I want to make you beg for mercy,
I need simply to speak
of your being guilty of every grievous
    wrong,
not that this is hidden from people,
but to make enraged
those who henceforth shall be nourished
    by love.

(10)
Dal secolo hai partita cortesia
e ciò ch'è in donna da pregiar vertute:
in gaia gioventute
distrutta hai l'amorosa leggiadria.
Più non voi discovrir qual donna sia
che per le propietà sue canosciute.

(10)
You have eliminated from the world
    courtesy
and that virtue which in a lady is prized:
in its joyful youthfulness
you have destroyed amorous gracefulness.
I will not reveal who this woman is
except by her known qualities.

Chapter VIII: *(cont.)*

(11)
Chi non merta salute
non speri mai d'aver sua compagnia.

(12) Questo sonetto si divide in quattro
parti: ne la prima parte chiamo la Morte
per certi suoi nomi propri; ne la seconda,
parlando a lei, dico la cagione per che io
mi muovo a biasimarla; ne la terza la
vitupero; ne la quarta mi volgo a parlare a
indiffinita persona, avvegna che quanto a
lo mio intendimento sia diffinita. La
seconda comincia quivi: *poi che hai data*;
la terza quivi: *E s'io di grazia*; la quarta
quivi: *Chi non merta salute.*

(11)
Whoever does not merit salvation
should not hope to keep her company.

(12) This sonnet is divided into four parts: in
the first part, I call on Death by certain
appropriate names; in the second, I say the
reasons why I blame him; in the third, I
revile him; in the fourth, I turn to speak to
an unspecified person, although defined in
my intention. The second begins here: "*poi
che hai data*: since you have given"; the third
here: "*E s'io di grazia*: And if I want"; the
fourth here: "*Chi non merta salute*: Whoever
does not merit salvation."

Chapter IX: *Love Appears on Road from Florence and Designates Another Screen Lady*

(1) Appresso la morte di questa donna
alquanti die avvenne cosa per la quale me
convenne partire de la sopradetta cittade
e ire verso quelle parti dov'era la gentile
donna ch'era stata mia difesa, avvegna che
non tanto fosse lontano lo termine de lo
mio andare quanto ella era.

(1) Several days after the death of this lady
something occurred that caused me to
depart from the above-mentioned city and
to go toward those parts where the gentle
lady was who had been my screen, although
the destination of my travel was not so far
away as hers.

(2) E tutto ch'io fosse a la compagnia di
molti quanto a la vista, l'andare mi
dispiacea sì, che quasi li sospiri non
poteano disfogare l'angoscia che lo cuore
sentia, però ch'io mi dilungava de la mia
beatitudine.

(2) And even though according to outward
appearance I was in the company of many,
the journey displeased me so much that my
sighs could hardly vent the anguish felt in
my heart because I was distancing myself
from my beatitude.

(3) E però lo dolcissimo segnore, lo quale
mi segnoreggiava per la vertù de la
gentilissima donna, ne la mia
imaginazione apparve come peregrino
leggeramente vestito e di vili drappi.

(3) And so the most sweet lord, who ruled
over me through the virtue of the most
gentle lady, appeared in my imagination as
a pilgrim scantily dressed and in vile clothes.

(4) Elli mi parea disbigottito, e guardava la
terra, salvo che talora li suoi occhi mi
parea che si volgessero ad uno fiume bello
e corrente e chiarissimo, lo quale sen gia
lungo questo cammino là ov'io era.

(4) He seemed to me to be distraught, and
looked at the earth, except that sometimes
his eyes seemed to me to turn to a lovely
river flowing and limpid, which coursed
alongside the way where I was.

Chapter IX: (*cont.*)

(5) A me parve che Amore mi chiamasse, e dicessemi queste parole: «Io vegno da quella donna la quale è stata tua lunga difesa, e so che lo suo rivenire non sarà a gran tempi; e però quello cuore che io ti facea avere a lei, io l'ho meco, e portolo a donna la quale sarà tua difensione, come questa era». E nominollami per nome, sì che io la conobbi bene.

(6) «Ma tuttavia, di queste parole ch'io t'ho ragionate se alcuna cosa ne dicessi, dille nel modo che per loro non si discernesse lo simulato amore che tu hai mostrato a questa e che ti converrà mostrare ad altri».

(7) E dette queste parole, disparve questa mia imaginazione tutta subitamente per la grandissima parte che mi parve che Amore mi desse di sé; e, quasi cambiato ne la vista mia, cavalcai quel giorno pensoso molto e accompagnato da molti sospiri.

(8) Appresso lo giorno cominciai di ciò questo sonetto, lo quale comincia: *Cavalcando.*

(9)
Cavalcando l'altr'ier per un cammino,
pensoso de l'andar che mi sgradia,
trovai Amore in mezzo de la via
in abito leggier di peregrino.

(10)
Ne la sembianza mi parea meschino,
come avesse perduto segnoria;
e sospirando pensoso venia,
per non veder la gente, a capo chino.

(11)
Quando mi vide, mi chiamò per nome,
e disse: «Io vegno di lontana parte,
ov'era lo tuo cor per mio volere;
e recolo a servir novo piacere».

(12)
Allora presi di lui sì gran parte,
ch'elli disparve, e non m'accorsi come.

(5) It seemed to me that Love called to me and said these words to me: "I come from that lady who has long been your screen, and I know that her return will not be made for a long time; and therefore, that heart which I made you have for her I have with me, and I bear it to another lady who will be your screen, even as this one was." And he named her by name, so that I knew well who she was.

(6) "Nevertheless, of these words that I have told you, if you say any of them, say them in such manner that the simulated love not be discerned that you have shown for one lady and that you now will show for another."

(7) And these words said, this imagining of mine suddenly disappeared because of the great part that it seemed to me that Love had given me of himself; and almost transformed in my appearance, I rode that day very pensive and accompanied by many sighs.

(8) The day after I began writing a sonnet about this, which begins: "*Cavalcando*: Riding."

(9)
Riding the other day along a way,
pensive about the journey, which I disliked,
I found Love in the middle of the road
dressed lightly as a pilgrim.

(10)
In his countenance he seemed wretched to me
as if he had lost his lordship;
and he came sighing and pensive
with bowed head so as to see no one.

(11)
When he saw me he called me by name,
and said: "I have come from afar,
where your heart was by my will;
and I bring it to serve a new pleasure."

(12)
Then I took so great a part in him
that he disappeared, and I did not
      perceive how.

Chapter IX: (*cont.*)

(13) Questo sonetto ha tre parti: ne la prima parte dico sì com'io trovai Amore, e quale mi parea; ne la seconda dico quello ch'elli mi disse, avvegna che non compiutamente per tema ch'avea di discovrire lo mio secreto; ne la terza dico com'elli mi disparve. La seconda comincia quivi: *Quando mi vide*; la terza: *Allora presi*.

(13) This sonnet has three parts: in the first part, I say how I found Love and how he appeared to me; in the second, I say what he said to me, although not completely, for fear of divulging my secret; in the third, I say how he disappeared. The second begins here: "*Quando mi vide*: When he saw me"; the third: "*Allora presi*: Then I took."

Chapter X: *Beatrice Denies Dante Her Greeting*

(1) Appresso la mia ritornata mi misi a cercare di questa donna che lo mio segnore m'avea nominata ne lo cammino de li sospiri; e acciò che lo mio parlare sia più brieve, dico che in poco tempo la feci mia difesa tanto, che troppa gente ne ragionava oltre li termini de la cortesia; onde molte fiate mi pensava duramente.

(1) After my return, I set about to search for this lady whom my lord had named in the way of the sighs; and in order that my speech be briefer, I say that in a short time I made her my screen, so much that many people talked about it beyond the bounds of courtesy; and this often made me sorely pensive.

(2) E per questa cagione, cioè di questa soverchievole voce che parea che m'infamasse viziosamente, quella gentilissima, la quale fue distruggitrice di tutti li vizi e regina de le virtudi, passando per alcuna parte, mi negò lo suo dolcissimo salutare, ne lo quale stava tutta la mia beatitudine.

(2) And for this reason, that is, this imperious rumor that seemed to defame me viciously, that most gentle one, who was the destroyer of vices and the queen of virtues, in passing by denied me her most sweet greeting, in which consisted all my blessedness.

(3) E uscendo alquanto del proposito presente, voglio dare a intendere quello che lo suo salutare in me vertuosamente operava.

(3) And digressing somewhat from the present purpose, I want to let it be understood how her greeting operated in me powerfully and virtuously.

Chapter XI: *Miraculous Effects of Beatrice's Greeting Described*

(1) Dico che quando ella apparia da parte alcuna, per la speranza de la mirabile salute nullo nemico mi rimanea, anzi mi giugnea

(1) I say that when she appeared anywhere, the hope of her miraculous greeting/ salvation meant that no enemy remained for

una fiamma di caritade, la quale mi facea perdonare a chiunque m'avesse offeso; e chi allora m'avesse domandato di cosa alcuna, la mia risponsione sarebbe stata solamente 'Amore', con viso vestito d'umilitade.

(2) E quando ella fosse alquanto propinqua al salutare, uno spirito d'amore, distruggendo tutti li altri spiriti sensitivi, pingea fuori li deboletti spiriti del viso, e dicea loro: «Andate a onorare la donna vostra»; ed elli si rimanea nel luogo loro. E chi avesse voluto conoscere Amore, fare lo potea mirando lo tremare de li occhi miei.

(3) E quando questa gentilissima salute salutava, non che Amore fosse tal mezzo che potesse obumbrare a me la intollerabile beatitudine, ma elli quasi per soverchio di dolcezza divenia tale, che lo mio corpo, lo quale era tutto allora sotto lo suo reggimento, molte volte si movea come cosa grave inanimata.

(4) Sì che appare manifestamente che ne le sue salute abitava la mia beatitudine, la quale molte volte passava e redundava la mia capacitade.

me; I was touched by a flame of charity that made me pardon whoever had offended me; and to whoever then had asked anything of me, my response would be only "Love," with a look clothed in humility.

(2) And when she was near the point of greeting me, a spirit of love, routing all other sensitive spirits, thrust out the weak spirits of sight and said to them: "Go honor your lady"; and it remained in their place. And whoever had wished to know Love could do so by looking at the palpitation of my eyes.

(3) And when this most gentle greeting/ salvation saluted/greeted, Love was not a means that could overshadow my unbearable bliss/beatitude, but almost by excess of sweetness he became such that my body, which was then completely under his governance, often moved as something heavy and inanimate.

(4) So that it manifestly appears that in her greeting dwelt my blessedness, which many times exceeded and evacuated my capacity.

Chapter XII: *Dream of God of Love as Young Man Dressed in White – and a Ballad*

(1) Ora, tornando al proposito, dico che poi che la mia beatitudine mi fue negata, mi giunse tanto dolore, che, partito me da le genti, in solinga parte andai a bagnare la terra d'amarissime lagrime.

(2) E poi che alquanto mi fue sollenato questo lagrimare, misimi ne la mia camera, là ov'io potea lamentarmi sanza essere udito; e quivi, chiamando misericordia a la donna de la cortesia,

(1) Now, returning to my purpose, I say that after my blessedness was denied to me, I was taken by such grief that separating myself from all people, I went to a solitary place to bathe the ground with most bitter tears.

(2) And after this weeping had subsided somewhat, I went to my chamber, where I could grieve and lament without being heard; and there, calling for mercy from the lady of all courtesy and saying, "Love,

Chapter XII: (cont.)

e dicendo «Amore, aiuta lo tuo fedele», m'addormentai come un pargoletto battuto lagrimando.

(3) Avvenne quasi nel mezzo de lo mio dormire che me parve vedere ne la mia camera lungo me sedere uno giovane vestito di bianchissime vestimenta, e pensando molto quanto a la vista sua, mi riguardava là ov'io giacea; e quando m'avea guardato alquanto, pareami che sospirando mi chiamasse, e diceami queste parole: «Fili mi, tempus est ut pretermictantur simulacra nostra».

(4) Allora mi parea che io lo conoscesse, però che mi chiamava così come assai fiate ne li miei sonni m'avea già chiamato: e riguardandolo, parvemi che piangesse pietosamente, e parea che attendesse da me alcuna parola; ond'io, assicurandomi, cominciai a parlare così con esso: «Segnore de la nobiltade, e perché piangi tu?». E quelli mi dicea queste parole: «Ego tanquam centrum circuli, cui simili modo se habent circumferentie partes; tu autem non sic».

(5) Allora, pensando a le sue parole, mi parea che m'avesse parlato molto oscuramente; sì ch'io mi sforzava di parlare, e diceali queste parole: «Che è ciò, segnore, che mi parli con tanta oscuritade?». E quelli mi dicea in parole volgari: «Non dimandare più che utile ti sia».

(6) E però cominciai allora con lui a ragionare de la salute la quale mi fue negata, e domandailo de la cagione; onde in questa guisa da lui mi fue risposto: «Quella nostra Beatrice udio da certe persone di te ragionando, che la donna la quale io ti nominai nel cammino de li sospiri, ricevea da te alcuna noia; e però

help your faithful follower," I fell asleep like a crying and beaten child.

(3) It happened nearly in the middle of my sleep that I seemed to see seated alongside me in my chamber a young man dressed in a most white garment, and in a deeply thoughtful attitude he watched me where I lay; and when he had looked at me for some time, it seemed that, sighing, he called to me and said to me these words: "*Fili mi, tempus est ut pretermictantur simulacra nostra*: My son, the time is come for us to put aside our simulations."

(4) Then it seemed to me that I knew him, since he called me as often enough in my sleep already he had called me; and looking at him, it seemed to me that he was piteously weeping, and he seemed to be waiting for some word from me; whence, reassuring myself, I began to speak thus to him: "Most noble Lord, why do you weep?" And he said these words to me: "*Ego tanquam centrum circuli, cui simili modo se habent circumferentie partes; tu autem non sic*: I am like the center of a circle, whose parts are all similarly related to the circumference; you, however, are not so."

(5) Then, as I thought about his words, he seemed to me to have spoken very obscurely; so much so that I forced myself to speak and said these words to him: "What is this that you speak, lord, so obscurely to me?" And he said to me in the vernacular language: "Do not ask more than is useful for you."

(6) And thus I began with him to reflect about the greeting that had been denied me and asked him the reason for it, and the response from him to me was in this manner: "Our Beatrice heard from certain persons speaking about you that the lady whom I named for you in the way of sighs received annoyance from you; and

questa gentilissima, la quale è contraria di tutte le noie, non degnò salutare la tua persona, temendo non fosse noiosa.

(7) Onde con ciò sia cosa che veracemente sia conosciuto per lei alquanto lo tuo secreto per lunga consuetudine, voglio che tu dichi certe parole per rima, ne le quali tu comprendi la forza che io tegno sopra te per lei, e come tu fosti suo tostamente da la tua puerizia. E di ciò chiama testimonio colui che lo sa, e come tu prieghi lui che li le dica; ed io, che son quelli, volentieri le ne ragionerò; e per questo sentirà ella la tua volontade, la quale sentendo, conoscerà le parole de li ingannati.

(8) Queste parole fa che siano quasi un mezzo, sì che tu non parli a lei immediatamente, che non è degno; e no le mandare in parte, sanza me, ove potessero essere intese da lei, ma falle adornare di soave armonia, ne la quale io sarò tutte le volte che farà mestiere».

(9) E dette queste parole, sì disparve, e lo mio sonno fue rotto. Onde io ricordandomi, trovai che questa visione m'era apparita ne la nona ora del die; e anzi ch'io uscisse di questa camera, propuosi di fare una ballata, ne la quale io seguitasse ciò che lo mio segnore m'avea imposto; e feci poi questa ballata, che comincia: *Ballata, i' voi.*

(10)
Ballata, i' voi che tu ritrovi Amore,
e con lui vade a madonna davante,
sì che la scusa mia, la qual tu cante,
ragioni poi con lei lo mio segnore.
(11)
Tu vai, ballata, sì cortesemente,
che sanza compagnia
dovresti avere in tutte parti ardire;
ma se tu vuoli andar sicuramente,

therefore this most gentle lady, who is contrary to all annoyances, did not deign to greet your person, fearing it might be noisome.

(7) Since in fact the truth of your secret is already somewhat known to her through long familiarity, I want you to say certain words in rhyme in which you include the power that I hold over you through her, and how you were hers from early in your boyhood. And for that purpose, call as witness him who knows, and beg him that he tell her this; and I, who am he, will willingly tell her of it; and by this means she will hear of your will, hearing which she will know for false the words of those who were deceived.

(8) Let these words be like an intermediary, so that you not speak directly to her, which is not seemly; and do not send them, without me, anywhere where they might be heard by her, but make them to be adorned with sweet harmony, in which I will be present as often as is necessary."

(9) And having said these words, he disappeared and my sleep was broken. When I reflected on it, I found that this vision had appeared to me in the ninth hour of the day, and before I left this chamber, I resolved to write a ballad in which I would carry out that which my lord had imposed on me; and later I composed this ballad, which begins: "*Ballata, i' voi*: Ballad, I want."

(10)
Ballad, I want you to find Love,
and to go with him before my lady,
so that my excuse, which you sing,
may be explained to her by my lord.
(11)
Go, ballad, so courteously
that without company
you should dare go anywhere;
but if you wish to go safely,

retrova l'Amor pria,
ché forse non è bon sanza lui gire;
però che quella che ti dee audire,
sì com'io credo, è ver di me adirata:
se tu di lui non fossi accompagnata,
leggeramente ti faria disnore.

(12)
Con dolze sono, quando se' con lui,
comincia este parole,
appresso che averai chesta pietate:
«Madonna, quelli che mi manda a vui,
quando vi piaccia, vole,
sed elli ha scusa, che la m'intendiate.
Amore è qui, che per vostra bieltate
lo face, come vol, vista cangiare:
dunque perché li fece altra guardare
pensatel voi, da che non mutò 'l core».

(13)
Dille: «Madonna, lo suo core è stato
con sì fermata fede,
che 'n voi servir l'ha 'mpronto onne pensero:
tosto fu vostro, e mai non s'è smagato».
Sed ella non ti crede,
dì che domandi Amor, che sa lo vero:
ed a la fine falle umil preghero,
lo perdonare se le fosse a noia,
che mi comandi per messo ch'eo moia,
e vedrassi ubidir ben servidore.

(14)
E dì a colui ch'è d'ogni pietà chiave,
avante che sdonnei,
che le saprà contar mia ragion bona:
«Per grazia de la mia nota soave
reman tu qui con lei,
e del tuo servo ciò che vuoi ragiona;
e s'ella per tuo prego li perdona,
fa che li annunzi un bel sembiante pace».

(15)
Gentil ballata mia, quando ti piace,
movi in quel punto che tu n'aggie onore.

first find Love,
without whom perhaps you should not go;
since she who must hear you,
as I believe, is angry against me:
if you were not accompanied by him,
she might lightly dishonor you.

(12)
With sweet sound, when you are
    with him,
begin these words,
after you have asked her pity:
"My lady, he who sends me to you,
if you please, wishes,
if he be excused, that you listen to me.
Love is here, who for your beauty
makes him, at will, change appearance:
therefore if it made him look at another,
realize that it did not change his heart."

(13)
Tell her: "My lady, his heart has been
in such firm faith,
that serving you has been impressed on
    every thought:
he was yours from the first and never
    strayed."
If she does not believe you,
tell her to ask for Love, who knows the truth:
and finally make humble prayer to her,
that she pardon if she was annoyed,
that she command me by a messenger to die,
and she will see her good servant obey.

(14)
And before you take your leave,
say to him who is key to all pity
and will know how to plead my good cause:
"By the grace of my sweet note
remain here with her,
and say what you will of your servant;
and if because of your prayer she
    pardons him,
make a lovely countenance announce
    peace to him."

(15)
Gentle my ballad, if you please,
go in a moment when you may have honor.

(16) Questa ballata in tre parti si divide: ne la prima dico a lei ov'ella vada, e confortola però che vada più sicura, e dico ne la cui compagnia si metta, se vuole sicuramente andare e sanza pericolo alcuno; ne la seconda dico quello che lei si pertiene di fare intendere; ne la terza la licenzio del gire quando vuole, raccomandando lo suo movimento ne le braccia de la fortuna. La seconda parte comincia quivi: *Con dolze sono*; la terza quivi: *Gentil ballata*.

(17) Potrebbe già l'uomo opporre contra me e dicere che non sapesse a cui fosse lo mio parlare in seconda persona, però che la ballata non è altro che queste parole ched io parlo: e però dico che questo dubbio io lo intendo solvere e dichiarare in questo libello ancora in parte più dubbiosa; e allora intenda qui chi qui dubita, o chi qui volesse opporre in questo modo.

(16) This ballad is divided into three parts: in the first, I say where it is to go and encourage it to go more safely, and I say in whose company to place itself should it wish to go safely and without any danger; in the second, I say that which it has to make understood; in the third, I give it license to go when it wishes, commending its movement into the arms of fortune. The second part begins here: "*Con dolze sono*: With sweet sound"; the third here: *Gentil ballata mia*: Gentle my ballad."

(17) One might already raise an objection against me and say that one cannot know to whom my speech in the second person is addressed, since the ballad is nothing other than these words that I speak: and so I say that I intend to resolve this doubt and to declare it in an even more doubtful part of this book; so then let whoever doubts here, or whoever objects in this manner, be advised.

Chapter XIII: *Thoughts of Love at War with One Another*

(1) Appresso di questa soprascritta visione, avendo già dette le parole che Amore m'avea imposte a dire, mi cominciaro molti e diversi pensamenti a combattere e a tentare, ciascuno quasi indefensibilemente; tra li quali pensamenti quattro mi parea che ingombrassero più lo riposo de la vita.

(2) L'uno de li quali era questo: buona è la signoria d'Amore, però che trae lo intendimento del suo fedele da tutte le vili cose.

(3) L'altro era questo: non buona è la signoria d'Amore, però che quanto lo suo fedele più fede li porta, tanto più gravi e dolorosi punti li conviene passare.

(4) L'altro era questo: lo nome d'Amore è sì dolce a udire, che impossibile mi

(1) After the vision written above, having already written the words that Love had required me to say, many and diverse thoughts began to struggle and contend within me, each one irresistibly; among them, four thoughts seemed to disrupt my life's tranquility.

(2) One of them was this: Love's lordship is good because it draws the mind of its faithful one away from vile things.

(3) Another was this: the lordship of Love is not good because the greater the trust the faithful bears him so much the heavier and the more painful are the trials he must pass through.

(4) Another was this: the name of Love is so sweet to hear that it seems to me impossible

pare che la sua propria operazione sia ne le più cose altro che dolce, con ciò sia cosa che li nomi seguitino le nominate cose, sì come è scritto: «Nomina sunt consequentia rerum».

(5) Lo quarto era questo: la donna per cui Amore ti stringe così, non è come l'altre donne, che leggeramente si muova del suo cuore.

(6) E ciascuno mi combattea tanto, che mi facea stare quasi come colui che non sa per qual via pigli lo suo cammino, e che vuole andare e non sa onde se ne vada; e se io pensava di volere cercare una comune via di costoro, cioè là ove tutti s'accordassero, questa era via molto inimica verso me, cioè di chiamare e di mettermi ne le braccia de la Pietà.

(7) E in questo stato dimorando, mi giunse volontade di scriverne parole rimate; e dissine allora questo sonetto, lo quale comincia: *Tutti li miei penser.*

(8)
Tutti li miei penser parlan d'Amore;
e hanno in lor sì gran varietate,
ch'altro mi fa voler sua potestate,
altro folle ragiona il suo valore,
altro sperando m'apporta dolzore,
altro pianger mi fa spesse fiate;
e sol s'accordano in cherer pietate,
tremando di paura che è nel core.

(9)
Ond'io non so da qual matera prenda;
e vorrei dire, e non so ch'io mi dica:
così mi trovo in amorosa erranza!
E se con tutti voi fare accordanza,
convenemi chiamar la mia nemica,
madonna la Pietà, che mi difenda.

(10) Questo sonetto in quattro parti si può dividere: ne la prima dico e soppongo che tutti li miei pensieri sono d'Amore; ne la seconda dico che

that its proper operation should be in most things other than sweet, since names follow from the things named, as it is written: "*Nomina sunt consequentia rerum*: Names are consequences of things."

(5) The fourth was this: the lady through whom Love has so strong a hold on me is not like other ladies, who are lightly moved in their hearts.

(6) And each of these besieged me so that I was made like someone who does not know which way to go, who wants to go but does not know whither; and if I thought to try and find a common way among them, in which all would agree, this was a way very inimical to me: it meant calling on and throwing myself into the arms of Pity.

(7) And while I was in this state of mind, a will to write rhymed words came to me; I then wrote this sonnet, which begins: "*Tutti li miei penser.* All of my thoughts."

(8)
All of my thoughts speak of Love
and have among themselves so great variety,
that one makes me will its lordship,
another judges its worthiness as folly,
another hopes to bring me sweetness,
another makes me weep repeatedly;
and all accord only in seeking pity,
trembling with fear in the heart.

(9)
So I do not know from which to take my theme;
I would like to speak, but do not know what
   to say:
thus I find myself in amorous errancy!
And if I wish to make you all concordant,
I am constrained to call on my enemy,
Madonna Pity, to defend me.

(10) This sonnet can be divided into four parts: in the first, I say and submit that all my thoughts are about Love; in the second, I say that they are diverse and narrate their diversity; in the third,

sono diversi, e narro la loro diversitade; ne la terza dico in che tutti pare che s'accordino; ne la quarta dico che volendo dire d'Amore, non so da qual parte pigli matera, e se la voglio pigliare da tutti, convene che io chiami la mia inimica, madonna la Pietade; e dico 'madonna' quasi per disdegnoso modo di parlare. La seconda parte comincia quivi: *e hanno in lor*; la terza quivi: *e sol s'accordano*; la quarta quivi: *Ond'io non so*.

I say in what all seem to agree; in the fourth, I say that wishing to speak of Love, I do not know from what to begin and am forced to call on my enemy, Madonna Pity; and I say "Madonna" as a disdainful mode of speech. The second part begins here: "*e hanno in lor*: and they have among themselves"; the third here: "*e sol s'accordano*: and all accord only"; the fourth here: "*Ond'io non so*: So I do not know."

Chapter XIV: *Dante Distraught ("Transfigured") and Mocked at Marriage Feast*

(1) Appresso la battaglia de li diversi pensieri avvenne che questa gentilissima venne in parte ove molte donne gentili erano adunate; a la qual parte io fui condotto per amica persona, credendosi fare a me grande piacere, in quanto mi menava là ove tante donne mostravano le loro bellezze.

(2) Onde io, quasi non sappiendo a che io fossi menato, e fidandomi ne la persona la quale uno suo amico a l'estremitade de la vita condotto avea, dissi a lui: «Perché semo noi venuti a queste donne?».

(3) Allora quelli mi disse: «Per fare sì ch'elle siano degnamente servite». E lo vero è che adunate quivi erano a la compagnia d'una gentile donna che disposata era lo giorno; e però, secondo l'usanza de la sopradetta cittade, convenia che le facessero compagnia nel primo sedere a la mensa che facea ne la magione del suo novello sposo. Sì che io, credendomi fare piacere di questo amico, propuosi di stare al servigio de le donne ne la sua compagnia.

(1) After the battle of diverse thoughts it happened that this most gracious one came to where many gentle ladies were gathered; I was led there by a friend who believed this was a great favor to me, since he led me to where so many ladies were displaying their beauty.

(2) Hence, hardly knowing where I was being led and trusting in the person who had conducted a friend of his to the extremity of life, I said to this person: "Why have we come to these ladies?"

(3) Then he said to me: "To ensure that they are worthily served." And the truth is that they were gathered in the company of a gentle lady who had been wedded that day; and so, observing the custom of the above-mentioned city, it was fitting that they keep her company in the first sitting at table for her in the house of her new husband. Thus, believing that I was pleasing this friend, I resolved to remain in the service of the ladies in her company.

Chapter XIV: (*cont.*)

(4) E nel fine del mio proponimento mi parve sentire uno mirabile tremore incominciare nel mio petto da la sinistra parte e distendersi di subito per tutte le parti del mio corpo. Allora dico che io poggiai la mia persona simulatamente ad una pintura la quale circundava questa magione; e temendo non altri si fosse accorto del mio tremare, levai li occhi, e mirando le donne, vidi tra loro la gentilissima Beatrice.

(4) And no sooner had I so resolved than I seemed to feel an extraordinary tremor begin in the left part of my chest and spread suddenly throughout all parts of my body. I say that I then leaned my body in dissimulation against a fresco painting that circled around this house; and fearing lest anyone notice my trembling, I raised my eyes, and gazing at the ladies, I saw among them the most gentle Beatrice.

(5) Allora fuoro sì distrutti li miei spiriti per la forza che Amore prese veggendosi in tanta propinquitade a la gentilissima donna, che non ne rimasero in vita più che li spiriti del viso; e ancora questi rimasero fuori de li loro istrumenti, però che Amore volea stare nel loro nobilissimo luogo per vedere la mirabile donna.

(5) Then my spirits were so destroyed by the power that Love exerted, seeing himself so near to the most gentle lady, that none other than the spirits of sight remained alive; and even these remained outside of their organs, since Love wanted to stay in their most noble place in order to see the miraculous lady.

(6) E avvegna che io fossi altro che prima, molto mi dolea di questi spiritelli, che si lamentavano forte e diceano: «Se questi non ci infolgorasse così fuori del nostro luogo, noi potremmo stare a vedere la maraviglia di questa donna così come stanno li altri nostri pari».

(6) And although I was in an altered state, I was greatly grieved for these little spirits, which lamented loudly and said: "If he had not lightning-bolted us out of our place, we would be able to stay and see the marvel of this lady as the other spirits, our peers, are doing."

(7) Io dico che molte di queste donne, accorgendosi de la mia trasfigurazione, si cominciaro a maravigliare, e ragionando si gabbavano di me con questa gentilissima; onde lo ingannato amico di buona fede mi prese per la mano, e traendomi fuori de la veduta di queste donne, sì mi domandò che io avesse.

(7) I say that many of these ladies, noticing my transfiguration, began to marvel, and they spoke mockingly of me with that most gentle one, whence the friend who had been deceived in good faith took me by the hand and leading me out of the view of these ladies, asked me what was the matter.

(8) Allora io, riposato alquanto, e resurressiti li morti spiriti miei, e li discacciati rivenuti a le loro possessioni, dissi a questo mio amico queste parole: «Io tenni li piedi in quella parte de la vita di là da la quale non si puote ire più per intendimento di ritornare».

(8) Once I had somewhat recovered, my mortal spirits resurrected and the banished ones having regained their possessions, I said to this friend of mine these words: "I held my feet in that part of life beyond which one cannot go with the intention of returning."

Chapter XIV: (*cont.*)

(9) E partitomi da lui, mi ritornai ne la camera de le lagrime; ne la quale, piangendo e vergognandomi, fra me stesso dicea: «Se questa donna sapesse la mia condizione, io non credo che così gabbasse la mia persona, anzi credo che molta pietade le ne verrebbe».

(9) And having left him, I returned to the chamber of my tears; in which, weeping and feeling ashamed, I said to myself: "If this lady knew of my condition, I do not believe that she would mock my person; on the contrary, I believe that she would feel much pity."

(10) E in questo pianto stando, propuosi di dire parole, ne le quali, parlando a lei, significasse la cagione del mio trasfiguramento, e dicesse che io so bene ch'ella non è saputa, e che se fosse saputa, io credo che pietà ne giugnerebbe altrui; e propuosile di dire desiderando che venissero per avventura ne la sua audienza. E allora dissi questo sonetto, lo quale comincia: *Con l'altre donne.*

(10) And in the midst of this weeping, I resolved to say words in which, speaking of her, I would signify the cause of my transfiguration and would say that I know well that it was not known, but that if it were, I believe that pity would come over others; and I resolved to speak, desiring that it should by chance come into her hearing. And then I wrote this sonnet, which begins: "*Con l'altre donne*: With the other ladies."

(11)
Con l'altre donne mia vista gabbate,
e non pensate, donna, onde si mova
ch'io vi rassembri sì figura nova
quando riguardo la vostra beltate.

(11)
With the other ladies you mock the sight
of me and think not, lady, whence it comes
that I cut such a strange figure
when I gaze upon your beauty.

(12)
Se lo saveste, non poria Pietate
tener più contra me l'usata prova,
ché Amor, quando sì presso a voi mi trova,
prende baldanza e tanta securtate,
che fere tra' miei spiriti paurosi,
e quale ancide, e qual pinge di fore,
sì che solo remane a veder vui:
ond'io mi cangio in figura d'altrui,
ma non sì ch'io non senta bene allore
li guai de li scacciati tormentosi.

(12)
If you knew why, Pity would not be able
to uphold the proof used against me,
since Love, when I find myself so near you,
acquires audacity and so much confidence
that he sets upon my frightened spirits
and kills some, puts others to flight,
so that he alone remains to view you:
whence I change into another form,
but not so that I do not then hear
well the wailings of these tormented outcasts.

(13) Questo sonetto non divido in parti, però che la divisione non si fa se non per aprire la sentenzia de la cosa divisa; onde con ciò sia cosa che per la sua ragionata cagione assai sia manifesto, non ha mestiere di divisione.

(13) This sonnet I will not divide into parts, since division is not made except to open the meaning of the thing divided; so since this thing is clear enough from its narrated cause, it does not need to be divided.

(14) Vero è che tra le parole dove si manifesta la cagione di questo sonetto,

(14) It is true that, among the words where the cause of this sonnet is made manifest, some

Chapter XIV: (*cont.*)

si scrivono dubbiose parole, cioè quando dico che Amore uccide tutti li miei spiriti, e li visivi rimangono in vita, salvo che fuori de li strumenti loro. E questo dubbio è impossibile a solvere a chi non fosse in simile grado fedele d'Amore; e a coloro che vi sono è manifesto ciò che solverebbe le dubitose parole: e però non è bene a me di dichiarare cotale dubitazione, acciò che lo mio parlare dichiarando sarebbe indarno, o vero di soperchio.

obscure words are written, particularly when I say that Love killed all my spirits, though the visual ones remained alive, albeit outside of their organs. And this doubt is impossible to resolve for whoever is not a similarly ranking devotee of Love; and to those who are, that which would resolve the dubious words is manifest, so that my speech of clarification would be in vain, or superfluous.

Chapter XV: *Why Dante Continues to Try to See His Lady*

(1) Appresso la nuova trasfigurazione mi giunse uno pensamento forte, lo quale poco si partia da me, anzi continuamente mi riprendea, ed era di cotale ragionamento meco: «Poscia che tu pervieni a così dischernevole vista quando tu se' presso di questa donna, perché pur cerchi di vedere lei? Ecco che tu fossi domandato da lei: che avrestù da rispondere, ponendo che tu avessi libera ciascuna tua vertude in quanto tu le rispondessi?»

(1) After this last strange transfiguration, a powerful thought began to obsess me, continually reproaching me with this reasoning: "Since you are reduced to such a pathetic figure when you are near to this lady, why do you still seek to see her? Were she to ask you this, what would you answer, supposing your faculties remained free to respond?"

(2) E a costui rispondea un altro, umile, pensero, e dicea: «S'io non perdessi le mie vertudi, e fossi libero tanto che io le potessi rispondere, io le direi che sì tosto com'io imagino la sua mirabile bellezza, sì tosto mi giunge uno desiderio di vederla, lo quale è di tanta vertude, che uccide e distrugge ne la mia memoria ciò che contra lui si potesse levare; e però non mi ritraggono le passate passioni da cercare la veduta di costei».

(2) And to this another humble thought answered and said: "If I did not lose my faculties and remained free to respond to her, I would tell her that as soon as I imagine her miraculous beauty I am taken by so strong a desire to see her that, in my mind, it kills and destroys that which could be opposed against it; therefore, my past sufferings do not prevent me from seeking the sight of her."

(3) Onde io, mosso da cotali pensamenti, propuosi di dire certe parole, ne le quali, escusandomi a lei da cotale riprensione, ponesse anche di quello che mi diviene presso di lei; e dissi questo sonetto, lo quale comincia: *Ciò che m'incontra*.

(4)
Ciò che m'incontra, ne la mente more,
quand'i' vegno a veder voi, bella gioia;
e quand'io vi son presso, i' sento Amore
che dice: «Fuggi, se 'l perir t'è noia».

(5)
Lo viso mostra lo color del core,
che, tramortendo, ovunque po' s'appoia;
e per la ebrietà del gran tremore
le pietre par che gridin: Moia, moia.

(6)
Peccato face chi allora mi vide,
se l'alma sbigottita non conforta,
sol dimostrando che di me li doglia,
per la pietà, che 'l vostro gabbo ancide,
la qual si cria ne la vista morta
de li occhi, c'hanno di lor morte voglia.

(7) Questo sonetto si divide in due parti: ne la prima dico la cagione per che non mi tengo di gire presso di questa donna; ne la seconda dico quello che mi diviene per andare presso di lei; e comincia questa parte quivi: *e quand'io vi son presso*.

(8) E anche si divide questa seconda parte in cinque, secondo cinque diverse narrazioni: che ne la prima dico quello che Amore, consigliato da la ragione, mi dice quando le sono presso; ne la seconda manifesto lo stato del cuore per essemplo del viso; ne la terza dico sì come onne sicurtade mi viene meno; ne la quarta dico

(3) So, motivated by these thoughts, I resolved to say certain words with which, excusing myself to her for this reproach, I would also describe what I become near to her; and I composed this sonnet, which begins: "*Ciò che m'incontra*: That meets me."

(4)
That which befalls me dies in memory
when I come to see you, beautiful joy,
and when I am near you, I hear Love
say: "Flee, if perishing is pernicious
   to you."

(5)
My face displays the color of my heart,
which, swooning fatally, props itself up
   wherever it can;
and due to the inebriation of the great
   quaking
the very stones seem to cry: Die, die.

(6)
Whoever sees me then commits a sin
if they do not comfort my distraught soul,
if only by showing themselves pained
   for me,
for pity's sake, which your mockery kills,
and which would be created by the
   deathly sight
of my eyes that desire their own death.

(7) This sonnet is divided into two parts: in the first, I tell the reason why I do not restrain myself from going near to this lady; in the second, I say what happens to me when I go near her; and this part begins: "*e quand'io vi son presso*: and when I am near you."

(8) And also this second part divides into five, according to five different narrations: in the first, I say what Love, counseled by reason, tells me when I am near her; in the second, I manifest the state of the heart by the example of the face; in the third, I say how every security is lost; in the fourth, I say that anyone sins who does

Chapter XV: (*cont.*)

che pecca quelli che non mostra pietà di me, acciò che mi sarebbe alcuno conforto; ne l'ultima dico perché altri doverebbe avere pietà, e ciò è per la pietosa vista che ne li occhi mi giugne; la quale vista pietosa è distrutta, cioè non pare altrui, per lo gabbare di questa donna, lo quale trae a sua simile operazione coloro che forse vederebbono questa pietà.

(9) La seconda parte comincia quivi: *Lo viso mostra*; la terza quivi: *e per la ebrietà*; la quarta: *Peccato face*; la quinta: *per la pietà*.

not show pity toward me, that it might be of some comfort; in the last, I say why others should take pity, and this is for the piteous look that fills my eyes; this piteous look is destroyed, or does not appear to others, due to the mockery of this lady, which induces a similar reaction in those who would perhaps see this pity.

(9) The second part begins here: "*Lo viso mostra*: My face displays"; the third here: "*e per la ebrietà*: and due to the inebriation"; the fourth: "*Peccato face*: Whoever sees"; the fifth: "*per la pietà*: for pity's sake."

Chapter XVI: *The State of Being in Love – Its Conflicts*

(1) Appresso ciò che io dissi questo sonetto, mi mosse una volontade di dire anche parole, ne le quali io dicesse quattro cose ancora sopra lo mio stato, le quali non mi parea che fossero manifestate ancora per me.

(2) La prima de le quali si è che molte volte io mi dolea, quando la mia memoria movesse la fantasia ad imaginare quale Amore mi facea.

(3) La seconda si è che Amore spesse volte di subito m'assalia sì forte, che 'n me non rimanea altro di vita se non un pensero che parlava di questa donna.

(4) La terza si è che quando questa battaglia d'Amore mi pugnava così, io mi movea quasi discolorito tutto per vedere questa donna, credendo che mi difendesse la sua veduta da questa battaglia, dimenticando quello che per appropinquare a tanta gentilezza m'addivenia.

(5) La quarta si è come cotale veduta non solamente non mi difendea, ma finalmente disconfiggea la mia poca vita.

(1) After I had written this sonnet, a will moved me to say further words in which I should speak of four things about my state that I seemed not yet to have made manifest.

(2) The first of these is that I was often pained when my memory moved my fantasy to imagine what Love was doing in me.

(3) The second is that Love often suddenly assailed me so strongly that nothing was left alive in me except the thought that spoke of this lady.

(4) The third is that this battle of Love fought so within me that I would go all pale to see this lady, believing that the sight of her would defend me from this battle, forgetting what became of me when I approached so much nobility.

(5) The fourth is how that sight not only did not defend me but finally defeated my little life.

Chapter XVI: (*cont.*)

(6) E però dissi questo sonetto, lo quale comincia: *Spesse fiate*.

(7)
Spesse fiate vegnonmi a la mente
le oscure qualità ch'Amor mi dona,
e venmene pietà, sì che sovente
io dico: «Lasso!, avviene elli a persona?»;

(8)
ch'Amor m'assale subitamente,
sì che la vita quasi m'abbandona:
campami un spirto vivo solamente,
e que' riman perché di voi ragiona.

(9)
Poscia mi sforzo, ché mi voglio atare;
e così smorto, d'onne valor voto,
vegno a vedervi, credendo guerire:

(10)
e se io levo li occhi per guardare,
nel cor mi si comincia uno tremoto,
che fa de' polsi l'anima partire.

(11) Questo sonetto si divide in quattro parti, secondo che quattro cose sono in esso narrate; e però che sono di sopra ragionate, non m'intrametto se non di distinguere le parti per li loro cominciamenti: onde dico che la seconda parte comincia quivi: *ch'Amor*; la terza quivi: *Poscia mi sforzo*; la quarta quivi: *e se io levo*.

(6) And so I wrote this sonnet, which begins: "*Spesse fiate*: Time and again."

(7)
Time and again the dark qualities that
Love imparts to me come into my mind,
and pity comes to me so that often I say:
"Alas, does this happen to anyone else?";

(8)
for Love assails me so suddenly
that life practically abandons me:
one spirit only survives in me,
and that remains because it speaks of you.

(9)
Then I force myself, for I want to help
    myself,
and so extinguished, voided of valor,
I come to see you, believing that the cure:

(10)
and if I lift my eyes to look,
a tremor in my heart begins
that makes the soul depart from my pulse.

(11) This sonnet is divided into four parts, according to the four things narrated in it; but since they are spoken of above, I will not intervene except to distinguish the parts and their beginnings: accordingly, I say that the second part begins here: "*ch'Amor*: for Love"; the third here: "*Poscia mi sforzo*: Then I force myself"; the fourth here: "*e se io levo*: and if I lift."

Chapter XVII: *A New and Nobler Theme*

(1) Poi che dissi questi tre sonetti, ne li quali parlai a questa donna però che fuoro narratori di tutto quasi lo mio stato, credendomi tacere e non dire più però che mi parea di me assai avere manifestato,

(1) After I had written these three sonnets, in which I spoke to this lady, given that they narrated nearly everything about my state, believing I would be silent and say no more, since it seemed to me that enough

Chapter XVII: (*cont.*)

avvegna che sempre poi tacesse di dire a lei, a me convenne ripigliare matera nuova e più nobile che la passata.	about me had been made manifest, although I should for ever after cease to write to her, I felt compelled to take up new matter and more noble than in the past.
(2) E però che la cagione de la nuova matera è dilettevole a udire, la dicerò, quanto potrò più brievemente.	(2) And since the cause of the new matter is delightful to hear, I will tell of it, as briefly as I can.

Chapter XVIII: *Interrogated by Ladies, Dante Discovers New Matter for His Poetry*

(1) Con ciò sia cosa che per la vista mia molte persone avessero compreso lo secreto del mio cuore, certe donne, le quali adunate s'erano dilettandosi l'una ne la compagnia de l'altra, sapeano bene lo mio cuore, però che ciascuna di loro era stata a molte mie sconfitte; e io passando appresso di loro, sì come da la fortuna menato, fui chiamato da una di queste gentili donne.	(1) Since many people had understood from seeing me the secret of my heart, certain ladies, who had gathered so as to delight in one another's company, knew my heart well because each of them had been present at many of my defeats; and passing nearby them, as if led by fortune, I was called to by one of these gentle ladies.
(2) La donna che m'avea chiamato era donna di molto leggiadro parlare; sì che quand'io fui giunto dinanzi da loro, e vidi bene che la mia gentilissima donna non era con esse, rassicurandomi le salutai, e domandai che piacesse loro.	(2) The lady who had called to me was a lady of very graceful speech; such that when I was standing before them and saw well that my most gentle lady was not with them, reassured, I greeted them and asked what might please them.
(3) Le donne erano molte, tra le quali n'avea certe che si rideano tra loro; altre v'erano che mi guardavano aspettando che io dovessi dire; altre v'erano che parlavano tra loro. De le quali una, volgendo li suoi occhi verso me e chiamandomi per nome, disse queste parole: «A che fine ami tu questa tua donna, poi che tu non puoi sostenere la sua presenza? Dilloci, ché certo lo fine di cotale amore conviene che sia novissimo». E poi che m'ebbe dette queste parole, non solamente ella, ma tutte l'altre cominciaro ad attendere in vista la mia risponsione.	(3) The ladies were many, among whom certain ones were laughing among themselves; there were others who gazed at me waiting for whatever I would say. One of them, turning her eyes toward me and, calling me by name, said these words: "To what purpose do you love this lady, since you cannot sustain her presence? Tell us, since certainly such a love must be very new and strange." And when she had said these words to me, not only she, but all the others appeared to be waiting for my response.

Chapter XVIII: (*cont.*)

(4) Allora dissi queste parole loro: «Madonne, lo fine del mio amore fue già lo saluto di questa donna, forse di cui voi intendete, e in quello dimorava la beatitudine, ché era fine di tutti li miei desiderii. Ma poi che le piacque di negarlo a me, lo mio segnore Amore, la sua merzede, ha posto tutta la mia beatitudine in quello che non mi puote venire meno».

(5) Allora queste donne cominciaro a parlare tra loro; e sì come talora vedemo cadere l'acqua mischiata di bella neve, così mi parea udire le loro parole uscire mischiate di sospiri.

(6) E poi che alquanto ebbero parlato tra loro, anche mi disse questa donna che m'avea prima parlato, queste parole: «Noi ti preghiamo che tu ne dichi ove sta questa tua beatitudine». Ed io, rispondendo lei, dissi cotanto: «In quelle parole che lodano la donna mia».

(7) Allora mi rispuose questa che mi parlava: «Se tu ne dicessi vero, quelle parole che tu n'hai dette in notificando la tua condizione, avrestù operate con altro intendimento».

(8) Onde io, pensando a queste parole, quasi vergognoso mi partio da loro, e venia dicendo fra me medesimo: «Poi che è tanta beatitudine in quelle parole che lodano la mia donna, perché altro parlare è stato lo mio?».

(9) E però propuosi di prendere per matera de lo mio parlare sempre mai quello che fosse loda di questa gentilissima; e pensando molto a ciò, pareami avere impresa troppo alta matera quanto a me, sì che non ardia di cominciare; e così dimorai alquanti dì con disiderio di dire e con paura di cominciare.

(4) Then I spoke these words to them: "My lady, the purpose of my love was once the greeting of this lady, perhaps you understand whom, and in that dwelt my blessedness, which was the end of all my desires. But since she has chosen to deny it to me, my lord Love, in his mercy, has placed all my blessedness in that which cannot fail me."

(5) Then those ladies began to speak among themselves; and as we sometimes see water falling mixed with lovely snow, so I seemed to hear their words being uttered mixed with sighs.

(6) And after they had spoken a little among themselves, the lady who had spoken to me first said these words to me: "We beseech you that you tell us in what this blessedness of yours consists." And I, responding to her, said this much: "In those words that praise my lady."

(7) Then she who spoke with me replied: "If you were speaking truly, those words that you uttered in making known your condition would have been proffered with some other meaning."

(8) Then I, reflecting on these words, feeling somewhat ashamed, left them and went along saying to myself: "Since there is so much blessedness in those words that praise my lady, why has any other sort of speaking (or writing) been mine?"

(9) And thus I resolved to take as matter of my speech always that which is praise of this most gentle one; and reflecting much about it, I seemed to have taken on a theme too elevated for me, so that I did not dare to begin; and thus I remained for several days with the desire to say (write) and the fear of beginning.

Chapter XIX: *First* Canzone *of Praise: "Ladies Who Have Intelligence of Love"*

(1) Avvenne poi che passando per uno cammino lungo lo quale sen gia uno rivo chiaro molto, a me giunse tanta volontade di dire, che io cominciai a pensare lo modo ch'io tenesse; e pensai che parlare di lei non si convenia che io facesse, se io non parlasse a donne in seconda persona, e non ad ogni donna, ma solamente a coloro che sono gentili e che non sono pure femmine.

(2) Allora dico che la mia lingua parlò quasi come per se stessa mossa, e disse: *Donne ch'avete intelletto d'amore.*

(3) Queste parole io ripuosi ne la mente con grande letizia, pensando di prenderle per mio cominciamento; onde poi, ritornato a la sopradetta cittade, pensando alquanti die, cominciai una canzone con questo cominciamento, ordinata nel modo che si vedrà di sotto ne la sua divisione. La canzone comincia: *Donne ch'avete.*

(4)
Donne ch'avete intelletto d'amore,
i' vo' con voi de la mia donna dire,
non perch'io creda sua laude finire,
ma ragionar per isfogar la mente.

(5)
Io dico che pensando il suo valore,
Amor sì dolce mi si fa sentire,
che s'io allora non perdessi ardire,
farei parlando innamorar la gente.

(6)
E io non vo' parlar sì altamente,
ch'io divenisse per temenza vile;
ma tratterò del suo stato gentile
a respetto di lei leggeramente,
donne e donzelle amorose, con vui,
ché non è cosa da parlarne altrui.

(1) Then it happened that passing down a path along which ran a very clear stream, so strong a will came over me to say (write) that I began to think about what means to use; and I thought that it was not appropriate for me to speak of her unless I spoke to ladies in the second person, and not to every lady but only to those who are gentle and not just women.

(2) Then I say that my tongue spoke, almost as if moved of its own accord and said: "*Donne ch'avete intelletto d'amore*: Ladies who have intelligence of love."

(3) I laid these words up in my memory with great joy, thinking I would take them for my beginning; wherefore, afterward, having returned to the above-mentioned city, reflecting for several days, I began a canzone with this beginning, ordered in the manner that will be seen below from its division. The canzone begins: "*Donne ch'avete*: Ladies who have."

(4)
Ladies who have intelligence of love,
I want to speak with you about my lady,
not because I believe I can exhaust her
      praise,
but to discharge my mind by speaking.

(5)
I say that when I think of her worth,
Love makes me feel such sweetness
that if I did not then cease to be bold,
my speaking would make people fall in
      love.

(6)
I do not want to speak so loftily
that, out of fear, I should become vile;
but I will speak of her graciousness
only lightly with respect to her being –
with you, ladies and loving maidens,
since it is not a thing to speak about with
      others.

Chapter XIX: (*cont.*)

(7)
Angelo clama in divino intelletto
e dice: «Sire, nel mondo si vede
maraviglia ne l'atto che procede
d'un'anima che 'nfin qua su risplende».
Lo cielo, che non have altro difetto
che d'aver lei, al suo segnor la chiede,
e ciascun santo ne grida merzede.

(8)
Sola Pietà nostra parte difende,
ché parla Dio, che di madonna intende:
«Diletti miei, or sofferite in pace
che vostra spene sia quanto me piace
là 'v' è alcun che perder lei s'attende,
e che dirà ne lo inferno: O mal nati,
io vidi la speranza de' beati».

(9)
Madonna è disiata in sommo cielo:
or voi di sua virtù farvi savere.
Dico, qual vuol gentil donna parere
vada con lei, che quando va per via,
gitta nei cor villani Amore un gelo,
per che onne lor pensero agghiaccia e pere;
e qual soffrisse di starla a vedere
diverria nobil cosa, o si morria.

(10)
E quando trova alcun che degno sia
di veder lei, quei prova sua vertute,
ché li avvien, ciò che li dona, in salute,
e sì l'umilia, ch'ogni offesa oblia.
Ancor l'ha Dio per maggior grazia dato
che non pò mal finir chi l'ha parlato.

(11)
Dice di lei Amor: «Cosa mortale
come esser pò sì adorna e sì pura?»
Poi la reguarda, e fra se stesso giura
che Dio ne 'ntenda di far cosa nova.
Color di perle ha quasi, in forma quale

(7)
An angel clamors in the divine intellect
and says: "Sir, in the world a marvel is seen
in the act that proceeds from a soul
who shines all the way up here on high."
Heaven, which has no other defect
but lack of her, requests her of its lord,
and every saint cries for this reward.

(8)
Pity alone defends our part,
so that God speaks, referring to my lady:
"My beloved, suffer now in peace
that your hope, for as long as it pleases me,
abide where someone is bound to lose her,
someone who will say in hell: O ill-born
  ones,
I saw the hope of the blessed."

(9)
My lady is desired in highest heaven:
now I want to make you know her virtue.
I say, whoever wants to appear a gentle
  lady
should go with her, since when she
  goes by,
Love throws a chill into uncouth hearts,
such that all their thoughts freeze and
  perish;
and anyone who could suffer to remain
  gazing at her
would become something noble, or else die.

(10)
And when she finds someone worthy
to look at her, he experiences her power,
which comes to him as given in her greeting,
and it so humbles him that every offense is
  forgotten.
Yet God has given a still greater grace:
that whoever has spoken with her cannot
  end badly.

(11)
Love says of her: "A mortal thing,
how can it be so lovely and so pure?"
Then he looks at her and to himself swears
that God intended to make something
  unique.

convene a donna aver, non for misura:
ella è quanto de ben pò far natura;
per essemplo di lei bieltà si prova.

(12)
De li occhi suoi, come ch'ella li mova,
escono spirti d'amore inflammati,
che feron li occhi a qual che allor la guati,
e passan sì che 'l cor ciascun retrova:
voi le vedete Amor pinto nel viso,
've non pote alcun mirarla fiso.

(13)
Canzone, io so che tu girai parlando
a donne assai, quand'io t'avrò avanzata.
Or t'ammonisco, perch'io t'ho allevata
per figliuola d'Amor giovane e piana,
che là 've giugni tu diche pregando:
«Insegnatemi gir, ch'io son mandata
a quella di cui laude so' adornata».

(14)
E se non vuoli andar sì come vana,
non restare ove sia gente villana:
ingegnati, se puoi, d'esser palese
solo con donne o con omo cortese,
che ti merranno là per via tostana.
Tu troverai Amor con esso lei;
raccomandami a lui come tu dei.

(15) Questa canzone, acciò che sia meglio
intesa, la dividerò più artificiosamente che
l'altre cose di sopra. E però prima ne fo tre
parti: la prima parte è proemio de le
sequenti parole; la seconda è lo intento
trattato; la terza è quasi una serviziale de le
precedenti parole. La seconda comincia
quivi: *Angelo clama*; la terza quivi:
Canzone, io so che.

(16) La prima parte si divide in quattro: ne
la prima dico a cu' io dicer voglio de la mia

She has the color of pearl in just the form
suited to a lady, not beyond measure.
She is all that nature can make well;
beauty proves itself by her example.

(12)
From her eyes, when she moves them,
issue flaming spirits of love
that wound the eyes of whoever then
    beholds her
and penetrate, so that each attains the heart:
you see Love painted on her face,
there where no one can keep a fixed gaze.

(13)
Canzone, I know that you will go about
    speaking
to many ladies, when I have sent you
    forth.
Now I admonish you, since I have
    raised you
as a daughter of Love, young and easy,
that wherever you wind up you say, praying:
"Show me where to go, since I am sent
to her with whose praise I am adorned."

(14)
And if you do not wish to go in vain,
do not remain where vulgar people are:
use your wit, if you can, to be plain
only to ladies or to courteous men,
who will lead you there by the quickest
    way.
You will find Love, and her with him:
commend me to him as you should.

(15) This canzone, in order that it may be
better understood, I will divide more
meticulously than the other compositions
above. And so I first distinguish three parts:
the first part is the proem for the words
following it; the second part is the theme
treated; the third part is like a servant to the
preceding words. The second begins here:
"*Angelo clama*: An angel clamors"; the third
here: "*Canzone, io so che*: Canzone, I know
that."

(16) The first part is divided into four: in
the first, I say to whom I wish to speak of

donna, e perché io voglio dire; ne la
seconda dico quale me pare avere a me
stesso quand'io penso lo suo valore,
e com'io direi s'io non perdessi
l'ardimento; ne la terza dico come credo
dire di lei, acciò ch'io non sia impedito da
viltà; ne la quarta, ridicendo anche a cui
ne intenda dire, dico la cagione per che
dico a loro. La seconda comincia quivi: *Io
dico*; la terza quivi: *E io non vo' parlar*; la
quarta: *donne e donzelle.*

(17) Poscia quando dico: *Angelo clama*,
comincio a trattare di questa donna.
E dividesi questa parte in due: ne la prima
dico che di lei si comprende in cielo; ne la
seconda dico che di lei si comprende in
terra, quivi: *Madonna è disiata.*

(18) Questa seconda parte si divide in due:
che ne la prima dico di lei quanto da la
parte de la nobilitade de la sua anima,
narrando alquanto de le sue vertudi
effettive che de la sua anima procedeano;
ne la seconda dico di lei quanto da la parte
de la nobilitade del suo corpo, narrando
alquanto de le sue bellezze, quivi: *Dice di
lei Amor.*

(19) Questa seconda parte si divide in
due; che ne la prima dico d'alquante
bellezze che sono secondo tutta la
persona; ne la seconda dico d'alquante
bellezze che sono secondo diterminata
parte de la persona, quivi: *De li occhi suoi.*

(20) Questa seconda parte si divide in due;
che ne l'una dico degli occhi, li quali sono
principio d'amore; ne la seconda dico de
la bocca, la quale è fine d'amore. E acciò
che quinci si lievi ogni vizioso pensiero,
ricordisi chi ci legge, che di sopra è scritto
che lo saluto di questa donna, lo quale era
de le operazioni de la bocca sua, fue fine de
li miei desiderii mentre ch'io lo potei
ricevere.

my lady and why I wish to speak; in
the second, I say what condition I seem to
be in when I think of her worth, and how
I would speak if I did not lose my ardor; in
the third, I say
how I believe I should speak in order not
to be impeded by timidity; in the fourth,
reiterating to whom I intend to speak, I say
the reason why I speak with them.
The second part begins with: "*Io dico*:
I say"; the third with: "*E io non vo' parlar*:
I would not speak"; the fourth: "*donne
e donzelle*: ladies and loving maidens."

(17) Then when I say: "*Angelo clama*: An
angel clamors," I begin to treat of this
lady. And this part divides in two: in the
first, I say what of her is understood in
heaven; in the second, I say what is
understood of her on earth, here:
"*Madonna è disiata*: My lady is desired."

(18) This second part is divided in two: in
the first, I speak of her with respect to the
nobility of her soul, narrating something of
the powers that effectively proceed from
her soul; in the second, I speak of her with
respect to the nobility of her body,
narrating something of its beauties, here:
"*Dice di lei Amor*: Love says of her."

(19) This second part is divided in two: in
the first, I speak of some beauties that are
in her whole person; in the second, I speak
of some beauties that are in certain parts
of her person, here: "*De li occhi suoi*: From
her eyes."

(20) This second part is divided in two: in
one, I speak of the eyes, which are the
beginning of love; in the second, of the
mouth, which is the end of love. And in
order that here every vicious thought be
removed, the one who reads is reminded
that it is written above that the greeting of
this lady, which was an operation of her
mouth, was the end of my desires while
I could receive it.

Chapter XIX: (*cont.*)

(21) Poscia quando dico: *Canzone, io so che tu*, aggiungo una stanza quasi come ancella de l'altre, ne la quale dico quello che di questa mia canzone desidero; e però che questa ultima parte è lieve a intendere, non mi travaglio di più divisioni.

(22) Dico bene che, a più aprire lo intendimento di questa canzone, si converrebbe usare di più minute divisioni; ma tuttavia chi non è di tanto ingegno che per queste che sono fatte la possa intendere, a me non dispiace se la mi lascia stare, ché certo io temo d'avere a troppi comunicato lo suo intendimento pur per queste divisioni che fatte sono, s'elli avvenisse che molti le potessero audire.

(21) Then where I say: "*Canzone, io so che tu*: Canzone, I know that you," I add a stanza as a handmaiden of the others in which I say what it is that I desire of my canzone; and since this last part is easy to understand, I will not take pains with more divisions.

(22) I know well that to open more the meaning of this canzone, more minute divisions would be necessary; nevertheless, I am not displeased that whoever does not have wits enough to understand from these that have been made should leave it be, since certainly I fear that I have communicated its meaning to too many by the divisions already made, if it should happen that many were able to hear it.

Chapter XX: *What Is Love? "Love and the Gentle Heart Are One Thing"*

(1) Appresso che questa canzone fue alquanto divolgata tra le genti, con ciò fosse cosa che alcuno amico l'udisse, volontade lo mosse a pregare me che io li dovesse dire che è Amore, avendo forse per l'udite parole speranza di me oltre che degna.

(2) Onde io, pensando che appresso di cotale trattato bello era trattare alquanto d'Amore, e pensando che l'amico era da servire, propuosi di dire parole ne le quali io trattassi d'Amore; e allora dissi questo sonetto, lo qual comincia: *Amore e 'l cor gentil.*

(3)
Amore e 'l cor gentil sono una cosa,
sì come il saggio in suo dittare pone,
e così esser l'un sanza l'altro osa
com'alma razional sanza ragione.

(1) After this canzone had become somewhat known among the people, it happened that a certain friend heard it and was moved to entreat me to say what Love is, conceiving perhaps from the words heard more hope in me than was merited.

(2) So, thinking that it would be a fine thing, after the previous theme, to treat something of Love, and thinking that the friend should be served, I resolved to say words in which I treated Love; and then I composed this sonnet, which begins: "*Amore e 'l cor gentil*: Love and the gentle heart."

(3)
Love and the gentle heart are one thing,
as the sage in his poem posits,
so that for one to be without the other
is like a rational soul without reason.

Chapter XX: (*cont.*)

(4)
Falli natura quand'è amorosa,
Amor per sire e 'l cor per sua magione,
dentro la qual dormendo si riposa
tal volta poca e tal lunga stagione.

(5)
Bieltate appare in saggia donna pui,
che piace a gli occhi sì, che dentro al core
nasce un disio de la cosa piacente;
e tanto dura talora in costui,
che fa svegliar lo spirito d'Amore.
E simil face in donna omo valente.

(6) Questo sonetto si divide in due parti:
ne la prima dico di lui in quanto è in
potenzia; ne la seconda dico di lui in
quanto di potenzia si riduce in atto. La
seconda comincia quivi: *Bieltate appare*.

(7) La prima si divide in due: ne la prima
dico in che suggetto sia questa potenzia; ne
la seconda dico sì come questo suggetto
e questa potenzia siano produtti in essere,
e come l'uno guarda l'altro come forma
materia.

(8) La seconda comincia quivi: *Falli
natura*. Poscia quando dico: *Bieltate
appare*, dico come questa potenzia si
riduce in atto; e prima come si riduce in
uomo, poi come si riduce in donna, quivi:
E simil face in donna.

(4)
Nature, when enamored, makes them both,
Love as lord and the heart for his house,
within which he reposes sleeping
sometimes a short while and sometimes long.

(5)
Beauty appears then in a sage lady,
so pleasant to the eyes, that inside the heart
a desire of the pleasing thing is born;
and it remains so long inside
until it arouses the spirit of Love.
And similarly on a lady works a valiant man.

(6) This sonnet is divided into two parts: in
the first, I speak of him [Love] as potential;
in the second, I speak of him as potential
realized in action. The second begins here:
"*Bieltate appare*: Beauty appears."

(7) The first is divided in two: in the first,
I say in what subject this potential inheres;
in the second, I say how this subject and this
potential are produced in being, and how
one relates to the other as form to matter.

(8) The second begins here: "*Falli natura*:
Nature takes." Afterwards, when I say:
"*Bieltate appare*," I say how this potential is
realized in action; and first how it is realized
in a man, then how it is realized in a lady,
here: "*E simil face in donna*: And similarly on
a lady."

Chapter XXI: *How Beatrice Awakens Love*

(1) Poscia che trattai d'Amore ne la
soprascritta rima, vennemi volontade di
volere dire anche, in loda di questa
gentilissima, parole, per le quali io
mostrasse come per lei si sveglia questo
Amore, e come non solamente si sveglia là

(1) After I had treated of Love in the rhyme
above, a will came to me to want to say also,
in praise of this most gentle one, words by
which I would show how this Love is
awoken through her, and how not only
where he already sleeps, but also where he is

ove dorme, ma là ove non è in potenzia,
ella, mirabilemente operando, lo fa venire.
E allora dissi questo sonetto, lo quale
comincia: *Ne li occhi porta.*

(2)
Ne li occhi porta la mia donna Amore,
per che si fa gentil ciò ch'ella mira;
ov'ella passa, ogn'om ver lei si gira,
e cui saluta fa tremar lo core,
sì che, bassando il viso, tutto smore,
e d'ogni suo difetto allor sospira:
fugge dinanzi a lei superbia ed ira.
Aiutatemi, donne, farle onore.

(3)
Ogne dolcezza, ogne pensero umile
nasce nel core a chi parlar la sente,
ond'è laudato chi prima la vide.

(4)
Quel ch'ella par quando un poco sorride,
non si pò dicer né tenere a mente,
sì è novo miracolo e gentile.

(5) Questo sonetto si ha tre parti: ne la
prima dico sì come questa donna riduce
questa potenzia in atto secondo la
nobilissima parte de li suoi occhi; e ne la
terza dico questo medesimo secondo la
nobilissima parte de la sua bocca; e intra
queste due parti è una particella, ch'è
quasi domandatrice d'aiuto a la
precedente parte e a la sequente,
e comincia quivi: *Aiutatemi, donne.* La
terza comincia quivi: *Ogne dolcezza.*

(6) La prima si divide in tre; che ne la
prima parte dico sì come virtuosamente
fae gentil tutto ciò che vede, e questo è
tanto a dire quanto inducere Amore in
potenzia là ove non è; ne la seconda dico
come reduce in atto Amore ne li cuori di
tutti coloro cui vede; ne la terza dico
quello che poi virtuosamente adopera ne'

not present potentially, she, by working
miraculously, makes him come. And then
I composed this sonnet, which begins: "*Ne
li occhi porta:* In her eyes . . . bears."

(2)
In her eyes, my lady bears Love,
by which whatever she sees is made noble;
where she passes, every man turns
     toward her,
and she make hearts tremble in those she
     greets;
so that, lowering their gaze, all cadaverous,
they sigh for all their defects:
pride and anger flee before her.
Help me, ladies, to pay her honor.

(3)
Every sweetness, every humble thought
is born in the heart of one who hears her
     speak:
therefore, whoever saw her first is lauded.

(4)
How she looks when she smiles a little
cannot be said nor held in mind,
so rare and noble a miracle it is.

(5) This sonnet has three parts: in the first,
I say how this lady realizes in action the
potential of the most noble feature, her
eyes; in the third, I say the same according
to the most noble feature, her mouth;
between these two parts there is a little part,
which asks for help from the preceding and
succeeding parts, and it begins here:
"*Aiutatemi, donne.* Help me, ladies." The
third begins here: "*Ogne dolcezza:* Every
sweetness."

(6) The first is divided into three; in the
first part, I say how powerfully she makes
noble all that she sees, and this is as much
as to say how she makes Love to exist
potentially where he is not; in the second,
I say how she realizes love in act in the
hearts of all who see her; in the third, I say
how powerfully she operates in their

loro cuori. La seconda comincia quivi: *ov'ella passa*; la terza quivi: *e cui saluta.*

hearts. The second begins here: "*ov'ella passa*: where she passes"; the third here: "*e cui saluta*: in those she greets."

(7) Poscia quando dico: *Aiutatemi, donne,* do a intendere a cui la mia intenzione è di parlare, chiamando le donne che m'aiutino onorare costei.

(7) Next, where I say "*Aiutatemi, donne*: Help me, ladies," I make known whom I intend to speak with, calling on ladies to help me pay honor to her.

(8) Poscia quando dico: *Ogne dolcezza,* dico quello medesimo che detto è ne la prima parte, secondo due atti de la sua bocca; l'uno de li quali è lo suo dolcissimo parlare, e l'altro lo suo mirabile riso; salvo che non dico di questo ultimo come adopera ne li cuori altrui, però che la memoria non puote ritenere lui né sua operazione.

(8) Then, where I say "*Ogne dolcezza*: Every sweetness," I say the same that is said in the first part, but according to the two acts of her mouth: one of which is her most sweet speech, and the other her marvelous smile; except that I do not say how the latter operates in the hearts of others because the memory cannot retain it, nor its operation.

Chapter XXII: *The Death of Beatrice's Father*

(1) Appresso ciò non molti dì passati, sì come piacque al glorioso sire lo quale non negoe la morte a sé, colui che era stato genitore di tanta maraviglia quanta si vedea ch'era questa nobilissima Beatrice, di questa vita uscendo, a la gloria etternale se ne gio veracemente.

(1) After not many days had passed, it pleased the glorious lord who did not deny death even to himself, that he who had been the father of so much marvel as was seen in this most noble Beatrice, leaving this life, truly went to eternal glory.

(2) Onde con ciò sia cosa che cotale partire sia doloroso a coloro che rimangono e sono stati amici di colui che se ne va; e nulla sia sì intima amistade come da buon padre a buon figliuolo e da buon figliuolo a buon padre; e questa donna fosse in altissimo grado di bontade, e lo suo padre, sì come da molti si crede e vero è, fosse bono in alto grado; manifesto è che questa donna fue amarissimamente piena di dolore.

(2) Since such a departure is sorrowful to those who remain and have been friends of the one who goes; and there is no more intimate friendship than that of good father to good son and of good son to good father; and this lady was of the highest degree of goodness, and her father, as is believed by many and is true, was good in high degree; it is evident that this lady was filled most bitterly with sorrow.

(3) E con ciò sia cosa che, secondo l'usanza de la sopradetta cittade, donne con donne e uomini con uomini s'adunino a cotale tristizia, molte donne s'adunaro colà dove questa Beatrice piangea pietosamente:

(3) And since following the custom of the above-mentioned city, women with women and men with men gathered in such sorrowing, many women gathered where this Beatrice was piteously weeping: so that

onde io veggendo ritornare alquante
donne da lei, udio dicere loro parole di
questa gentilissima, com'ella si lamentava;
tra le quali parole udio che diceano:
«Certo ella piange sì, che quale la mirasse
doverebbe morire di pietade».

(4) Allora trapassaro queste donne; e io
rimasi in tanta tristizia, che alcuna lagrima
talora bagnava la mia faccia, onde io mi
ricopria con porre le mani spesso a li miei
occhi; e se non fosse ch'io attendea audire
anche di lei, però ch'io era in luogo onde
se ne giano la maggiore parte di quelle
donne che da lei si partiano, io mi sarei
nascoso incontanente che le
lagrime m'aveano assalito.

(5) E però dimorando ancora nel
medesimo luogo, donne anche passaro
presso di me, le quali andavano
ragionando tra loro queste parole: «Chi
dee mai essere lieta di noi, che avemo
udita parlare questa donna così
pietosamente?».

(6) Appresso costoro passaro altre donne,
che veniano dicendo: «Questi ch'è qui
piange né più né meno come se l'avesse
veduta, come noi avemo». Altre dipoi
diceano di me: «Vedi questi che non pare
esso, tal è divenuto!».

(7) E così passando queste donne, udio
parole di lei e di me in questo modo che
detto è. Onde io poi, pensando, proposi
di dire parole, acciò che degnamente avea
cagione di dire, ne le quali parole io
conchiudesse tutto ciò che inteso avea da
queste donne; e però che volentieri l'averei
domandate se non mi fosse stata
riprensione, presi tanta matera di dire
come s'io l'avesse domandate ed
elle m'avessero risposto.

(8) E feci due sonetti; che nel primo
domando, in quello modo che voglia mi
giunse di domandare; ne l'altro dico la
loro risponsione, pigliando ciò ch'io udio
da loro sì come lo mi avessero detto

I, seeing some ladies return from her, heard
them say words of this most gentle one
about how she lamented; among which
words I heard them saying: "Surely, she
weeps so, that whoever saw her would die of
pity."

(4) Then those ladies passed by; and
I remained in such sorrow that some tears
sometimes bathed my face, whence I often
covered my eyes with my hands; and had
I not waited to hear more about her, since
I was in a place where the majority of those
women coming from her passed, I would
have hidden myself as soon as the tears had
assaulted me.

(5) So, while I remained still in the same
place, ladies who passed nearby me went
along saying among themselves these
words: "Who shall ever be happy again
among us, now that we have heard this lady
speak so piteously?"

(6) After these, other ladies passed, who
came along saying: "This man here weeps
neither more nor less than he would had he
seen her as we have." Others afterwards said
of me: "Look at this man who has become
such that he does not seem to be himself!"

(7) And so, with these ladies passing,
I heard words about her and about me in
the manner that has been said. Afterwards,
upon reflection, I resolved to write words,
since I had a worthy cause for it, in which
I would include all that I had heard from
these ladies; and since I would have
questioned them, had that not been
reprehensible, I conceived the matter just as
if I had asked them and they had
responded.

(8) And I made two sonnets; in the first, I ask
in that manner in which the will to question
came to me; in the other, I give their response,
taking that which I heard from them as if they
had said it responding to me. And the first

rispondendo. E comincia lo primo: *Voi che portate la sembianza umile*, e l'altro: *Se' tu colui c'hai trattato sovente.*

begins: "*Voi che portate la sembianza umile*: You who bear a humble look," and the other: "*Se' tu colui c'hai trattato sovente*: Are you he who has often treated."

(9)
Voi che portate la sembianza umile,
con li occhi bassi, mostrando dolore,
onde venite che 'l vostro colore
par divenuto de pietà simile?
Vedeste voi nostra donna gentile
bagnar nel viso suo di pianto Amore?
Ditelmi, donne, che 'l mi dice il core,
perch'io vi veggio andar sanz'atto vile.

(9)
You who bear a humble look,
with lowered eyes, displaying grief,
whence do you come that your color
seems to have become that of pity?
Have you seen our gentle lady
bathing her face with tears of Love?
Tell me, ladies, for so my heart tells me,
since I see you proceeding with no base act.

(10)
E se venite da tanta pietate,
piacciavi di restar qui meco alquanto,
e qual che sia di lei, nol mi celate.
Io veggio li occhi vostri c'hanno pianto,
e veggiovi tornar sì sfigurate,
che 'l cor mi triema di vederne tanto.

(10)
And if you come from so much sorrow,
may it please you to abide by me a moment,
and not to conceal from me how it goes
with her.
I see that your eyes have wept,
and I see you return so disfigured,
that my heart trembles to have seen so much.

(11) Questo sonetto si divide in due parti: ne la prima chiamo e domando queste donne se vegnono da lei, dicendo loro che io lo credo, però che tornano quasi ingentilite; ne la seconda le prego che mi dicano di lei. La seconda comincia quivi: *E se venite.*

(11) This sonnet is divided into two parts: in the first, I call and ask these ladies if they come from her, telling them that I believe they do, since they return as if ennobled; in the second, I beseech them to tell me of her. The second begins here: "*E se venite*: And if you come."

(12) Qui appresso è l'altro sonetto, sì come dinanzi avemo narrato.

(12) Here, following after, is the other sonnet, as we have mentioned above.

(13)
Se' tu colui c'hai trattato sovente
di nostra donna, sol parlando a nui?
Tu risomigli a la voce ben lui,
ma la figura ne par d'altra gente.

(13)
Are you he who has often treated
of our lady, speaking only with us?
You resemble him in voice,
but your face seems to be someone else's.

(14)
E perché piangi tu sì coralmente,
che fai di te pietà venire altrui?
Vedestù pianger lei, che tu non pui
punto celar la dolorosa mente?

(14)
And why do you weep so heart-rendingly
that you cause in others pity of yourself?
Did you see her weep, that you cannot
in the least conceal your sorrowing mind?

(15)
Lascia piangere noi e triste andare
(e fa peccato chi mai ne conforta),
che nel suo pianto l'udimmo parlare.

(15)
Let us weep and go sadly by
(and whoever should comfort us sins)
for we have heard her speak in her weeping.

Chapter XXII: (*cont.*)

(16)
Ell'ha nel viso la pietà sì scorta,
che qual l'avesse voluta mirare
sarebbe innanzi lei piangendo morta.

(17) Questo sonetto ha quattro parti,
secondo che quattro modi di parlare
ebbero in loro le donne per cui rispondo;
e però che sono di sopra assai manifesti,
non m'intrametto di narrare la sentenzia
de le parti, e però le distinguo solamente.
La seconda comincia quivi: *E perché
piangi*; la terza: *Lascia piangere noi*; la
quarta: *Ell'ha nel viso*.

(16)
She has pity so displayed in her face
that whoever had dared to look
would have died of weeping in front of her.

(17) This sonnet has four parts
corresponding to the four modes of speech
in the ladies for whom I speak; and since
they are made sufficiently manifest above,
I do not intervene to detail the meaning of
the parts, and so I simply distinguish them.
The second begins here: "*E perché piangi*:
And why do you weep"; la terza: "*Lascia
piangere noi*: Let us weep"; la quarta: "*Ell'ha
nel viso*: She has . . . in her face.*"

Chapter XXIII: *Dante's Delirious Premonition of Beatrice's Death (Second* Canzone*)*

(1) Appresso ciò per pochi dì avvenne che in
alcuna parte de la mia persona mi giunse
una dolorosa infermitade, onde io
continuamente soffersi per nove dì
amarissima pena; la quale mi condusse
a tanta debolezza, che me convenia stare
come coloro li quali non si possono
muovere.

(2) Io dico che ne lo nono giorno,
sentendome dolere quasi
intollerabilmente, a me giunse uno
pensero lo quale era de la mia donna.

(3) E quando ei pensato alquanto di lei, ed
io ritornai pensando a la mia debilitata vita;
e veggendo come leggiero era lo suo durare,
ancora che sana fosse, sì cominciai
a piangere fra me stesso di tanta miseria.
Onde, sospirando forte, dicea fra me
medesimo: «Di necessitade convene che la
gentilissima Beatrice alcuna volta si muoia».

(4) E però mi giunse uno sì forte
smarrimento, che chiusi li occhi
e cominciai a travagliare sì come farnetica

(1) A few days after this, it happened that in
part of my body a painful illness inflicted
me, from which I suffered continuously for
nine days a most bitter agony; which
brought me into such weakness that I was
constrained to stay like those who cannot
move.

(2) I say that on the ninth day, feeling
myself in almost intolerable pain, a thought
came to me that was about my lady.

(3) And when I had thought about her
a while, I returned to thinking of my
debilitated life; and seeing how fragile its
duration was, even when it was healthy,
I began to weep within myself over so much
misery. Then, sighing deeply, I said to
myself: "Of necessity, it must be that the
most gentle Beatrice will die some day."

(4) And thus I was overcome by such a
strong sense of lostness that I closed my eyes
and began to be travailed like a delirious

persona ed a imaginare in questo manner: che ne lo incominciamento de lo errare che fece la mia fantasia, apparvero a me certi visi di donne scapigliate, che mi diceano: «Tu pur morrai»; e poi, dopo queste donne, m'apparvero certi visi diversi e orribili a vedere, li quali mi diceano: «Tu se' morto».

(5) Così cominciando ad errare la mia fantasia, venni a quello ch'io non sapea ove io mi fosse; e vedere mi parea donne andare scapigliate piangendo per via, maravigliosamente triste; e pareami vedere lo sole oscurare, sì che le stelle si mostravano di colore ch'elle mi faceano giudicare che piangessero; e pareami che li uccelli volando per l'aria cadessero morti, e che fossero grandissimi tremuoti.

(6) E maravigliandomi in cotale fantasia, e paventando assai, imaginai alcuno amico che mi venisse a dire: «Or non sai? la tua mirabile donna è partita di questo secolo». Allora cominciai a piangere molto pietosamente; e non solamente piangea ne la imaginazione, ma piangea con li occhi, bagnandoli di vere lagrime.

(7) Io imaginava di guardare verso lo cielo, e pareami vedere moltitudine d'angeli li quali tornassero in suso, ed aveano dinanzi da loro una nebuletta bianchissima. A me parea che questi angeli cantassero gloriosamente, e le parole del loro canto mi parea udire che fossero queste: *Osanna in excelsis*; e altro non mi parea udire.

(8) Allora mi parea che lo cuore, ove era tanto amore, mi dicesse: «Vero è che morta giace la nostra donna». E per questo mi parea andare per vedere lo corpo ne lo quale era stata quella nobilissima e beata anima; e fue sì forte la erronea fantasia, che mi mostrò questa donna morta: e pareami

person and to imagine in this manner: in the beginning of the errancy of my fantasy, certain faces of women with disheveled hair appeared to me, who were saying to me: "You, too, will die." And then, after these women, certain faces, diverse and horrible to see, appeared to me, which were saying to me: "You are dead."

(5) With my fantasy thus beginning to stray, I came to the point where I did not know where I was; and I seemed to see disheveled women go weeping along the way, disturbingly sad; and I seemed to see the sun darken, so that the stars showed themselves to be of such color as made me judge that they were weeping; and it seemed to me that the birds flying in the air fell dead, and that there were enormous earthquakes.

(6) And astonished at such a fantasy, and very frightened, I imagined a friend who came to me to say: "Now, don't you know? Your miraculous lady is departed out of this world." Then I began to weep most piteously; and I wept not only in my imagination but also with my eyes, bathing them with true tears.

(7) I imagined that I was looking toward the heaven, and I seemed to see a multitude of angels who were returning above, and they had in front of them a little cloud of whitest white. And it appeared to me that these angels were singing gloriously, and the words of their song that I seemed to hear were these: "*Osanna in excelsis*: Hosanna in the highest"; and more than this I seemed not to hear.

(8) Then it seemed to me that the heart, where there was so much love, said to me: "True it is that our lady lies dead." And at that I seemed to go to see the body in which that most noble and blessed soul had been; and my erring fantasy was so strong that it showed me this lady dead; and it seemed to me that women covered her, that is, her

Chapter XXIII: (*cont.*)

che donne la covrissero, cioè la sua testa, con uno bianco velo; e pareami che la sua faccia avesse tanto aspetto d'umilitade, che parea che dicesse: «Io sono a vedere lo principio de la pace».

(9) In questa imaginazione mi giunse tanta umilitade per vedere lei, che io chiamava la Morte, e dicea: «Dolcissima Morte, vieni a me, e non m'essere villana, però che tu dei essere gentile, in tal parte se' stata! Or vieni a me, che molto ti disidero; e tu lo vedi, ché io porto già lo tuo colore».

(10) E quando io avea veduto compiere tutti li dolorosi mestieri che a le corpora de li morti s'usano di fare, mi parea tornare ne la mia camera, e quivi mi parea guardare verso lo cielo; e sì forte era la mia imaginazione, che piangendo incominciai a dire con verace voce: «Oi anima bellissima, come è beato colui che ti vede!».

(11) E dicendo io queste parole con doloroso singulto di pianto, e chiamando la Morte che venisse a me, una donna giovane e gentile, la quale era lungo lo mio letto, credendo che lo mio piangere e le mie parole fossero solamente per lo dolore de la mia infermitade, con grande paura cominciò a piangere.

(12) Onde altre donne che per la camera erano s'accorsero di me, che io piangea, per lo pianto che vedeano fare a questa; onde faccendo lei partire da me, la quale era meco di propinquissima sanguinitade congiunta, elle si trassero verso me per isvegliarmi, credendo che io sognasse, e diceanmi: «Non dormire più», e «Non ti sconfortare».

(13) E parlandomi così, sì mi cessò la forte fantasia entro in quello punto ch'io volea dire: «O Beatrice, benedetta sie tu»; e già detto avea «O Beatrice», quando riscotendomi apersi li occhi, e vidi che io era ingannato. E con tutto che io chiamasse questo nome, la mia voce era sì rotta dal singulto del piangere, che queste donne

head, with a white veil; and it seemed to me that her face had such a look of humility that it seemed to say: "I am looking at the beginning of all peace."

(9) In this imagining, I was overcome by such a sense of humility, seeing her, that I called on Death and said: "Sweetest Death, come to me, do not be mean to me, since you must be gentle, having been in such a place! Now come to me, who desire you greatly; you can see that I already bear your color."

(10) And when I had seen the sorrowful duties that are customarily paid to the bodies of the dead accomplished, I seemed to return to my chamber, and there I seemed to look toward the heaven; and my imagination was so strong, that, weeping, I began to say with a real voice: "O most beautiful soul, how blessed is he who sees you!"

(11) And while I was saying these words in a painful sob of tears, and calling on Death to come to me, a young and gentle lady, who was at my bedside, believing that my weeping and my words were only because of the pain of my infirmity, began to weep with great fear.

(12) Whereby other ladies who were about in the room took notice of me and my weeping because of the weeping that they saw in her; so that making her, who was related to me by closest consanguinity, leave me, they drew near me to wake me, believing that I was dreaming, and said to me: "Sleep no more," and "Do not be troubled."

(13) And by their speaking thus to me, the powerful fantasy ceased in me right at the point where I wanted to say: "O Beatrice, you are blessed"; and I had already said "O Beatrice," when, with a start, I opened my eyes and saw that I was deceived. And although I called this name, my voice was so broken by the sob of my weeping that, in

non mi pottero intendere, secondo il mio parere; e avvegna che io vergognasse molto, tuttavia per alcuno ammonimento d'Amore mi rivolsi a loro.

(14) E quando mi videro, cominciaro a dire: «Questi pare morto», e a dire tra loro: «Proccuriamo di confortarlo»; onde molte parole mi diceano da confortarmi, e talora mi domandavano di che io avesse avuto paura.

(15) Onde io, essendo alquanto riconfortato, e conosciuto lo fallace imaginare, rispuosi a loro: «Io vi diroe quello ch'i' hoe avuto». Allora, cominciandomi dal principio infino a la fine, dissi loro quello che veduto avea, tacendo lo nome di questa gentilissima.

(16) Onde poi, sanato di questa infermitade, propuosi di dire parole di questo che m'era addivenuto, però che mi parea che fosse amorosa cosa dire; e però ne dissi questa canzone: *Donna pietosa e di novella etate*, ordinata sì come manifesta la infrascritta divisione.

(17)
Donna pietosa e di novella etate,
adorna assai di gentilezze umane,
ch'era là 'v'io chiamava spesso Morte,
veggendo li occhi miei pien di pietate,
e ascoltando le parole vane,
si mosse con paura a pianger forte.

(18)
E altre donne, che si fuoro accorte
di me per quella che meco piangia,
fecer lei partir via,
e appressarsi per farmi sentire.
Qual dicea: «Non dormire»,
e qual dicea: «Perché sì ti sconforte?»
Allor lassai la nova fantasia,
chiamando il nome de la donna mia.

(19)
Era la voce mia sì dolorosa
e rotta sì da l'angoscia del pianto,
ch'io solo intesi il nome nel mio core;

my opinion, the ladies were not able to understand me; and although I was very ashamed, nevertheless, following Love's admonition, I turned toward them.

(14) And when they saw me, they began to say, "This man appears to be dead" and to say among themselves: "Let us undertake to comfort him"; whereupon they said many things to comfort me, and at times they asked me what had so frightened me.

(15) Whence I, being somewhat comforted and aware of my false imagining, responded to them: "I will tell you what I had." Then, from the beginning to the end, I told them what I had seen, keeping silent the name of this most gentle one.

(16) Afterward, being recovered from this illness, I resolved to compose words about what had happened to me, since it seemed to me to be a love-ly (amorous) thing to hear; and so I composed this canzone: "*Donna pietosa e di novella etate*: A lady, compassionate and young," ordered as the division below makes manifest.

(17)
A lady, compassionate and young,
well-endowed with human gentleness,
who was where I often called on death,
seeing my eyes full of pity
and hearing my vain words,
was moved by fear to weep aloud.

(18)
And other ladies, who became aware
of me because of her weeping with me,
made her go away
and gathered round to rouse me to awareness.
One said: "Do not sleep,"
and one said: "Why are you so troubled?"
Then I left off my strange fantasy,
calling out the name of my lady.

(19)
My voice was so tormented
and so broken by my anguished weeping,
that I alone heard the name in my heart;

Chapter XXIII: (*cont.*)

e con tutta la vista vergognosa
ch'era nel viso mio giunta cotanto,
mi fece verso lor volgere Amore.

(20)
Elli era tale a veder mio colore,
che facea ragionar di morte altrui:
«Deh, consoliam costui»
pregava l'una l'altra umilemente;
e dicevan sovente:
«Che vedestù, che tu non hai valore?»
E quando un poco confortato fui,
io dissi: «Donne, dicerollo a vui.

(21)
Mentr'io pensava la mia frale vita,
e vedea 'l suo durar com'è leggiero,
piansemi Amor nel core, ove dimora;
per che l'anima mia fu sì smarrita,
che sospirando dicea nel pensero:
– Ben converrà che la mia donna mora –.

(22)
Io presi tanto smarrimento allora,
ch'io chiusi li occhi vilmente gravati,
e furon sì smagati
li spirti miei, che ciascun giva errando;
e poscia imaginando,
di caunoscenza e di verità fora,
visi di donne m'apparver crucciati,
che mi dicean pur: – Morra'ti, morra'ti –.

(23)
Poi vidi cose dubitose molte,
nel vano imaginar ov'io entrai;
ed esser mi parea non so in qual loco,
e veder donne andar per via disciolte,
qual lagrimando, e qual traendo guai,
che di tristizia saettavan foco.

(24)
Poi mi parve vedere a poco a poco
turbar lo sole e apparir la stella,
e pianger elli ed ella;
cader li augelli volando per l'are,
e la terra tremare;
ed omo apparve scolorito e fioco,
dicendomi: – Che fai?

and in spite of the shameful look
that was so evident in my face,
Love made me turn toward them.

(20)
They saw my color to be such
that it made them talk of someone's death:
"Well, let's try to console him"
the one urged the other humbly;
and often they said:
"What did you see, that has shattered you?"
And when I was somewhat comforted,
I said: "Ladies, I will tell you.

(21)
While I was reflecting on my frail life,
and seeing how fleeting its duration is,
Love wept within my heart, where he dwells;
such that my spirit was so confounded,
that, sighing, it said in thought:
'Surely, my lady will have to die.'

(22)
Then I was beset by such distress
that I closed my vilely burdened eyes,
and my spirits were so confounded
that each one wandered aimlessly;
and then, in imagining,
outside of knowledge and truth,
faces of women appeared to me distraught,
which also said to me: 'You will die, you
        will die.'

(23)
Then I saw many doubtful things,
in the vain imagining into which I entered;
and I seemed to be I know not where,
and to see disheveled women going their
        way, some weeping,
some wailing in grief,
who shot forth fiery arrows of sadness.

(24)
Then I seemed to see little by little
the sun grow dim and the star appear,
and the one and the others weep;
the birds flying through the air fell down,
the earth trembled;
and a man appeared, pale and hoarse,
saying to me: 'What are you doing?

Non sai novella?
morta è la donna tua, ch'era sì bella –.

(25)
Levava li occhi miei bagnati in pianti,
e vedea, che parean pioggia di manna,
li angeli che tornavan suso in cielo,
e una nuvoletta avean davanti,
dopo la qual gridavan tutti: *Osanna*;
e s'altro avesser detto, a voi dire'lo.

(26)
Allor diceva Amor: – Più nol ti celo;
vieni a veder nostra donna che giace –.
Lo imaginar fallace
mi condusse a veder madonna morta;
e quand'io l'avea scorta,
vedea che donne la covrian d'un velo;
ed avea seco umilità verace,
che parea che dicesse: – Io sono in pace –.

(27)
Io divenia nel dolor sì umile,
veggendo in lei tanta umiltà formata,
ch'io dicea: – Morte, assai dolce ti tegno;
tu dei omai esser cosa gentile,
poi che tu se' ne la mia donna stata,
e dei aver pietate e non disdegno.
Vedi che sì desideroso vegno
d'esser de' tuoi, ch'io ti somiglio in fede.
Vieni, ché 'l cor te chiede.–

(28)
Poi mi partia, consumato ogne duolo;
e quand'io era solo,
dicea, guardando verso l'alto regno:
– Beato, anima bella, chi te vede! –
Voi mi chiamaste allor, vostra merzede.»

(29) Questa canzone ha due parti: ne la
prima dico, parlando a indiffinita
persona, come io fui levato d'una vana
fantasia da certe donne, e come promisi
loro di dirla; ne la seconda dico come io
dissi a loro. La seconda comincia quivi:
Mentr'io pensava.

Do you not know the news?
She is dead, your lady, who was so lovely.'

(25)
I raised my eyes bathed in tears
and saw, appearing like a rain of manna,
angels returning to heaven above,
and a little cloud going before them,
after which they all cried out: 'Hosanna';
and if they had said more, I would tell you.

(26)
Then Love said: 'I will no longer conceal it
    from you;
come and see our lady lying.'
The fallacious imagining
led me to see my lady dead;
and when I had seen her,
I saw the ladies covering her with a veil;
and she had true humility about her,
which seemed to say: 'I am in peace.'

(27)
I became so humble in my grief,
seeing so much humility displayed in her,
that I said: 'Death, I hold you for exceedingly
sweet; you must now be a gentle thing,
since you have been in my lady,
and must have pity and not disdain.
See how I come, desirous to be one of
yours, since I truly resemble you.
Come, since my heart asks for you.'

(28)
Then I left, all mourning being accomplished;
and when I was alone,
I said, looking toward the high kingdom:
'Lovely soul, blessed is the one who
    sees you!'
Then you (ladies) called me, by your
    mercy."

(29) This canzone has two parts: in the first,
I say, speaking to an unspecified person,
how I was disabused of a vain fantasy by
certain ladies, and how I promised to tell
them of it; in the second, I say what I told
them. The second begins here: "*Mentr'io
pensava*: When I was reflecting."

Chapter XXIII: (*cont.*)

(30) La prima parte si divide in due: ne la prima dico quello che certe donne, e che una sola, dissero e fecero per la mia fantasia quanto è dinanzi che io fossi tornato in verace condizione; ne la seconda dico quello che queste donne mi dissero poi che io lasciai questo farneticare; e comincia questa parte quivi: *Era la voce mia.*

(31) Poscia quando dico: *Mentr'io pensava*, dico come io dissi loro questa mia imaginazione. Ed intorno a ciò foe due parti: ne la prima dico per ordine questa imaginazione; ne la seconda, dicendo a che ora mi chiamaro, le ringrazio chiusamente; e comincia quivi questa parte: *Voi mi chiamaste.*

(30) The first part is divided in two: in the first, I say what certain ladies, and particularly one, because of my delirium, said and did before I returned to awareness of reality; in the second, I say what the ladies said to me after I came out of my hallucinations; and this part begins here: "*Era la voce mia*: My voice was."

(31) Then when I say: "*Mentr'io pensava*: While I was reflecting," I say how I told them my imagining. And I do so in two parts: in the first, I recount this imagining in order; in the second, saying at what moment they called to me, I thank the ladies in a covert way; and this part begins here: "*Voi mi chiamaste*: Then you called me."

Chapter XXIV: *Allegorical Procession Featuring Giovanna and Beatrice*

(1) Appresso questa vana imaginazione, avvenne uno die che, sedendo io pensoso in alcuna parte, ed io mi sentio cominciare un tremuoto nel cuore, così come se io fosse stato presente a questa donna.

(2) Allora dico che mi giunse una imaginazione d'Amore; che mi parve vederlo venire da quella parte ove la mia donna stava, e pareami che lietamente mi dicesse nel cor mio: «Pensa di benedicere lo dì che io ti presi, però che tu lo dei fare». E certo me parea avere lo cuore sì lieto, che me non parea che fosse lo mio cuore, per la sua nuova condizione.

(3) E poco dopo queste parole, che lo cuore mi disse con la lingua d'Amore, io vidi venire verso me una gentile donna, la quale era di famosa bieltade, e fue già molto donna di questo primo mio amico. E lo nome di questa donna era Giovanna,

(1) After this vain imagining, it came to pass one day that, sitting somewhere deep in thought, I felt a tremor begin in my heart, as if I were in the presence of that lady.

(2) Then I say that an imagination came to me of Love; I seemed to see him come from that part where my lady was, and he seemed joyfully to say to me in my heart: "Think to bless the day on which I took you captive, since you ought to do so." And certainly I seemed to have a heart so happy that it seemed not to be my heart, so new was its condition.

(3) And a little after these words, which my heart spoke in the language of Love, I saw coming toward me a gentle lady, who was famous for her beauty, and who had long been the lady of that best friend of mine. And the name of this lady was

salvo che per la sua bieltade, secondo che altri crede, imposto l'era nome Primavera; e così era chiamata. E appresso lei, guardando, vidi venire la mirabile Beatrice.

(4) Queste donne andaro presso di me così l'una appresso l'altra, e parve che Amore mi parlasse nel cuore, e dicesse: «Quella prima è nominata Primavera solo per questa venuta d'oggi; ché io mossi lo imponitore del nome a chiamarla così Primavera, cioè prima verrà lo die che Beatrice si mosterrà dopo la imaginazione del suo fedele. E se anche vogli considerare lo primo nome suo, tanto è quanto dire 'prima verrà', però che lo suo nome Giovanna è da quello Giovanni lo quale precedette la verace luce, dicendo: 'Ego vox clamantis in deserto: parate viam Domini'».

(5) Ed anche mi parve che mi dicesse, dopo, queste parole: «E chi volesse sottilmente considerare, quella Beatrice chiamerebbe Amore per molta simiglianza che ha meco».

(6) Onde io poi, ripensando, propuosi di scrivere per rima a lo mio primo amico (tacendomi certe parole le quali pareano da tacere), credendo io che ancor lo suo cuore mirasse la bieltade di questa Primavera gentile; e dissi questo sonetto, lo quale comincia: *Io mi senti' svegliar.*

(7)
Io mi senti' svegliar dentro a lo core
un spirito amoroso che dormia:
e poi vidi venir da lungi Amore
allegro sì, che appena il conoscia,
dicendo: «Or pensa pur di farmi onore»;
e 'n ciascuna parola sua ridia.

Giovanna, except that because of her beauty, as people believe, she was given the name Primavera (Spring); and was so called. And coming after her, as I watched, I saw the miraculous Beatrice.

(4) These ladies passed close by me one after the other and it seemed that Love spoke to me in my heart and said: "That first one is named Primavera only in view of her coming today; for I moved the imposer of the name to call her thus, Primavera, that is, 'will come first' ('prima verrà') on the day that Beatrice will show herself after the imagination of her faithful one. And if you want to consider also her first name, it says as much as 'will come first' because her name Giovanna is from Giovanni (John), who preceded the true light, saying 'Ego vox clamantis in deserto: parate viam Domini': 'I am a voice of one crying in the wilderness: prepare ye the way of the Lord.'"

(5) And it also seemed to me that afterwards he said these words to me: "And who would consider subtly, would call that Beatrice Love for the great similarity she has with me."

(6) Wherefore, reflecting more, I resolved to write in rhyme to my best friend (holding back certain words which it seemed should be held back), believing that his heart still gazed on the beauty of that gentle Primavera; and I composed this sonnet, which begins: "*Io mi senti' svegliar:* I felt awakening within."

(7)
I felt awakening within my heart
an amorous spirit that was sleeping:
and then I saw Love come from afar
so joyful that I hardly recognized him,
saying: "Now think only of honoring me";
and in every word of his he smiled.

Chapter XXIV: (*cont.*)

(8)
E poco stando meco il mio segnore,
guardando in quella parte onde venia,
io vidi monna Vanna e monna Bice
venire inver lo loco là 'v'io era,
l'una appresso de l'altra maraviglia;

(9)
e sì come la mente mi ridice,
Amor mi disse: «Quell'è Primavera,
e quell'ha nome Amor, sì mi somiglia».

(10) Questo sonetto ha molte parti: la
prima delle quali dice come io mi senti'
svegliare lo tremore usato nel cuore,
e come parve che Amore m'apparisse
allegro nel mio cuore da lunga parte; la
seconda dice come me parea che Amore
mi dicesse nel mio cuore, e quale mi parea;
la terza dice come, poi che questi fue
alquanto stato meco cotale, io vidi e udio
certe cose. La seconda parte comincia
quivi: *dicendo: Or pensa*; la terza quivi:
E poco stando.

(11) La terza parte si divide in due: ne la
prima dico quello che io vidi; ne la
seconda dico quello che io udio. La
seconda comincia quivi: *Amor mi disse*.

(8)
And while my lord stayed briefly with me,
I, looking to that part whence he had come,
saw lady Vanna and lady Bice
come toward the place where I was,
the one following the other miracle;

(9)
and as my memory re-tells it to me,
Love told me: "That is Primavera (Spring),
and this other so resembles me that she is
named Love."

(10) This sonnet has many parts: the first
of which says how I felt the usual tremor
wakened in my heart and how it seemed
that Love appeared to me in my heart joyful
from afar; the second says how it seemed to
me that Love spoke to me in my heart and
how he appeared to me; the third says how,
after he had been with me a while, I saw and
heard certain things. The second part
begins here: "*dicendo: Or pensa*: saying:
Now think"; the third here: "*E poco stando*:
And while."

(11) The third part divides into two: in the
first, I say that which I saw; in the second,
I say that which I heard. The second begins
here: "*Amor mi disse*: Love told me."

Chapter XXV: *Philosophical Justification of Treating Love Rhetorically as a Substance*

(1) Potrebbe qui dubitare persona degna
da dichiararle onne dubitazione, e dubitare
potrebbe di ciò, che io dico d'Amore come
se fosse una cosa per sé, e non solamente
sustanzia intelligente, ma sì come fosse
sustanzia corporale: la quale cosa, secondo
la veritate, è falsa; ché Amore non è per sé sì
come sustanzia, ma è uno accidente in
sustanzia.

(1) At this point, a person worthy of having
every doubt clarified might have a doubt
about my speaking of Love as if it were
a thing on its own and not only an intelligent
substance but also a corporeal substance;
which is clearly false; since Love is not in itself
a substance but rather an accident in
a substance.

(2) E che io dica di lui come se fosse corpo, ancora sì come se fosse uomo, appare per tre cose che dico di lui. Dico che lo vidi venire; onde, con ciò sia cosa che venire dica moto locale, e localmente mobile per sé, secondo lo Filosofo, sia solamente corpo, appare che io ponga Amore essere corpo. Dico anche di lui che ridea, e anche che parlava; le quali cose paiono essere proprie de l'uomo, e spezialmente essere risibile; e però appare ch'io ponga lui essere uomo.

(3) A cotale cosa dichiarare, secondo che è buono a presente, prima è da intendere che anticamente non erano dicitori d'amore in lingua volgare, anzi erano dicitori d'amore certi poete in lingua latina; tra noi dico, avvegna forse che tra altra gente addivenisse, e addivegna ancora, sì come in Grecia, non volgari ma litterati poete queste cose trattavano.

(4) E non è molto numero d'anni passati, che appariro prima questi poete volgari; ché dire per rima in volgare tanto è quanto dire per versi in latino, secondo alcuna proporzione. E segno che sia picciolo tempo, è che se volemo cercare in lingua d'*oco* e in quella di *sì*, noi non troviamo cose dette anzi lo presente tempo per cento e cinquanta anni.

(5) E la cagione per che alquanti grossi ebbero fama di sapere dire, è che quasi fuoro li primi che dissero in lingua di *sì*.

(6) E lo primo che cominciò a dire sì come poeta volgare, si mosse però che volle fare intendere le sue parole a donna, a la quale era malagevole d'intendere li versi latini. E questo è contra coloro che rimano sopra altra matera che amorosa, con ciò sia cosa che cotale modo di parlare fosse dal principio trovato per dire d'amore.

(2) And that I speak of Love as if it were a body and, furthermore, as if it were a man, appears from three things that I say about it. I say that I saw him approaching; and since coming entails locomotion, and since according to the Philosopher only a body is in itself locally mobile, it appears that I posit Love as a body. I also say of Love that it laughs and also that it speaks, which things appear to be proper to humans, especially being capable of laughing; and thus I appear to make him human.

(3) To clarify this matter as is fitting at present, first it is necessary to understand that anciently there were no versifiers of love in the vulgar tongue; instead, certain poets in the Latin language wrote love poetry; among us, I say – although perhaps among other peoples it happened and still happens, as in Greece – not vernacular but literary poets treated these matters.

(4) And not many years ago the first of these vernacular poets appeared; I say "poets," since to compose rhymes in the vernacular is comparable to composing verses in Latin, keeping due proportions. And a sign that this happened not long ago can be found in the language of *oc* and in that of *sì*, where we find no such poetry before the present time more than a hundred and fifty years.

(5) And the reason that certain uncouth individuals were famous for knowing how to versify is that they were practically the first to compose in the language that uses *sì*.

(6) And the first who began to write as a vernacular poet was motivated by the desire to make his words understood by a lady, for whom Latin verses were difficult. And this is contrary to those who rhyme about other than amorous subjects, since such a mode of composition was from the first found for treating of love.

(7) Onde, con ciò sia cosa che a li poete sia conceduta maggiore licenza di parlare che a li prosaici dittatori, e questi dicitori per rima non siano altro che poete volgari, degno e ragionevole è che a loro sia maggiore licenzia largita di parlare che a li altri parlatori volgari: onde, se alcuna figura o colore rettorico è conceduto a li poete, conceduto è a li rimatori.

(8) Dunque, se noi vedemo che li poete hanno parlato a le cose inanimate, sì come se avessero senso e ragione, e fattele parlare insieme; e non solamente cose vere, ma cose non vere, cioè che detto hanno, di cose le quali non sono, che parlano, e detto che molti accidenti parlano, sì come se fossero sustanzie e uomini; degno è lo dicitore per rima di fare lo somigliante, ma non sanza ragione alcuna, ma con ragione la quale poi sia possibile d'aprire per prosa.

(9) Che li poete abbiano così parlato come detto è, appare per Virgilio; lo quale dice che Iuno, cioè una dea nemica de li Troiani, parloe ad Eolo, segnore de li venti, quivi nel primo de lo Eneida: *Eole, nanque tibi*, e che questo segnore le rispuose, quivi: *Tuus, o regina, quid optes explorare labor; michi iussa capessere fas est*. Per questo medesimo poeta parla la cosa che non è animata a le cose animate, nel terzo de lo Eneida, quivi: *Dardanide duri*. Per Lucano parla la cosa animata a la cosa inanimata, quivi: *Multum, Roma, tamen debes civilibus armis*. Per Orazio parla l'uomo a la scienzia medesima sì come ad altra persona; e non solamente sono parole d'Orazio, ma dicele quasi recitando lo modo del buono Omero, quivi ne la sua Poetria: *Dic michi, Musa, virum*. Per Ovidio parla Amore, sì come se fosse persona umana, ne lo principio de lo libro c'ha nome Libro di Remedio d'Amore, quivi: *Bella michi, video, bella parantur, ait*. E per questo puote essere manifesto a chi dubita in alcuna parte di questo mio libello.

(7) Thus, since greater license is granted to poets than to prose writers, and since those who speak in rhyme are nothing other than vernacular poets, it is worthy and reasonable that greater license to compose be granted to them than to other vernacular writers: so that, if any figure or rhetorical color is allowed to the (Latin) poets, it should be allowed also to (vernacular) rhymers.

(8) Therefore, if we see that the poets have addressed inanimate things as if they had sense and reason, and have made them talk to one another; and have done so not only with real things but also with unreal ones, so that they have said of things that are not that they speak, and have said that many accidents speak as if they were substances and humans; worthy is the composer in rhyme to do the like, yet not without some reason, but only with a rational intention that can then be opened up in prose.

(9) That the poets have spoken as stated here is apparent from Virgil, who says of Juno, a goddess inimical to the Trojans, that she spoke to Aeolus, lord of the winds, in the first book of the *Aeneid*: "*Eole, nanque tibi*: For to you, Aeolus," and that this lord responded to her thus: "*Tuus, o regina, quid optes explorare labor; michi iussa capessere fas est*: Your work, o queen, is to discover what you wish; my duty is to execute your commands." Through this same poet an inanimate thing (the oracle of Apollo) speaks to animate things in the third book of the *Aeneid*, here: "*Dardanide duri*: You hard Trojans." In Lucan, an animate thing speaks to an inanimate thing, here: "*Multum, Roma, tamen debes civilibus armis*: Much you owe, Rome, nevertheless to civil wars." In Horace, a man speaks to his own poetic faculty as if to another person; and not only are they Horace's words, but he utters them as if reciting in the manner of the good Homer, here in his *Ars poetica*: "*Dic michi, Musa, virum*: Tell me, Muse, of the man." In

Ovid, Love speaks as if it were a human person, at the beginning of the book called *The Book of the Remedy of Love,* here: "*Bella michi, video, bella parantur, ait:* Wars, I see, wars are being prepared against me, he says." And this should make things plain for whoever doubts concerning any part of my little book.

(10) E acciò che non ne pigli alcuna baldanza persona grossa, dico che né li poete parlavano così sanza ragione, né quelli che rimano deono parlare così non avendo alcuno ragionamento in loro di quello che dicono; però che grande vergogna sarebbe a colui che rimasse cose sotto vesta di figura o di colore rettorico, e poscia, domandato, non sapesse denudare le sue parole da cotale vesta, in guisa che avessero verace intendimento. E questo mio primo amico e io ne sapemo bene di quelli che così rimano stoltamente.

(10) So that an ignorant person not be emboldened, I say that the (Latin) poets did not speak without reason, nor should those who compose (vernacular) rhymes speak without having any justification of their own for what they speak; for great would be the shame on him who should rhyme about things with figures of speech and rhetorical colors if, when asked, he should not then be able to strip his words of that garment so as to show their true meaning. This best friend of mine and I know well of some who rhyme thus stupidly.

Chapter XXVI: *Height of Praise Poetry – "Tanto Gentile e Tanto Onesta Pare"*

(1) Questa gentilissima donna, di cui ragionato è ne le precedenti parole, venne in tanta grazia de le genti, che quando passava per via, le persone correano per vedere lei; onde mirabile letizia me ne giungea. E quando ella fosse presso d'alcuno, tanta onestade giungea nel cuore di quello, che non ardia di levare li occhi, né di rispondere a lo suo saluto; e di questo molti, sì come esperti, mi potrebbero testimoniare a chi non lo credesse.

(1) This most gentle lady, of whom the preceding words have spoken, came into such favor among the folk that when she passed by people ran to see her; which brought marvelous joy to me. And when she was near to anyone, so much purity entered their heart that they did not dare to raise their eyes, nor to respond to her greeting; and many, having experienced this, could testify to whoever did not believe it.

(2) Ella coronata e vestita d'umilitade s'andava, nulla gloria mostrando di ciò ch'ella vedea e udia. Diceano molti, poi che passata era: «Questa non è femmina, anzi è uno de li bellissimi angeli del cielo».

(2) She went along crowned and clothed in humility, manifesting no conceit from what she saw and heard. Many said, after she had passed by: "This was not a woman but rather one of the most beautiful angels

Chapter XXVI: (*cont.*)

E altri diceano: «Questa è una maraviglia; che benedetto sia lo Segnore, che sì mirabilemente sae adoperare!».

(3) Io dico ch'ella si mostrava sì gentile e sì piena di tutti li piaceri, che quelli che la miravano comprendeano in loro una dolcezza onesta e soave, tanto che ridicere non lo sapeano; né alcuno era lo quale potesse mirare lei, che nel principio nol convenisse sospirare.

(4) Queste e più mirabili cose da lei procedeano virtuosamente: onde io pensando a ciò, volendo ripigliare lo stilo de la sua loda, propuosi di dicere parole, ne le quali io dessi ad intendere de le sue mirabili ed eccellenti operazioni; acciò che non pur coloro che la poteano sensibilemente vedere, ma li altri sappiano di lei quello che le parole ne possono fare intendere. Allora dissi questo sonetto, lo quale comincia: *Tanto gentile*.

(5)
Tanto gentile e tanto onesta pare
la donna mia quand'ella altrui saluta,
ch'ogne lingua deven tremando muta,
e li occhi no l'ardiscon di guardare.

(6)
Ella si va, sentendosi laudare,
benignamente d'umiltà vestuta;
e par che sia una cosa venuta
da cielo in terra a miracol mostrare.

(7)
Mostrasi sì piacente a chi la mira,
che dà per li occhi una dolcezza al core,
che 'ntender no la può chi no la prova:
e par che de la sua labbia si mova
un spirito soave pien d'amore,
che va dicendo a l'anima: Sospira.

(8) Questo sonetto è sì piano ad intendere, per quello che narrato è dinanzi, che non

of heaven." And others said: "This is a marvel; blessed be the Lord, who knows how to work such wonders."

(3) I say that she showed herself so gentle and so full of all that is pleasing that those who looked on her experienced within themselves such a pure and soothing sweetness that they were unable to describe it; nor could anyone look on her without at once needing to sigh.

(4) These and other marvelous things proceeded from her virtuous power: and I, thinking of this, wanting to take up again my style of praising her, resolved to compose words in which I would let something of her miraculous and excellent effects be known; in order that not only those who could see her physically, but also others, might know of her that which can be understood through words. Then I composed this sonnet, which begins "*Tanto gentile*: So gentle."

(5)
So gentle and so pure appears
my lady when she greets others
that every tongue trembles into muteness,
and eyes do not dare look at her.

(6)
She goes along, hearing herself praised,
benignly dressed in humility;
and she seems a thing come down
from heaven to earth to manifest
     a miracle.

(7)
She shows herself so pleasing to all who
     behold
that through the eyes she grants
     a sweetness to the heart,
which no one can understand who has not
     experienced it:
and it seems that from her lips there moves
a gracious spirit full of love
that goes forth saying to the soul: Sigh.

(8) This sonnet is so plain to understand from that which has been narrated before

Chapter XXVI: (*cont.*)

abbisogna d'alcuna divisione; e però lassando lui, dico che questa mia donna venne in tanta grazia, che non solamente ella era onorata e laudata, ma per lei erano onorate e laudate molte.

(9) Ond'io, veggendo ciò e volendo manifestare a chi ciò non vedea, propuosi anche di dire parole, ne le quali ciò fosse significato; e dissi allora questo altro sonetto, che comincia: *Vede perfettamente onne salute*, lo quale narra di lei come la sua vertude adoperava ne l'altre, sì come appare ne la sua divisione.

(10)
Vede perfettamente onne salute
chi la mia donna tra le donne vede;
quelle che vanno con lei son tenute
di bella grazia a Dio render merzede.

(11)
E sua bieltate è di tanta vertute,
che nulla invidia a l'altre ne procede,
anzi le face andar seco vestute
di gentilezza, d'amore e di fede.

(12)
La vista sua fa onne cosa umile;
e non fa sola sé parer piacente,
ma ciascuna per lei riceve onore.

(13)
Ed è ne li atti suoi tanto gentile,
che nessun la si può recare a mente,
che non sospiri in dolcezza d'amore.

(14) Questo sonetto ha tre parti: ne la prima dico tra che gente questa donna più mirabile parea; ne la seconda dico sì come era graziosa la sua compagnia; ne la terza dico di quelle cose che vertuosamente operava in altrui. La seconda parte

that it has no need of any division; and thus, leaving it, I say that this lady of mine came into so much grace, that not only was she honored and praised but many other ladies were also honored and praised because of her.

(9) Having seen this, and wishing to make it manifest to whoever had not seen, I resolved to write something in which I would signify this; and then I composed this other sonnet, which begins: "*Vede perfettamente onne salute*: He sees perfectly all salvation," narrating of her how her virtuous power operated in other ladies, as appears from its division.

(10)
He sees perfectly all salvation
whoever sees my lady among the ladies;
those who go with her are bound
    to render thanks to God for this lovely
        grace.

(11)
Her beauty is of such power of virtue
that no envy in others can arise from it;
on the contrary, it makes them go
    with her
dressed in gentleness, love, and faith.

(12)
The sight of her makes every thing
    humble;
and does not make her alone appear
    pleasing;
every individual receives honor
    through her.

(13)
And she is so gentle in her acts
that no one can call her back to mind
without sighing for the sweetness of love.

(14) This sonnet has three parts: in the first, I say among what people this lady appeared most miraculous; in the second, I say how gracious was her company; in the third, I speak of the effects that her virtue operated in others. The second part begins here: "*quelle che vanno*: those who

comincia quivi: *quelle che vanno*; la terza quivi: *E sua bieltate*.

(15) Questa ultima parte si divide in tre: ne la prima dico quello che operava ne le donne, cioè per loro medesime; ne la seconda dico quello che operava in loro per altrui; ne la terza dico come non solamente ne le donne, ma in tutte le persone, e non solamente ne la sua presenzia, ma ricordandosi di lei, mirabilemente operava. La seconda comincia quivi: *La vista sua*; la terza quivi: *Ed è ne li atti*.

go"; and third here: "*E sua bieltate*: Her beauty."

(15) This last part is divided into three: in the first, I say what effects she brought about in ladies through themselves; in the second, I say what she brought about in them through others; in the third, I say how not only in ladies but in all persons, and not only in her presence but even just remembering her, she operated miraculously. The second part begins here: "*La vista sua*: The sight of her"; the third here: "*Ed è ne li atti*: And she is so gentle."

Chapter XXVII: *Beatrice's Effects on Dante and a* Canzone *Fragment*

(1) Appresso ciò, cominciai a pensare uno giorno sopra quello che detto avea de la mia donna, cioè in questi due sonetti precedenti; e veggendo nel mio pensero che io non avea detto di quello che al presente tempo adoperava in me, pareami defettivamente avere parlato.

(1) After this, I began to reflect one day on that which I had said of my lady in these two preceding sonnets; and seeing in my reflection that I had not told of that which she was bringing about within me at the present time, I seemed to have spoken defectively.

(2) E però proposi di dire parole, ne le quali io dicesse come me parea essere disposto a la sua operazione, e come operava in me la sua vertude; e non credendo potere ciò narrare in brevitade di sonetto, cominciai allora una canzone, la quale comincia: *Sì lungiamente*.

(2) And, therefore, I decided to write words in which I would say how I seemed to be susceptible to her influence and how her virtue worked in me; and not believing that I could do this in the brevity of a sonnet, I then began a canzone, which begins: "*Sì lungiamente*: So long a time."

(3)
Sì lungiamente m'ha tenuto Amore
e costumato a la sua segnoria,
che sì com'elli m'era forte in pria,
così mi sta soave ora nel core.

(3)
So long a time has Love held me
and accustomed me to his lordship,
that just as he was harsh to me before,
so now is he tender in my heart.

(4)
Però quando mi tolle sì 'l valore,
che li spiriti par che fuggan via,

(4)
But when he so takes my valor from me
that my spirits appear to flee away,

allor sente la frale anima mia	then my frail soul feels
tanta dolcezza, che 'l viso ne smore,	so much sweetness that my face turns wan,
poi prende Amore in me tanta vertute,	and then Love assumes such power over me,
che fa li miei spiriti gir parlando,	that he makes my spirits go about talking,
ed escon for chiamando	and they go out calling on
la donna mia, per darmi più salute.	my lady to give me more salutation/salvation.
(5)	(5)
Questo m'avvene ovunque ella mi vede,	This happens to me whenever she sees me,
e sì è cosa umil, che nol si crede.	and it is so humbling as not to be believed.

Chapter XXVIII: *The Death of Beatrice*

(1) *Quomodo sedet sola civitas plena populo! facta est quasi vidua domina gentium.* Io era nel proponimento ancora di questa canzone, e compiuta n'avea questa soprascritta stanzia, quando lo segnore de la giustizia chiamoe questa gentilissima a gloriare sotto la insegna di quella regina benedetta virgo Maria, lo cui nome fue in grandissima reverenzia ne le parole di questa Beatrice beata.	(1) "*Quomodo sedet sola civitas plena populo! facta est quasi vidua domina gentium*: How the city sits solitary that was full of people! She is made as a widow, she who was great among the nations." I was still intent on composing this canzone, and had completed the stanza transcribed above, when the lord of justice called this most gentle one to glory under the banner of that blessed queen, the virgin Mary, whose name was held in the greatest reverence in the words of this blessed Beatrice.
(2) E avvegna che forse piacerebbe a presente trattare alquanto de la sua partita da noi, non è lo mio intendimento di trattarne qui per tre ragioni: la prima è che ciò non è del presente proposito, se volemo guardare nel proemio che precede questo libello; la seconda si è che, posto che fosse del presente proposito, ancora non sarebbe sufficiente la mia lingua a trattare come si converrebbe di ciò; la terza si è che, posto che fosse l'uno e l'altro, non è convenevole a me trattare di ciò, per quello che, trattando, converrebbe essere me laudatore di me medesimo, la quale cosa è al postutto	(2) And although it might perhaps be pleasing at present to treat some things concerning her departure from us, it is not my intention to treat it here for three reasons: the first is that it is not within the present purpose if we want to look at the proem that precedes this book; the second is that, even were it within the present purpose, still my tongue would not be sufficient to treat of it in the way it would require; the third is that, even assuming the one and the other, it is not suitable for me to treat of this because I would have to be the praiser of myself, which is after all a blameworthy thing for whoever does it;

biasimevole a chi lo fae; e però lascio cotale trattato ad altro chiosatore.

(3) Tuttavia, però che molte volte lo numero del nove ha preso luogo tra le parole dinanzi, onde pare che sia non sanza ragione, e ne la sua partita cotale numero pare che avesse molto luogo, convenesi di dire quindi alcuna cosa, acciò che pare al proposito convenirsi. Onde prima dicerò come ebbe luogo ne la sua partita, e poi n'assegnerò alcuna ragione per che questo numero fue a lei cotanto amico.

therefore, I leave such treatment for another glossator.

(3) Nevertheless, since the number nine has many times occurred among the foregoing words, which is evidently not without a reason, and since in her departing this number seems to have an important place, it is therefore appropriate that something be said, inasmuch as it appears to suit the purpose. So, first, I will say how her departure took place, and then I will give a certain reason for why this number was so much friend to her.

Chapter XXIX: *Her Miraculous Number – She was Nine (Analogically)*

(1) Io dico che, secondo l'usanza d'Arabia, l'anima sua nobilissima si partio ne la prima ora del nono giorno del mese; e secondo l'usanza di Siria, ella si partio nel nono mese de l'anno, però che lo primo mese è ivi Tisirin primo, lo quale a noi è Ottobre; e secondo l'usanza nostra, ella si partio in quello anno de la nostra indizione, cioè de li anni Domini, in cui lo perfetto numero nove volte era compiuto in quello centinaio nel quale in questo mondo ella fue posta, ed ella fue de li cristiani del terzodecimo centinaio.

(1) I say that, according to the Arabian custom, her most noble soul departed in the first hour of the ninth day of the month; and according to the Syrian custom, she departed in the ninth month of the year [June], since the first month there is Tixryn the first, which for us is October; and according to our custom, she departed in that year of our dispensation, that is, the years of the Lord, in which the perfect number [ten] was completed nine times in that century in which she had been placed in this world, and she was a Christian of the thirteenth century.

(2) Perché questo numero fosse in tanto amico di lei, questa potrebbe essere una ragione: con ciò sia cosa che, secondo Tolomeo e secondo la cristiana veritade, nove siano li cieli che si muovono, e, secondo comune oppinione astrologa, li detti cieli adoperino qua giuso secondo la loro abitudine insieme, questo numero fue amico di lei per dare ad intendere che ne la sua generazione tutti e nove li mobili cieli perfettissimamente s'aveano insieme.

(2) As to why this number was so much a friend to her, one reason could be this: that according to Ptolemy, and following the Christian truth, nine are the heavens that move, and according to common astrological opinion, these heavens operate here below according to their relations with one another; this number was her friend in order to make it understood that, in her engendering, all nine mobile heavens were perfectly related together.

Chapter XXIX: (*cont.*)

(3) Questa è una ragione di ciò; ma più sottilmente pensando, e secondo la infallibile veritade, questo numero fue ella medesima; per similitudine dico, e ciò intendo così. Lo numero del tre è la radice del nove, però che, sanza numero altro alcuno, per se medesimo fa nove, sì come vedemo manifestamente che tre via tre fa nove. Dunque se lo tre è fattore per se medesimo del nove, e lo fattore per se medesimo de li miracoli è tre, cioè Padre e Figlio e Spirito Santo, li quali sono tre e uno, questa donna fue accompagnata da questo numero del nove a dare ad intendere ch'ella era uno nove, cioè uno miracolo, la cui radice, cioè del miracolo, è solamente la mirabile Trinitade.

(4) Forse ancora per più sottile persona si vederebbe in ciò più sottile ragione; ma questa è quella ch'io ne veggio, e che più mi piace.

(3) This is one reason, but reflecting more subtly, and according to an infallible truth, she was herself this number – by similitude, I say, and so intend. The number three is the root of nine, since without any other number, of itself it makes nine, as we see manifestly that three times three is nine. Therefore, if the three is in itself a factor of nine, and the maker in itself of miracles is three, that is, Father, Son, and Holy Spirit, which are three in one, this lady was accompanied by that number nine in order to make it understood that she was a nine, that is, a miracle, whose root, that is, the root of the miracle, is solely the miraculous Trinity.

(4) Perhaps again a subtler person might see in it a more subtle reason; but this is the one I see and that most pleases me.

Chapter XXX: *Dante's Letter to the Leaders of the Land*

(1) Poi che fue partita da questo secolo, rimase tutta la sopradetta cittade quasi vedova dispogliata da ogni dignitade; onde io, ancora lagrimando in questa desolata cittade, scrissi a li principi de la terra alquanto de la sua condizione, pigliando quello cominciamento di Geremia profeta che dice: *Quomodo sedet sola civitas.* E questo dico, acciò che altri non si maravigli perché io l'abbia allegato di sopra, quasi come entrata de la nuova materia che appresso vene.

(2) E se alcuno volesse me riprendere di ciò, ch'io non scrivo qui le parole che seguitano a quelle allegate, escusomene, però che lo intendimento mio non fue dal principio di scrivere altro che per volgare; onde, con ciò sia cosa che le parole che seguitano a quelle

(1) After she had departed from this world, the entire above-mentioned city remained like a widow stripped of every dignity; whence I, still weeping in this desolate city, wrote to the leaders of the land something about its condition, taking my beginning from Jeremiah the prophet who says: "*Quomodo sedet sola civitas*: How the city sits solitary." And this I say, in order that no one wonder why I have introduced it above almost as an entry into the new material that comes after.

(2) And if anyone should wish to reprimand me for not transcribing the words following those cited, I excuse myself because my intention from the beginning was to write nothing except in the vulgar tongue; and since the words

Chapter XXX: *(cont.)*

che sono allegate, siano tutte latine, sarebbe fuori del mio intendimento se le scrivessi.

(3) E simile intenzione so ch'ebbe questo mio primo amico a cui io ciò scrivo, cioè ch'io li scrivessi solamente volgare.

following those cited are all in Latin it would be outside my scope if I were to write them.

(3) And I know that my best friend, to whom I write this, had a similar intention, namely, that I should write to him only in the vernacular.

Chapter XXXI: *The* Canzone *(Third) of Mourning for Beatrice*

(1) Poi che li miei occhi ebbero per alquanto tempo lagrimato, e tanto affaticati erano che non poteano disfogare la mia tristizia, pensai di volere disfogarla con alquante parole dolorose; e però propuosi di fare una canzone, ne la quale piangendo ragionassi di lei per cui tanto dolore era fatto distruggitore de l'anima mia; e cominciai allora una canzone, la qual comincia: *Li occhi dolenti per pietà del core.*

(2) E acciò che questa canzone paia rimanere più vedova dopo lo suo fine, la dividerò prima che io la scriva; e cotale modo terrò da qui innanzi.

(3) Io dico che questa cattivella canzone ha tre parti: la prima è proemio; ne la seconda ragiono di lei; ne la terza parlo a la canzone pietosamente. La seconda parte comincia quivi: *Ita n'è Beatrice*; la terza quivi: *Pietosa mia canzone.*

(4) La prima parte si divide in tre: ne la prima dico perché io mi muovo a dire; ne la seconda dico a cui io voglio dire; ne la terza dico di cui io voglio dire. La seconda comincia quivi: *E perché me ricorda*; la terza quivi: *e dicerò.*

(1) After my eyes had wept for some time and were so fatigued that they could not discharge my sorrow, I thought I would like to discharge it with a few dolorous verses; and therefore I purposed to write a canzone in which, weeping, I would speak of her who through so much pain had become the destroyer of my soul; and I then began a canzone that begins: "*Li occhi dolenti per pietà del core*: The eyes grieving for pity in the heart."

(2) And so that this canzone might appear to remain the more a widow after its end, I will divide it before I transcribe it; and this mode I will observe from this point forward.

(3) I say that this mournful canzone has three parts: the first is the proem; in the second, I speak of her; in the third, I speak to the canzone piteously. The second part begins here: "*Ita n'è Beatrice*; Beatrice has gone"; the third here: "*Pietosa mia canzone*: My pitiful song."

(4) The first part is divided into three: in the first, I say why I was moved to write; in the second, I say to whom I wanted to write; in the third, I say of what I wanted to write. The second begins here: "*E perché me ricorda*: And because I remember"; the third here: "*e dicerò*: I will say."

(5) Poscia quando dico: *Ita n'è Beatrice*, ragiono di lei; e intorno a ciò foe due parti: prima dico la cagione per che tolta ne fue; appresso dico come altri si piange de la sua partita, e comincia questa parte quivi: *Partissi de la sua*.

(6) Questa parte si divide in tre: ne la prima dico chi non la piange; ne la seconda dico chi la piange; ne la terza dico de la mia condizione. La seconda comincia quivi: *ma ven tristizia e voglia*; la terza quivi: *Dannomi angoscia*.

(7) Poscia quando dico: *Pietosa mia canzone*, parlo a questa canzone, disignandole a quali donne se ne vada, e steasi con loro.

(8)
Li occhi dolenti per pietà del core
hanno di lagrimar sofferta pena,
sì che per vinti son remasi omai.
Ora, s'i' voglio sfogar lo dolore,
che a poco a poco a la morte mi mena,
convenemi parlar traendo guai.

(9)
E perché me ricorda ch'io parlai
de la mia donna, mentre che vivia,
donne gentili, volentier con vui,
non voi parlare altrui,
se non a cor gentil che in donna sia;
e dicerò di lei piangendo, pui
che si n'è gita in ciel subitamente,
e ha lasciato Amor meco dolente.

(10)
Ita n'è Beatrice in l'alto cielo,
nel reame ove li angeli hanno pace,
e sta con loro, e voi, donne, ha lassate:
no la ci tolse qualità di gelo
né di calore, come l'altre face,
ma solo fue sua gran benignitate;
ché luce de la sua umilitate
passò li cieli con tanta vertute,
che fé maravigliar l'etterno sire,
sì che dolce disire

(5) There where I say "*Ita n'è Beatrice*: Beatrice has gone," I speak of her; and out of that I make two parts: first I say the reason why she has been taken from us; afterwards, I say how others weep for her departure, and this part begins here: "*Partissi de la sua*: Once departed."

(6) That part is divided into three: in the first, I say who does not weep for her; in the second, I say who does weep; in the third, I tell of my condition. The second begins here: "*ma ven tristizia e voglia*: but let sorrow and will come"; the third here: "*Dannomi angoscia*: Sighs give me."

(7) Then when I say: "*Pietosa mia canzone*: My pitiful canzone," I speak to this canzone, designating which ladies it should go to and remain with.

(8)
The eyes grieving for the heart's pity
have suffered pain of weeping,
so that at length they are left vanquished.
Now, if I wish to vent the sorrow
that little by little leads to death,
I need to speak, expressing woes.

(9)
And since I remember how I spoke
about my lady, while she lived,
gentle ladies, willingly with you,
I do not wish to speak with others,
but only to gentle hearts in ladies;
and I will speak of her, weeping,
since she has gone suddenly to heaven,
and left Love with me grieving.

(10)
Beatrice has gone to the highest heaven,
in the realm where angels are in peace,
and abides with them, having left you, ladies:
no degree of cold has taken her from us
nor of heat, as happens with others:
it was only her great benevolence;
for the light of her humility
penetrated the heavens with such power
that it made marvel the eternal lord,
so that sweet desire

Chapter XXXI: (*cont.*)

lo giunse di chiamar tanta salute;
e fella di qua giù a sé venire,
perché vedea ch'esta vita noiosa
non era degna di sì gentil cosa.

(11)
Partissi de la sua bella persona
piena di grazia l'anima gentile,
ed èssi gloriosa in loco degno.
Chi no la piange, quando ne ragiona,
core ha di pietra sì malvagio e vile,
ch'entrar no i puote spirito benegno.
Non è di cor villan sì alto ingegno,
che possa imaginar di lei alquanto,
e però no li ven di pianger doglia:

(12)
ma ven tristizia e voglia
di sospirare e di morir di pianto,
e d'onne consolar l'anima spoglia
chi vede nel pensero alcuna volta
quale ella fue, e com'ella n'è tolta.

(13)
Dannomi angoscia li sospiri forte,
quando 'l pensero ne la mente grave
mi reca quella che m'ha 'l cor diviso:
e spesse fiate pensando a la morte,
venemene un disio tanto soave,
che mi tramuta lo color nel viso.

(14)
E quando 'l maginar mi ven ben fiso,
giugnemi tanta pena d'ogne parte,
ch'io mi riscuoto per dolor ch'i' sento;
e sì fatto divento,
che da le genti vergogna mi parte.
Poscia piangendo, sol nel mio lamento
chiamo Beatrice, e dico: «Or se' tu morta?»;
e mentre ch'io la chiamo, me conforta.

(15)
Pianger di doglia e sospirar d'angoscia
mi strugge 'l core ovunque sol mi trovo,
sì che ne 'ncrescerebbe a chi m'audesse:
e quale è stata la mia vita, poscia
che la mia donna andò nel secol novo,
lingua non è che dicer lo sapesse:

came over him to summon such a blessedness;
and he had her come to him from here below
because he saw that this noisome life
was not worthy of anything so noble.

(11)
Departed from her lovely body is
her gentle soul, full of grace:
it dwells gloriously in a worthy place.
Whoever does not weep, speaking of her,
has a heart of stone, so malicious and vile
that no benign spirit can enter it.
A rude heart lacks sufficient wit
to be able to imagine anything about her,
and therefore pain of weeping comes not
    to it:

(12)
but sadness and the will
to sigh and to die of weeping,
and to strip the soul of every consolation,
come to whoever once sees in thought
what she was, and how she is taken from us.

(13)
Sighs give me great anguish,
when thought within the heavy mind
recalls her for whom my heart is split:
and often thinking of death,
so sweet a desire comes to me
that it changes the color of my face.

(14)
And when this imagining becomes fixed
    in me,
so much pity comes to me from every side,
that I am shaken by the pain I feel;
and I become such
that shame separates me from other people.
Then, weeping, alone in my lament,
I call on Beatrice, and say: "Are you now
    dead?";
and while I call on her, I am comforted.

(15)
Weeping with grief and sighing with anguish
my heart pines wherever I find myself alone,
so that whoever heard me would be sorry:
and what my life has been since
my lady went to the everlasting life
no tongue knows how to say:

(16)

e però, donne mie, pur ch'io volesse,
non vi saprei io dir ben quel ch'io sono,
sì mi fa travagliar l'acerba vita;
la quale è sì 'nvilita,
che ogn'om par che mi dica: «Io
    t'abbandono»,
veggendo la mia labbia tramortita.
Ma qual ch'io sia la mia donna il si vede,
e io ne spero ancor da lei merzede.

(17)

Pietosa mia canzone, or va piangendo;
e ritruova le donne e le donzelle
a cui le tue sorelle
erano usate di portar letizia;
e tu, che se' figliuola di tristizia,
vatten disconsolata a star con elle.

(16)

and therefore, my ladies, even if I wished to,
I would not know how to say what I am,
my bitter life makes me suffer so;
it is so abased,
that everyone seems to tell me: "I abandon
    you,"
seeing my lifeless lips.
But my lady sees what I am,
and still I hope for recompense from her.

(17)

My pitiful canzone, go now weeping;
and find the ladies and the maidens
to whom your sisters
were accustomed to bear happiness;
and you, who are a daughter of distress,
go away disconsolate to stay with them.

Chapter XXXII: *A Poem on Sighs for One of Beatrice's Brothers*

(1) Poi che detta fue questa canzone, sì venne a me uno, lo quale, secondo li gradi de l'amistade, è amico a me immediatamente dopo lo primo; e questi fue tanto distretto di sanguinitade con questa gloriosa, che nullo più presso l'era.

(2) E poi che fue meco a ragionare, mi pregoe ch'io li dovessi dire alcuna cosa per una donna che s'era morta; e simulava sue parole, acciò che paresse che dicesse d'un'altra, la quale morta era certamente: onde io, accorgendomi che questi dicea solamente per questa benedetta, sì li dissi di fare ciò che mi domandava lo suo prego.

(3) Onde poi, pensando a ciò, propuosi di fare uno sonetto, nel quale mi lamentasse alquanto, e di darlo a questo mio amico, acciò che paresse che per lui l'avessi fatto; e dissi allora questo sonetto, che comincia: *Venite a intender li sospiri miei*.

(1) After this canzone was composed, a man came to me who in degrees of friendship was my friend immediately after the first; and he was of such close kinship with this glorious one, that no one was nearer.

(2) And after speaking with me, he asked me to write something for a lady who had died; and he disguised his words so as to seem to be talking about another, who had certainly died: and I, realizing that he spoke only of this blessed one, said that I would do what he asked of me in his request.

(3) Then, thinking about it, I decided to write a sonnet in which I would grieve somewhat and give it to my friend, so that it would appear that I had written it for him; and then I composed this sonnet, which begins: "*Venite a intender li sospiri miei*: Come to hear my sighs."

(4) Lo quale ha due parti: ne la prima chiamo li fedeli d'Amore che mi intendano; ne la seconda narro de la mia misera condizione. La seconda comincia quivi: *li quai disconsolati.*

(4) It has two parts: in the first, I call on Love's faithful, that they hear me; in the second, I tell of my miserable condition. The second begins here: "*li quai disconsolate*: they go disconsolately."

(5)
Venite a intender li sospiri miei,
oi cor gentili, ché pietà 'l disia:
li quai disconsolati vanno via,
e s'e' non fosser, di dolor morrei;
però che gli occhi mi sarebber rei,
molte fiate più ch'io non vorria,
lasso!, di pianger sì la donna mia,
che sfogasser lo cor, piangendo lei.

(5)
Come and listen to my sighs
you gentle hearts, since pity desires it:
they go disconsolately forth,
and were it not so, I would die of grief;
since my eyes would be offenders,
many times more than I would wish,
alas!, with weeping so for my lady,
to relieve my heart by crying for her.

(6)
Voi udirete lor chiamar sovente
la mia donna gentil, che si n'è gita
al secol degno de la sua vertute;
e dispregiar talora questa vita
in persona de l'anima dolente
abbandonata de la sua salute.

(6)
You will hear them often calling on
my gentle lady, who has gone away
to the life that is worthy of her virtue;
and sometimes they scorn this life
in the person of the grieving soul
abandoned by its salvation.

Chapter XXXIII: *Two Stanzas of a* Canzone

(1) Poi che detto ei questo sonetto, pensandomi chi questi era a cui lo intendea dare quasi come per lui fatto, vidi che povero mi parea lo servigio e nudo a così distretta persona di questa gloriosa.

(1) Once I had composed this sonnet, thinking of who he was to whom I intended to give it, as if made by him, I saw that it seemed to be a poor and bare service for a person so closely related to that glorious one.

(2) E però, anzi ch'io li dessi questo soprascritto sonetto, sì dissi due stanzie d'una canzone, l'una per costui veracemente, e l'altra per me, avvegna che paia l'una e l'altra per una persona detta, a chi non guarda sottilmente; ma chi sottilmente le mira vede bene che diverse persone parlano, acciò che l'una non chiama sua donna costei, e l'altra sì, come appare manifestamente.

(2) And so, before I gave him the sonnet written above, I composed two stanzas of a canzone, one for him in truth and the other for me, although the one and the other appear to be spoken by one person; but whoever subtly considers, clearly sees that diverse persons speak, since one does not call her his lady, while the other does, as plainly appears.

(3) Questa canzone e questo soprascritto sonetto li diedi, dicendo io lui che per lui solo fatto l'avea.

(4) La canzone comincia: *Quantunque volte*, e ha due parti: ne l'una, cioè ne la prima stanzia, si lamenta questo mio caro e distretto a lei; ne la seconda mi lamento io, cioè ne l'altra stanzia, che comincia: *E' si raccoglie ne li miei*. E così appare che in questa canzone si lamentano due persone, l'una de le quali si lamenta come frate, l'altra come servo.

(5)
Quantunque volte, lasso!, mi rimembra
ch'io non debbo già mai
veder la donna ond'io vo sì dolente,
tanto dolore intorno 'l cor m'assembra
la dolorosa mente,
ch'io dico: «Anima mia, ché non ten vai?
ché li tormenti che tu porterai
nel secol, che t'è già tanto noioso,
mi fan pensoso di paura forte».

(6)
Ond'io chiamo la Morte,
come soave e dolce mio riposo;
e dico «Vieni a me» con tanto amore,
che sono astioso di chiunque more.

(7)
E' si raccoglie ne li miei sospiri
un sono di pietate,
che va chiamando Morte tuttavia:
a lei si volser tutti i miei disiri,
quando la donna mia
fu giunta da la sua crudelitate;

(8)
perché 'l piacere de la sua bieltate,
partendo sé da la nostra veduta,
divenne spirital bellezza grande,
che per lo cielo spande
luce d'amor, che li angeli saluta
e lo intelletto loro alto, sottil
face maravigliar, sì v'è gentile.

(3) I gave him this canzone and the sonnet written above, saying that I had done it only for him.

(4) The canzone begins: "*Quantunque volte*: How many times" and has two parts: in one, the first stanza, this dear friend and close relation of hers laments; in the second, I lament, that is, in the other stanza, which begins: "*E' si raccoglie ne li miei*: And in my." And thus it appears that in this canzone two persons lament, one of them as brother, the other as servant (lover).

(5)
How many times, alas!, I remember
that I must never more
see the lady for whom I so grieve;
such grief is gathered around the heart
by the grieving mind,
so that I say: "My soul, why don't you leave?
since the torments that you will bear
in the world, which is already so noxious
    to you,
make me pensive with dreadful fear."

(6)
Then I call on Death,
as my suave and sweet rest;
and say: "Come to me" with so much love,
that I am bitter toward whoever dies.

(7)
And in my sighs gathers
a sound of pity,
which goes on calling on Death
    continually:
to Death all my desires turned
when my lady
was struck by its cruelty;

(8)
because the pleasure of her loveliness,
taking leave of our sight
became great spiritual beauty,
which through the heaven spreads
the light of love; it greets the angels
and makes their high intellect
subtly marvel, so noble is she.

Chapter XXXIV: *Drawing an Angel on the Anniversary of Beatrice's Death*

(1) In quello giorno nel quale si compiea l'anno che questa donna era fatta de li cittadini di vita eterna, io mi sedea in parte ne la quale, ricordandomi di lei, disegnava uno angelo sopra certe tavolette; e mentre io lo disegnava, volsi li occhi, e vidi lungo me uomini a li quali si convenia di fare onore.

(2) E' riguardavano quello che io facea; e secondo che me fu detto poi, elli erano stati già alquanto anzi che io me ne accorgesse. Quando li vidi, mi levai, e salutando loro dissi: «Altri era testé meco, però pensava».

(3) Onde partiti costoro, ritornaimi a la mia opera, cioè del disegnare figure d'angeli: e faccendo ciò, mi venne uno pensero di dire parole, quasi per annovale, e scrivere a costoro li quali erano venuti a me; e dissi allora questo sonetto, lo quale comincia: *Era venuta*; lo quale ha due cominciamenti, e però lo dividerò secondo l'uno e secondo l'altro.

(4) Dico che secondo lo primo questo sonetto ha tre parti: ne la prima dico che questa donna era già ne la mia memoria; ne la seconda dico quello che Amore però mi facea; ne la terza dico de gli effetti d'Amore. La seconda comincia quivi: *amor, che*; la terza quivi: *Piangendo uscivan for*.

(5) Questa parte si divide in due: ne l'una dico che tutti li miei sospiri uscivano parlando; ne la seconda dico che alquanti diceano certe parole diverse da gli altri.

(6) La seconda comincia quivi: *Ma quei*. Per questo medesimo modo si divide secondo l'altro cominciamento, salvo che ne la prima parte dico quando questa donna era così venuta ne la mia memoria, e ciò non dico ne l'altro.

(7)
Primo cominciamento
Era venuta ne la mente mia

(1) On the day on which one year was completed since this lady had become a citizen of eternal life, I was sitting in a place where, reminiscing about her, I was designing an angel on certain tablets; and while I was drawing, I turned my eyes and saw beside me men to whom honor was due.

(2) And they were observing what I was doing; and as I was told later, they had been there already for a while before I was aware of them. When I saw them, I got up and, greeting them, said: "Another was with me just now, therefore I was steeped in thought."

(3) Once they had left, I returned to my work, that of drawing figures of angels: and doing so, the idea came to me of composing words for an anniversary poem and to write them to those men who had come to me; and then I composed this sonnet, which begins: "*Era venuta*: There came," which has two beginnings, and thus I will divide it according to one and the other.

(4) I say that, according to the first, this sonnet has three parts: in the first, I say that this lady was already in my memory; in the second, I say that which Love, therefore, did to me; in the third, I tell of the effects of Love. The second begins here: "*amor, che*: love who"; the third here: "*Piangendo uscivan for*: Weeping they went out."

(5) This part divides in two: in one, I say that all my sighs issued in speaking; in the second, I say that some said certain words different from the others.

(6) The second begins here: "*Ma quei*: But those." The sonnet divides in the same way with the other beginning, except that in the first part I say when this lady had come to my memory, which I do not say in the other (first version).

(7)
First beginning:
There came into my mind

Chapter XXXIV: (*cont.*)

la gentil donna che per suo valore
fu posta da l'altissimo signore
nel ciel de l'umiltate, ov'è Maria.

the gentle lady who for her worth
was placed by the highest Lord
in the heaven of humility, where Mary is.

(8)
Secondo cominciamento
Era venuta ne la mente mia
quella donna gentil cui piange Amore,
entro 'n quel punto che lo suo valore
vi trasse a riguardar quel ch'eo facia.

(8)
Second beginning:
There came into my mind
that gentle lady for whom Love sheds tears
at just that moment in which her worth
drew you to look at what I was doing.

(9)
Amor, che ne la mente la sentia,
s'era svegliato nel destrutto core,
e diceva a' sospiri: «Andate fore»;
per che ciascun dolente si partia.

(9)
Love, who felt her in my mind,
had awoken in my destroyed heart,
and said to my sighs: "Get out";
so that each departed grieving.

(10)
Piangendo uscivan for de lo mio petto
con una voce che sovente mena
le lagrime dogliose a li occhi tristi.

(10)
They went out weeping from my chest
with a voice that often brings
mournful tears to my sad eyes.

(11)
Ma quei che n'uscian for con maggior pena,
venian dicendo: «Oi nobile intelletto,
oggi fa l'anno che nel ciel salisti».

(11)
But those that went out with the greatest pain,
came saying: "O noble intellect,
today it's one year since you rose to heaven."

Chapter XXXV: *The Gentle Lady at the Window Takes Pity on Dante*

(1) Poi per alquanto tempo, con ciò fosse cosa che io fosse in parte ne la quale mi ricordava del passato tempo, molto stava pensoso, e con dolorosi pensamenti, tanto che mi faceano parere de fore una vista di terribile sbigottimento.

(1) Then after some time, since I happened to be in a place that recalled past time to me, I was pensive and abided long with painful thoughts, so long that it made me appear on the outside to be terribly distressed.

(2) Onde io, accorgendomi del mio travagliare, levai li occhi per vedere se altri mi vedesse. Allora vidi una gentile donna giovane e bella molto, la quale da una finestra mi riguardava sì pietosamente, quanto a la vista, che tutta la pietà parea in lei accolta.

(2) Becoming conscious of my tribulation, I raised my eyes to see if others saw me. Then I saw a gentle lady, young and very beautiful, who was watching me from a window so piteously, as it appeared, that all pity seemed to be gathered into her.

(3) Onde, con ciò sia cosa che quando li miseri veggiono di loro compassione altrui, più tosto si muovono a lagrimare, quasi come di se stessi avendo pietade, io senti'

(3) Since, when the miserable see compassion for them in others, they are more easily moved to tears, as if taking pity on themselves, I then felt my eyes begin to

Chapter XXXV: (*cont.*)

allora cominciare li miei occhi a volere
piangere; e però, temendo di non mostrare
la mia vile vita, mi partio dinanzi da li
occhi di questa gentile; e dicea poi fra me
medesimo: «E' non puote essere che con
quella pietosa donna non sia nobilissimo
amore».

(4) E però propuosi di dire uno sonetto, ne
lo quale io parlasse a lei, e conchiudesse in
esso tutto ciò che narrato è in questa
ragione. E però che per questa ragione è
assai manifesto, sì nollo dividerò. Lo
sonetto comincia: *Videro li occhi miei.*

(5)
Videro li occhi miei quanta pietate
era apparita in la vostra figura,
quando guardaste li atti e la statura
ch'io faccio per dolor molte fiate.

(6)
Allor m'accorsi che voi pensavate
la qualità de la mia vita oscura,
sì che mi giunse ne lo cor paura
di dimostrar con li occhi mia viltate.

(7)
E tolsimi dinanzi a voi, sentendo
che si movean le lagrime dal core,
ch'era sommosso da la vostra vista.

(8)
Io dicea poscia ne l'anima trista:
«Ben è con quella donna quello Amore
lo qual mi face andar così piangendo».

want to weep; and fearing to show my vile
life, I removed myself from the gaze of this
gentle one; and then I said within myself:
"It cannot but be that there is a most noble
love with this compassionate lady."

(4) And so I decided to write a sonnet in
which I would speak with her and include
all that is narrated in this account. And
since by this account its meaning is
sufficiently manifest, I will not divide it.
The sonnet begins: "*Videro li occhi miei*: My
eyes saw."

(5)
My eyes saw how much pity
had appeared in your face,
when you regarded the looks and bearing
that I expressed many times in pain.

(6)
Then I realized that you were thinking
of the quality of my concealed life,
so that my heart was invaded by fear
of showing with my eyes my wretchedness.

(7)
And I withdrew from before you, feeling
the tears that were moved from my heart,
which was stirred up by your looking.

(8)
Then I said in my sad soul:
"Surely with that lady is Love,
which makes me go along weeping so."

Chapter XXXVI: *A Further Sonnet of Infatuation with the Lady at the Window*

(1) Avvenne poi che là ovunque questa
donna mi vedea, sì si facea d'una vista
pietosa e d'un colore palido quasi come
d'amore; onde molte fiate mi ricordava

(1) It then happened that wherever this
lady saw me, she was made to look full of
pity and pallid as if from love; as a result,
she often reminded me of my most noble

Chapter XXXVI: *(cont.)*

de la mia nobilissima donna, che di simile colore si mostrava tuttavia.

(2) E certo molte volte non potendo lagrimare né disfogare la mia tristizia, io andava per vedere questa pietosa donna, la quale parea che tirasse le lagrime fuori de li miei occhi per la sua vista.

(3) E però mi venne volontade di dire anche parole, parlando a lei, e dissi questo sonetto, lo quale comincia: *Color d'amore*; ed è piano sanza dividerlo, per la sua precedente ragione.

(4)
Color d'amore e di pietà sembianti
non preser mai così mirabilmente
viso di donna, per veder sovente
occhi gentili o dolorosi pianti,
come lo vostro, qualora davanti
vedetevi la mia labbia dolente;
sì che per voi mi ven cosa a la mente,
ch'io temo forte non lo cor si schianti.

(5)
Eo non posso tener li occhi distrutti
che non reguardin voi spesse fiate,
per desiderio di pianger ch'elli hanno:
e voi crescete sì lor volontate,
che de la voglia si consuman tutti;
ma lagrimar dinanzi a voi non sanno.

lady, who always showed a similar coloring.

(2) And certainly many times, not being able to weep nor to relieve my sadness, I went to see this pitying lady, whose sight appeared to draw the tears from my eyes.

(3) And thus the will to compose some words came to me, and I composed this sonnet, which begins: "*Color d'amore*: Color of love"; and it is plain without division from the preceding account.

(4)
Color of love and looks of compassion
have never possessed so miraculously
the face of a lady, due to frequent seeing
of gentle eyes or painful tears,
as they do yours, whenever you see
before me my grieving countenance;
so that because of you thoughts come to mind
that make me sorely fear lest my heart burst.

(5)
I cannot keep my devastated eyes
from gazing at you frequently,
out of their desire to weep:
and you increase their yearning,
so that they are consumed with longing
but do not know how to weep in front of you.

Chapter XXXVII: *Dante Reproves His Own Pleasure in the Pitying Lady at the Window*

(1) Io venni a tanto per la vista di questa donna, che li miei occhi si cominciaro a dilettare troppo di vederla; onde molte volte me ne crucciava nel mio cuore ed aveamene per vile assai.

(2) Onde più volte bestemmiava la vanitade de li occhi miei, e dicea loro nel mio

(1) I came to such a point through the sight of this lady that my eyes began to delight too much in seeing her; whence I many times was tormented in my heart and considered myself as rather loathsome.

(2) So repeatedly I cursed the vanity of my eyes and told them in my thoughts: "You

Chapter XXXVII: (*cont.*)

pensero: «Or voi solavate fare piangere chi vedea la vostra dolorosa condizione, e ora pare che vogliate dimenticarlo per questa donna che vi mira; che non mira voi, se non in quanto le pesa de la gloriosa donna di cui piangere solete; ma quanto potete fate, ché io la vi pur rimembrerò molto spesso, maladetti occhi, ché mai, se non dopo la morte, non dovrebbero le vostre lagrime avere restate».

(3) E quando così avea detto fra me medesimo a li miei occhi, e li sospiri m'assalivano grandissimi e angosciosi. E acciò che questa battaglia che io avea meco non rimanesse saputa pur dal misero che la sentia, propuosi di fare un sonetto, e di comprendere in ello questa orribile condizione. E dissi questo sonetto, lo quale comincia: *L'amaro lagrimar.*

(4) Ed hae due parti: ne la prima parlo a li occhi miei sì come parlava lo mio cuore in me medesimo; ne la seconda rimuovo alcuna dubitazione, manifestando chi è che così parla; e comincia questa parte quivi: *Così dice.*

(5) Potrebbe bene ancora ricevere più divisioni, ma sariano indarno, però che è manifesto per la precedente ragione.

(6)
«L'amaro lagrimar che voi faceste,
oi occhi miei, così lunga stagione,
facea lagrimar l'altre persone
de la pietate, come voi vedeste.

(7)
Ora mi par che voi l'obliereste,
s'io fosse dal mio lato sì fellone,
ch'i' non ven disturbasse ogne cagione,
membrandovi colei cui voi piangeste.

(8)
La vostra vanità mi fa pensare,
e spaventami sì, ch'io temo forte
del viso d'una donna che vi mira.

used to make weep who ever saw your sad condition, and now it seems you want to forget that for this lady who gazes on you; she gazes only because she is grieved for the glorious lady for whom you were wont to lament; but do what you can, cursed eyes, since I will remind you constantly that never, except after death, should you cease from your tears."

(3) And when I had thus spoken within myself to my eyes, great and anguished sighs assailed me. And in order that this battle within me not remain known only to the miserable man who felt it, I decided to make a sonnet and to describe in it this horrible condition. And I wrote this sonnet, which begins: "*L'amaro lagrimar*: The bitter weeping."

(4) It has two parts: in the first, I speak to my eyes as if I spoke to the heart within me; in the second, I remove all doubt, making manifest who is speaking thus; and this part begins here: "*Così dice*: So speaks."

(5) Perhaps it could receive still further divisions, but they would be in vain, since it is manifest from the preceding account.

(6)
"The bitter weeping that you made,
oh eyes of mine, for so long a time,
made other persons weep
with pity, as you have seen.

(7)
Now it seems to me you would forget her,
if I for my part were so faithless
as not to come and deprive you of every
    cause,
reminding you of her for whom you weep.

(8)
Your vanity worries me,
and frightens me so that I tremble much
for the face of a lady who gazes on you.

Chapter XXXVII: (*cont.*)

Voi non dovreste mai, se non per morte,	You should never, save for death,
la vostra donna, ch'è morta, obliare».	forget your lady, who is dead."
Così dice 'l meo core, e poi sospira.	So speaks my heart, and then sighs.

Chapter XXXVIII: *Battle of Heart versus Soul, Eyes versus Remembrance*

(1) Ricovrai la vista di quella donna in sì nuova condizione, che molte volte ne pensava sì come di persona che troppo mi piacesse; e pensava di lei così: «Questa è una donna gentile, bella, giovane e savia, e apparita forse per volontade d'Amore, acciò che la mia vita si riposi». E molte volte pensava più amorosamente, tanto che lo cuore consentiva in lui, cioè nel suo ragionare.

(2) E quando io avea consentito ciò, e io mi ripensava sì come da la ragione mosso, e dicea fra me medesimo: «Deo, che pensero è questo, che in così vile modo vuole consolare me e non mi lascia quasi altro pensare?».

(3) Poi si rilevava un altro pensero, e diceame: «Or tu se' stato in tanta tribulazione, perché non vuoli tu ritrarre te da tanta amaritudine? Tu vedi che questo è uno spiramento d'Amore, che ne reca li disiri d'amore dinanzi, ed è mosso da così gentil parte com'è quella de li occhi de la donna che tanto pietosa ci s'hae mostrata».

(4) Onde io, avendo così più volte combattuto in me medesimo, ancora ne volli dire alquante parole; e però che la battaglia de' pensieri vinceano coloro che per lei parlavano, mi parve che si convenisse di parlare a lei; e dissi questo sonetto, lo quale comincia: *Gentil pensero*; e dico 'gentile' in quanto ragionava di gentile donna, ché per altro era vilissimo.

(1) I returned to the sight of that lady in such an unusual condition that many times I thought of her as a person who pleased me too much; for I thought of her thus: "This is a gentle lady, beautiful, young, and wise, and appearing perhaps by the will of Love, in order that my life be comforted." And many times I thought even more lovingly, so much so that the heart consented to it, that is, to this reasoning.

(2) And when I had consented to this and had reflected, as if moved by reason, I said to myself: "God, what thought is this that so vilely wants to console me and hardly lets me think of anything else?"

(3) Then another thought rose up and said to me: "Now that you have been in such tribulation, why do you not want to withdraw yourself from such bitterness? You see that this is an inspiration of Love, who brings before us the desires of love, and it is moved from so gentle a place as the eyes of the lady who has shown herself to be so compassionate toward us."

(4) So, having struggled repeatedly within myself, again I wished to compose words about it; and since in the battle of thoughts, those speaking for her were winning, it seemed to me that I should speak to her; and I composed this sonnet, which begins: "*Gentil pensero*: Gentle thought"; and I say "gentle" with regard to its reasoning of a gentle lady, for it was otherwise most vile.

(5) In questo sonetto fo due parti di me, secondo che li miei pensieri erano divisi. L'una parte chiamo cuore, cioè l'appetito; l'altra chiamo anima, cioè la ragione; e dico come l'uno dice con l'altro. E che degno sia di chiamare l'appetito cuore, e la ragione anima, assai è manifesto a coloro a cui mi piace che ciò sia aperto.

(6) Vero è che nel precedente sonetto io fo la parte del cuore contra quella de li occhi, e ciò pare contrario di quello che io dico nel presente; e però dico che ivi lo cuore anche intendo per lo appetito, però che maggiore desiderio era lo mio ancora di ricordarmi de la gentilissima donna mia, che di vedere costei, avvegna che alcuno appetito n'avessi già, ma leggiero parea: onde appare che l'uno detto non è contrario a l'altro.

(7) Questo sonetto ha tre parti: ne la prima comincio a dire a questa donna come lo mio desiderio si volge tutto verso lei; ne la seconda dico come l'anima, cioè la ragione, dice al cuore, cioè a lo appetito; ne la terza dico com'e' le risponde. La seconda parte comincia quivi: *L'anima dice*; la terza quivi: *Ei le risponde.*

(8)
Gentil pensero che parla di vui
sen vene a dimorar meco sovente,
e ragiona d'amor sì dolcemente,
che face consentir lo core in lui.

(9)
L'anima dice al cor: «Chi è costui,
che vene a consolar la nostra mente,
ed è la sua vertù tanto possente,
ch'altro penser non lascia star con nui?»

(10)
Ei le risponde: «Oi anima pensosa,
questi è uno spiritel novo d'amore,
che reca innanzi me li suoi desiri;
e la sua vita, e tutto 'l suo valore,
mosse de li occhi di quella pietosa
che si turbava de' nostri martiri».

(5) In this sonnet, I make two parts of myself, even as my thoughts were divided. One part I call heart, that is, appetite; the other I call soul, that is, reason; and I say how one speaks with the other. And that it is appropriate to call appetite heart and to call reason soul is sufficiently manifest to those to whom I wish it to be accessible.

(6) It is true that in the preceding sonnet I take the part of the heart against the eyes, and that seems contrary to what I say at present; and therefore I say that here I understand the heart also as the appetite, since my greater desire was still to remember my most gentle lady rather than to see the other, even though I already had some appetite for her; whence it is evident that the one saying is not contrary to the other.

(7) This sonnet has three parts: in the first, I begin to say to this lady how my desire turns wholly toward her; in the second, I say how the soul, that is, reason, speaks to the heart, that is, the appetite; in the third, I say how it responds. The second part begins here: "*L'anima dice*: The soul says"; the third here: "*Ei le risponde*: It responds."

(8)
A gentle thought that speaks of you
comes frequently to dwell with me,
and discourses of love so sweetly
that it secures the heart's consent.

(9)
The soul says to the heart: "Who is this,
who comes to console our mind,
and is of such great power that he
allows no other thought to stay with us?"

(10)
The heart responds: "O thoughtful soul,
this is a new little spirit of love
that brings its desire before me;
and its life and all of its worth
issue from the eyes of that piteous lady
who was so troubled by our suffering."

Chapter XXXIX: *A Strong Imagination of Beatrice Fortifies Dante against Temptation*

(1) Contra questo avversario de la ragione si levoe un die, quasi ne l'ora de la nona, una forte imaginazione in me, che mi parve vedere questa gloriosa Beatrice con quelle vestimenta sanguigne co le quali apparve prima a li occhi miei; e pareami giovane in simile etade in quale io prima la vidi.

(2) Allora cominciai a pensare di lei; e ricordandomi di lei secondo l'ordine del tempo passato, lo mio cuore cominciò dolorosamente a pentere de lo desiderio a cui sì vilmente s'avea lasciato possedere alquanti die contra la costanzia de la ragione: e discacciato questo cotale malvagio desiderio, sì si rivolsero tutti li miei pensamenti a la loro gentilissima Beatrice.

(3) E dico che d'allora innanzi cominciai a pensare di lei sì con tutto lo vergognoso cuore, che li sospiri manifestavano ciò molte volte; però che tutti quasi diceano nel loro uscire quello che nel cuore si ragionava, cioè lo nome di quella gentilissima, e come si partio da noi. E molte volte avvenia che tanto dolore avea in sé alcuno pensero, ch'io dimenticava lui e là dov'io era.

(4) Per questo raccendimento de' sospiri si raccese lo sollenato lagrimare in guisa che li miei occhi pareano due cose che disiderassero pur di piangere; e spesso avvenia che per lo lungo continuare del pianto, dintorno loro si facea uno colore purpureo, lo quale suole apparire per alcuno martirio che altri riceva.

(5) Onde appare che de la loro vanitade fuoro degnamente guiderdonati; sì che d'allora innanzi non potero mirare persona che li guardasse sì che loro potesse trarre a simile intendimento.

(6) Onde io, volendo che cotale desiderio malvagio e vana tentazione paresse distrutto, sì che alcuno dubbio non

(1) Against this adversary of reason, there arose one day, about the ninth hour, a strong imagination in me that I seemed to see this glorious Beatrice with that crimson garment with which she had appeared first to my eyes; and she appeared in the same young age as when I first saw her.

(2) Then I began to think of her; and remembering her according to the order of past time, my heart began dolorously to repent of the desire that it had so vilely allowed to possess it for some days contrary to the constancy of reason: and banishing this so evil desire, all my thoughts turned back to their most gentle Beatrice.

(3) And I say that from then on I began to think of her so much with my whole shameful heart that sighs often made it manifest; since nearly all of them said in their issuing forth that which was being said in my heart: the name of that most gentle one and how she had departed from us. And often it occurred that some thought had so much pain in it that I forgot it and where I was.

(4) Through this rekindling of my sighs, the subsided weeping was rekindled in such guise that my eyes appeared to be two things that desired only to weep; and often it happened that because of the long continuation of the weeping, a purple color ringed them round, as typically appears in someone who has suffered afflictions.

(5) So it seemed that their vanities were worthily rewarded; so that from that time on they were not able to look at anyone who might look back at them and draw them to a similar intent.

(6) Then I, wishing that so evil a desire and vain temptation appear destroyed, such that the rhymed words I had written before could

Chapter XXXIX: (*cont.*)

potessero inducere le rimate parole ch'io avea dette innanzi, propuosi di fare uno sonetto ne lo quale io comprendesse la sentenzia di questa ragione. E dissi allora: *Lasso! per forza di molti sospiri*; e dissi 'lasso' in quanto mi vergognava di ciò, che li miei occhi aveano così vaneggiato.

(7) Questo sonetto non divido, però che assai lo manifesta la sua ragione.

(8)
Lasso! per forza di molti sospiri,
che nascon de' penser che son nel core,
li occhi son vinti, e non hanno valore
di riguardar persona che li miri.

(9)
E fatti son che paion due disiri
di lagrimare e di mostrar dolore,
e spesse volte piangon sì, ch'Amore
li 'ncerchia di corona di martìri.

(10)
Questi penseri, e li sospir ch'eo gitto,
diventan ne lo cor sì angosciosi,
ch'Amor vi tramortisce, sì lien dole;
però ch'elli hanno in lor li dolorosi
quel dolce nome di madonna scritto,
e de la morte sua molte parole.

induce no doubt, I resolved to make a sonnet that would contain the essence of this account. And then I said: "*Lasso! per forza di molti sospiri*: Alas! By the force of many sighs"; and I said "Alas" because I was ashamed that my eyes had vainly strayed.

(7) I do not divide this sonnet because its reasoned account makes it clear.

(8)
Alas! By the force of many sighs
that are born of thoughts in the heart,
the eyes are conquered and have no power
to gaze back at a person who looks at them.

(9)
They are made to resemble two desires
to weep and to show pain,
and often they weep so, that Love
encircles them with martyrs' crowns.

(10)
These thoughts and the sighs I expulse
become so anguished in the heart
that Love faints there, so grieved is he;
since they have in their grievings
written that sweet name of my lady
and many words about her death.

Chapter XL: *Pilgrims to Rome Made to Participate in Civic Mourning*

(1) Dopo questa tribulazione avvenne, in quello tempo che molta gente va per vedere quella imagine benedetta la quale Iesu Cristo lasciò a noi per essemplo de la sua bellissima figura, la quale vede la mia donna gloriosamente, che alquanti peregrini passavano per una via la quale è quasi mezzo de la cittade ove nacque e vivette e morio la gentilissima donna.

(2) Li quali peregrini andavano, secondo che mi parve, molto pensosi; ond'io, pensando a loro, dissi fra me medesimo:

(1) After this tribulation took place, in the time when many people go to see that blessed image that Jesus Christ has left us as an exemplar of his most beautiful countenance, which my lady gloriously sees, there were some pilgrims passing through the street that is nearly the middle of the city where the most gentle lady was born and lived and died.

(2) These pilgrims seemed to me to go along very pensively; thus, thinking of them, I said to myself: "These pilgrims

«Questi peregrini mi paiono di lontana parte, e non credo che anche udissero parlare di questa donna, e non ne sanno neente; anzi li loro penseri sono d'altre cose che di queste qui, ché forse pensano de li loro amici lontani, li quali noi non conoscemo».

(3) Poi dicea fra me medesimo: «Io so che s'elli fossero di propinquo paese, in alcuna vista parrebbero turbati passando per lo mezzo de la dolorosa cittade».

(4) Poi dicea fra me medesimo: «Se io li potesse tenere alquanto, io li pur farei piangere anzi ch'elli uscissero di questa cittade, però che io direi parole le quali farebbero piangere chiunque le intendesse».

(5) Onde, passati costoro da la mia veduta, propuosi di fare uno sonetto, ne lo quale io manifestasse ciò che io avea detto fra me medesimo; e acciò che più paresse pietoso, propuosi di dire come se io avesse parlato a loro; e dissi questo sonetto, lo quale comincia: *Deh peregrini che pensosi andate.*

(6) E dissi 'peregrini' secondo la larga significazione del vocabulo; ché peregrini si possono intendere in due modi, in uno largo e in uno stretto: in largo, in quanto è peregrino chiunque è fuori de la sua patria; in modo stretto non s'intende peregrino se non chi va verso la casa di sa' Iacopo o riede.

(7) E però è da sapere che in tre modi si chiamano propriamente le genti che vanno al servigio de l'Altissimo: chiamansi palmieri in quanto vanno oltremare, là onde molte volte recano la palma; chiamansi peregrini in quanto vanno a la casa di Galizia, però che la sepultura di sa' Iacopo fue più lontana de la sua patria che d'alcuno altro apostolo; chiamansi romei in

seem to me to come from afar, and I do not believe that they have ever heard about this lady; they know nothing of her; their thoughts, instead, are about other things than what is happening here; perhaps they are thinking of their faraway friends, whom we do not know."

(3) Then I said to myself: "I know that if they were from a near country, they would in some regard appear perturbed passing through the center of the grieving city."

(4) Then I said to myself: "If I could detain them a while, I would make them, too, weep before they left this city, since I would speak words that would make anyone who heard them weep."

(5) So, after they had passed from my sight, I resolved to compose a sonnet in which I would express that which I had spoken within myself; and in order that it appear more pathetic, I decided to speak as if I had spoken with them; and I composed this sonnet, which begins: "*Deh peregrini che pensosi andate*: Ah, pilgrims who go pensively."

(6) And I said "pilgrims" according to the broad sense of the word: since pilgrims can be understood in two ways, in a broad and in a narrow sense; in the broad one, a pilgrim is whoever is outside their country; in the narrow sense, a pilgrim is understood only to be one who is headed toward, or returning from, the house of St. James.

(7) However, it should be realized that there are three ways in which people who travel in the service of the Most High are properly called: they are called *palmers* inasmuch as they go overseas, whence they often bring back palms; they are called *pilgrims* inasmuch as they go to the sanctuary in Galicia, since the sepulcher of St. James was further from his fatherland than that of any other apostle; and they are

Chapter XL: (*cont.*)

quanto vanno a Roma, là ove questi cu' io chiamo peregrini andavano.

called *romers* if they go to Rome, where these whom I call pilgrims were going.

(8) Questo sonetto non divido, però che assai lo manifesta la sua ragione.

(8) I have not divided this sonnet because its reasoned account makes it sufficiently clear.

(9)
Deh peregrini che pensosi andate,
forse di cosa che non v'è presente,
venite voi da sì lontana gente,
com'a la vista voi ne dimostrate,
che non piangete quando voi passate
per lo suo mezzo la città dolente,
come quelle persone che neente
par che 'ntendesser la sua gravitate?

(9)
Ah, pilgrims who go pensively,
thinking perhaps of things not present,
do you come from people so far away,
as is demonstrated by your appearance,
that you do not weep when you pass
through the center of the grieving city,
like persons who seem to know
nothing of its heavy sorrow?

(10)
Se voi restaste per volerlo audire,
certo lo cor de' sospiri mi dice
che lagrimando n'uscireste pui.
Ell'ha perduta la sua beatrice;
e le parole ch'om di lei pò dire
hanno vertù di far piangere altrui.

(10)
If you would stay and be willing to hear,
my heart of sighs surely tells me
that you would then leave weeping.
For [this city] has lost its beatifier;
and the words that man can say of her
have power to make others weep.

Chapter XLI: *Poem for Two Gentle Ladies: "Oltre la Spera"*

(1) Poi mandaro due donne gentili a me pregando che io mandasse loro di queste mie parole rimate; onde io, pensando la loro nobilitade, propuosi di mandare loro e di fare una cosa nuova, la quale io mandasse a loro con esse, acciò che più onorevolmente adempiesse li loro prieghi. E dissi allora uno sonetto, lo quale narra del mio stato, e manda'lo a loro co lo precedente sonetto accompagnato, e con un altro che comincia: *Venite a intender.*

(1) Later, two gentle ladies sent word to me requesting that I send them some of these rhymed verses of mine; so I, considering their nobility, proposed to do so and also to compose something new, which I would send as well, in order that their request be honorably fulfilled. And then I composed a sonnet, which narrates my state, and I sent it with the preceding sonnet accompanying, and with another that begins: "*Venite a intender.* Come and listen."

(2) Lo sonetto lo quale io feci allora, comincia: *Oltre la spera*; lo quale ha in sé cinque parti.

(2) The sonnet that I then made begins: "*Oltre la spera*: Beyond the sphere" and contains five parts.

(3) Ne la prima dico ove va lo mio pensero, nominandolo per lo nome d'alcuno suo effetto.

(3) In the first, I say where my thought goes, naming it by the name of one of its effects.

(4) Ne la seconda dico perché va là suso, cioè chi lo fa così andare.

(5) Ne la terza dico quello che vide, cioè una donna onorata là suso; e chiamolo allora 'spirito peregrino', acciò che spiritualmente va là suso, e sì come peregrino lo quale è fuori de la sua patria, vi stae.

(6) Ne la quarta dico come elli la vede tale, cioè in tale qualitade, che io non lo posso intendere, cioè a dire che lo mio pensero sale ne la qualitade di costei in grado che lo mio intelletto no lo puote comprendere; con ciò sia cosa che lo nostro intelletto s'abbia a quelle benedette anime sì come l'occhio debole a lo sole: e ciò dice lo Filosofo nel secondo de la Metafisica.

(7) Ne la quinta dico che, avvegna che io non possa intendere là ove lo pensero mi trae, cioè a la sua mirabile qualitade, almeno intendo questo, cioè che tutto è lo cotale pensare de la mia donna, però ch'io sento lo suo nome spesso nel mio pensero: e nel fine di questa quinta parte dico 'donne mie care', a dare ad intendere che sono donne coloro a cui io parlo.

(8) La seconda parte comincia quivi: *intelligenza nova*; la terza quivi: *Quand'elli è giunto*; la quarta quivi: *Vedela tal*; la quinta quivi: *So io che parla*.

(9) Potrebbesi più sottilmente ancora dividere, e più sottilmente fare intendere; ma puotesi passare con questa divisa, e però non m'intrametto di più dividerlo.

(10)
Oltre la spera che più larga gira
passa 'l sospiro ch'esce del mio core:
intelligenza nova, che l'Amore
piangendo mette in lui, pur su lo tira.

(11)
Quand'elli è giunto là dove disira,
vede una donna, che riceve onore,

(4) In the second, I say why it goes on high, that is, who makes it go there.

(5) In the third, I say what it sees, that is, an honored lady on high; and I call it then "pilgrim spirit," because it journeys upward spiritually and sojourns there like a pilgrim who is outside his homeland.

(6) In the fourth, I say how it sees her to be such and with such qualities that I cannot understand, that is to say, that my thought rises toward her essence to a degree that my intellect cannot comprehend because our intellect in relation to those blessed souls is like the weak eye before the sun: and this the Philosopher says in the second book of the Metaphysics.

(7) In the fifth, I say that although I cannot understand that to which my thought has taken me, namely, to her miraculous essence, at least I understand this, that such a thought is wholly about my lady, since I hear her name often in my thought: and at the end of this fifth part I say "my dear ladies," in order to make it known that those to whom I speak are ladies.

(8) The second part begins here: "*intelligenza nova*: new intelligence"; the third here: "*Quand'elli è giunto*: When it arrives"; the fourth: "*Vedela tal*: Seeing her thus"; the fifth here: "*So io che parla*: I know that it speaks."

(9) It could be divided still more subtly and be made to be understood more subtly; but it can pass with this division, and so I do not undertake to divide it further.

(10)
Beyond the sphere that circles widest
passes the sigh that issues from my heart:
new intelligence, which Love
weeping instills in it draws it upward.

(11)
When it arrives where it desires,
it sees a lady, who receives honor,

Chapter XLI: (*cont.*)

e luce sì, che per lo suo splendore lo peregrino spirito la mira.	and shines so that by her splendor the pilgrim spirit can behold her.
(12) Vedela tal, che quando 'l mi ridice, io no lo intendo, sì parla sottile al cor dolente, che lo fa parlare.	(12) It sees her such that when it recounts to me I do not understand, so subtly it speaks to the aching heart, which makes it speak.
(13) So io che parla di quella gentile, però che spesso ricorda Beatrice, sì ch'io lo 'ntendo ben, donne mie care.	(13) I know that it speaks of that gentle one because it often remembers Beatrice, so that I understand it well, my dear ladies.

Chapter XLII: *Marvelous Vision of Beatrice in Glory and Suspension of Dante's Writing*

(1) Appresso questo sonetto apparve a me una mirabile visione, ne la quale io vidi cose che mi fecero proporre di non dire più di questa benedetta infino a tanto che io potesse più degnamente trattare di lei.	(1) After writing this sonnet, a marvelous vision appeared to me in which I saw things that made me resolve to say nothing more about this blessed lady until I should be able to treat of her more worthily.
(2) E di venire a ciò io studio quanto posso, sì com'ella sae veracemente. Sì che, se piacere sarà di colui a cui tutte le cose vivono, che la mia vita duri per alquanti anni, io spero di dicer di lei quello che mai non fue detto d'alcuna.	(2) And to reach that state I apply myself as much as I can, as she truly knows. So that, if it will please him by whom all things live that my life endure some years, I hope to say of her what has never been said of any woman.
(3) E poi piaccia a colui che è sire de la cortesia, che la mia anima se ne possa gire a vedere la gloria de la sua donna, cioè di quella benedetta Beatrice, la quale gloriosamente mira ne la faccia di colui *qui est per omnia secula benedictus*.	(3) And may it then please him who is the lord of courtesy that my soul should journey to see the glory of its lady, that is, of the blessed Beatrice, who gloriously gazes on the face of him *qui est per omnia secula benedictus* (who is blessed throughout all ages).

Index

true, 80

names not arbitrary signs, 125
narcissism, 51, 53, 103
narrative, 10
  as open to future, 10
  as openness, 72
  autobiographical, 1, 128
  epic, 19
  textual archeology of, 18
negative theology, xiv, 60, 64
Neo-Platonic, 29
  philosophy, 141
Nerval, Gérard de, 152
new
  as young, 2
  life, 2
  life for all, 29
  sun, 27
New Testament, 7, 27, 40
  as model of theologically revelatory
    literature, 14
  as supra-historical, 157
  canticles, 17
  critical study of, 8
  hymns, 76
Nietzsche, Friedrich, 122
nihilism, xiv
Noakes, Susan, 86
Nolan, Barbara, 11
Norton, Charles Eliot, 95
noumenon, 42, 74, 75
Nunc dimittis, 27

objectification, logic of, 46
ontological identity through similitude, 125
Other, 43, 44, 54, 56, 58, 60
  as absolute, 63
  as unsayable, 60
  otherness in dream, 154–55
  problem of access to, 75
  revelation of, through hermeneusis, 75
  symbolic language of, 155

Paden, William, 26
painting the *Vita nuova*, 97–107
Paul, Saint, 2
  I Corinthians 12, 5
  II Corinthians 5, 6
  Philippians 2. 6-11, 20, 23, 36
  Philippians 3: 11–14, 76
  Romans 8, 6
Pazzaglia, Mario, 5, 7, 26
performative, xii, xiii, 94, 97
Petrarca, Francesco. *See* Petrarch, Francesco

Petrarch, Francesco, 73
  and lyric closure, 72
  and lyric stubborness, 10
phenomenology, 9, 35
  back to the things themselves, 68
  new, 13
  of dream, 153
  theological, 13
  theological turn, 13
philology, future of, 87
Picone, Michelangelo, 8
Pihas, Gabriel, 5
pilgrimage, 38, 57
pilgrims through Florence, 126
Pirovano, Donato, 126
Poe, Elizabeth Wilson, 30
poetic
  epiphany, 38
  language, xii, 9
  making and transmission, 15
  prophecy, 25
  solipsism, 10
poetics of praise, xiii, 40, 54, 55
poetry
  and parallelism, 19
  and prose, 18–21
  as confessional and existential, 73
  as expression of individual experience, 73
  as originary interpretation, 73
  as Other-directed, 54
  as self-reflexive, 54
  as witness, 75
  biographical context of, 124
  in evangelical key, 54
  its own fulfillment, 56
  more noble matter for, 54
  narrativization of verse, 19
  not superseded by prose, 129
  vs. prose, 30–31
political theology, 85
popular culture, 143
Porete, Marguerite, 16
postmodern, 64
  democracy, xi
post-secular, xi
Pound, Ezra, 99
  Cantos, 137
Pre-Raphaelite, 84–89, 102
primacy of perception, 71
Primavera, 3
prose, 73
  as an overcoming of the poetry, 72
  commentary, 30
  ragioni, 31, 71
prosimetrum, 9, 16, 30

Milton Keynes UK
Ingram Content Group UK Ltd.
UKHW022225090923
428399UK00021B/132